Modern Technology
on
Vegetable Production

Modern Technology on Vegetable Production

Dr. Nem Pal Singh
Professor, Vegetable Science,
G.B.P.U.A. & T., Pantnagar,
Udham Singh Nagar, Uttranchal

Dr. A.K. Bhardwaj
Senior Research Officer,
Deptt. of Agronomy,
G.B.P.U.A. & T., Pantnagar,
Udham Singh Nagar, Uttranchal

Dr. Abnish Kumar
Senior Research Fellow,
Deptt. of Agronomy,
G.B.P.U.A. & T., Pantnagar,
Udham Singh Nagar, Uttranchal

Dr. K.M. Singh
Senior Research Fellow,
Deptt. of Agronomy,
G.B.P.U.A. & T., Pantnagar,
Udham Singh Nagar, Uttranchal

CBS

CBS Publishers & Distributors Pvt. Ltd.

New Delhi • Bengaluru • Chennai • Kochi • Kolkata • Mumbai
Hyderabad • Nagpur • Patna • Pune • Vijayawada

Modern Technology on Vegetable Production

ISBN: 978-93-86478-62-7

First CBS Reprint: 2017

Published by **Satish Kumar Jain** and produced by **Varun Jain** for
CBS Publishers & Distributors Pvt. Ltd.,
4819/XI Prahlad Street, 24 Ansari Road, Daryaganj, New Delhi - 110002
delhi@cbspd.com, cbspubs@airtelmail.in • www.cbspd.com
Ph.: 23289259, 23266861, 23266867 • Fax: 011-23243014

Corporate Office: 204 FIE, Industrial Area, Patparganj, Delhi - 110 092
Ph: 49344934 • Fax: 011-49344935
E-mail: publishing@cbspd.com • publicity@cbspd.com

Branches:
- *Bengaluru:* 2975, 17th Cross, K.R. Road, Bansankari 2nd Stage,
  Bengaluru - 70 • Ph: +91-80-26771678/79 • Fax: +91-80-26771680
  E-mail: cbsbng@gmail.com, bangalore@cbspd.com
- *Chennai:* No. 7, Subbaraya Street, Shenoy Nagar, Chennai - 600030
  Ph: +91-44-26681266, 26680620 • Fax: +91-44-42032115
  E-mail: chennai@cbspd.com
- *Kochi:* Ashana House, 39/1904, A.M. Thomas Road, Valanjambalam,
  Ernakulum, Kochi • Ph: +91-484-4059061-65
  Fax: +91-484-4059065 • E-mail: cochin@cbspd.com
- *Kolkata:* 6-B, Ground Floor, Rameshwar Shaw Road, Kolkata - 700014
  Ph: +91-33-22891126/7/8 • E-mail: kolkata@cbspd.com
- *Mumbai:* 83-C, Dr. E. Moses Road, Worli, Mumbai - 400018
  Ph: +91-9833017933, 022-24902340/41 • E-mail: mumbai@cbspd.com

Representatives:

- Hyderabad: 0-9885175004
- Patna: 0-9334159340
- Vijayawada: 0-9000660880
- Nagpur: 0-9021734563
- Pune: 0-9623451994

Printed at:
Neekunj Print Process, Delhi

PREFACE

Vegetable growing is one of the important branches of horticulture from economic as well as nutrition points of view. During the last few decades, interest in vegetable growing and marketing has increased rapidly as a result of greater appreciation of the value of vegetable food and of the place of vegetables in the nation's agriculture. Due to this fact, there is increase in the demand of suitable literature in the form of a suitable book dealing with recent technology *vis-a-vis* vegetable cultivation on small as well as large scale. To meet the increasing demand of a book on scientific cultivation "*Modern Vegetable Production*" has been written for the use of agriculture students as well as farmers and teachers.

The main aim of this book is to provide essential scientific knowledge on the problems and practices of vegetable crops, marketing, storage, preservation, exhibition and cultivation, etc. Many sources such as books, bulletins, scientific papers, journals etc. related with vegetable growing have been consulted. The modern/improved varieties and their characters, modern methods of controlling insect pests and diseases and recent methods of cultivation for vegetable crops have also been included in the book. Its content is based upon the scientific principles and is illustrated from practical view points.

Cultivation of 38 vegetable crops has been described in detail in the book. We hope that the book will be of great use to the students of agriculture and horticulture, farmers, seed growing agencies, seed dealers, extension workers and kitchen gardeners interested in vegetable production. The book is written in a very simple language and an easy to understand style. The publication of this book is not only timely but has a significance which is more than academic.

We take this opportunity to gratefully acknowledge the contribution made by various persons in the preparation of this book. We warmly acknowledge the various sources and publications from which valuable materials for this book were drawn. We feel highly indebted to the highly experienced and senior-most Professor of Horticulture, Dr. Raj Pal Singh, G.B. Pant University of Agriculture & Technology, Pantnagar (U.S. Nagar) for editing the entire manuscript and for his valuable suggestions and help rendered during the preparation of this book. We are also thankful to the entire staff of the Department of Horticulture of this University.

We also wish to acknowledge and express our sincere thanks and gratitude to the Vice-Chancellor of G.B. Pant University of Agriculture & Technology, Pantnagar; Dean, College of Agriculture; Director Extension; Head, Department of Agronomy and Horticulture at the same University, for providing the necessary encouragement to complete this work.

CONTENTS

Importance of Vegetables

According to L.H. Bailey, a vegetable is considered, in the common usage, as the edible portion of an herbaceous annual, biennial and perennial. In technical sense all plants are vegetables. The term, however, is usually applied to the edible plants which store up reserve food in roots, tubers, bulbs, stems, petioles, leaves, buds, flowers, fruits and seeds which are eaten cooked or raw. An exact definition is, however, impossible. Vegetables constitute a large and varied group of plants of considerable importance in the world's commerce. Vegetable growing is one of the major and important branches of horticulture from the point of view of value of the products.

Growing of vegetables is not only important for providing the protective food but also because these are important subsidiary foods playing a more significant role in the pattern of agriculture. These form the most nutritive menu of man and help in toning up energy and vigour. The importance of vegetables and their growing may be considered from many aspects. The presently available literature in our country relating to the science of vegetable production is scanty. For successful vegetable production, better seeds, improved varieties, improved cultural practices and better plant protection methods are necessary. So, for its better success allied services, like, transport, marketing, storage and preservation facilities and availability of technical guidance must be ascertained.

In India, where vegetarianism has been a way of life since the early days of recorded history, vegetables are very important in the daily diet. Vegetables contribute vitally to the general well being due to the reasons given below:-

1. Rich source of basic and protective elements like minerals, carbohydrates, vitamins, proteins and other chemical substances, which are required for human body.

2. More yield per unit area.

3. More net return per unit area per day.

4. Role in agro-forestry.

5. Employment of greater number of man power per unit area.

6. Suitability for succession and intercropping resulting in greater intensity of cropping.

7. Suitability for smaller as well as bigger fields.

Vegetables are a rich source of human nutrition

Vegetables play an important role in human nutrition. They provide proteins, carbohydrates, minerals, vitamins and roughages which constitute the essentials of balanced diet. They are important for neutralising the acidic effect produced during digestion of meat, cheese and other fatty foods and roughages promote digestion and help to prevent constipation. The vitamins which occur in almost all kinds of vegetables produce profound and specific physiological effects. During recent years, the interest in vegetable production has increased rapidly as a result of greater appreciation of the food value of vegetables and of the place of vegetables in the nation's food requirements.

The causes of nutrient deficiencies, their symptoms and ways of correcting them are given below:

Minerals

Ten mineral elements are required for proper growth and development of the human body. Out of these calcium, iron and phosphorus are required in larger quantities but they are not present in sufficient amount in other food materials except vegetables. Iodine and sodium elements are also supplied by vegetables. These minerals are present in minute quantities but they are most valuable for better growth and development of human health. Due to availability of minerals, vegetables are treated as protective food and are supposed to be very useful for vegetarians.

Calcium

Indian diet lacks calcium which is most important for bones, teeth, for preventing blood clotting, and for resistance to infection. In its absence children suffer from rickets, pigeon chest, irritability and retarded growth. In women it may cause trouble in child-birth due to osteomalacia after repeated pregnancies. Calcium co-ordinates with other minerals in the body and helps to correct proportion of other elements. Curry, amaranth and drumstick leaves, methi, turnip green, mustard green, coriander, spinach, cabbage, carrot, cauliflower, lettuce, onion, peas and tomatoes provide this element to the body.

Iron

Iron is an essential part of the red blood corpuscles and is the best known oxygen carrier in the body. Anaemia, pale smooth tongue, pale lips, eyes and skin, spoon shaped nails and frequent exhaustion are the main consequences of iron deficiency. Moringa leaves, amaranthus, methi, mint, coriander, drumstick (leaves and fruits), spinach and mustard green are good sources of iron.

Phosphorus

It helps in cell multiplication of both bones and soft tissues, and in proper maintenance of liquid content of the tissues. It also plays an important role in the oxidation of carbohydrates which produce energy. Potatoes, carrot, tomatoes, cucumber, spinach, cauliflower and lettuce are the best source of phosphorus.

Carbohydrates

The tuber vegetables are the cheapest source of carbohydrates, their yield being three to four times more than the yield from cereals per unit area, and are thus possible substitutes for cereals. While most vegetables make their contribution to the diet as a source of minerals and vitamins rather than as source of calorie energy and protein in which they are deficient, a few of them such as potatoes, sweet potatoes, tapioca, peas and dried seeds of beans are significant as energy food or sources of calories.

Vitamin 'A'

It is fat soluble and essential for growth and reproduction. Its deficiency in the diet causes inability to see in twilight, sensitivity to bright light, foamy white patches on the conjunctive (Bitot spots); softening of the cornea, eventually leading to blindness, frequent respiratory infections, formation of stones in kidney and bladder, dryness, pimpling, roughness and eruptions of skin and rough skin in children. Growth of children is also retarded and they are constantly susceptible to diseases.

It can be obtained from carrot, spinach, turnip green, palak, mustard green, amaranthus, coriander, colocasia leaves, sweet potato (yellow) and pumpkin (yellow). Though its availability in green vegetables varies according to the variety and the season but on an average 120 g of green vegetables contain 2000 to 12000 international units of vitamin 'A'.

Vitamin B complex

i) Thiamine (B_1) - The deficiency of thiamine causes beriberi; loss of appetite.

ii) Riboflavin (B_2) - Its deficiency may cause cracks at the corners of the mouth, raw-red cracked lips, glossy tongue, ulcers in the oral cavity.

iii) Nicotinic acid - Its deficiency may cause sore tongue (scarlet coloured), "Pellagra" showing skin changes in hands, feet, legs and neck, and mental changes in severe conditions.

iv) Pyridoxin (B_6) - Its deficiency may cause ulceration of oral cavity. It is associated with anaemia also. Peas, broadbean, lima bean, garlic, asparagus, corns, tomatoes are rich in Vitamin B complex.

Vitamin 'C'

It is a water soluble vitamin and essential for general growth and resistance against diseases. Its deficiency may cause scurvy, bleeding gums and mucous membranes, and susceptibility to infection as common cold, loss of energy, delay in wound healing, enlargement of heart and damage to heart muscles. Turnip green, green chillies, Brussel's sprouts, mustard green, amaranthus, coriander, drumstick leaves, cauliflower, knolkhol, spinach, cabbage, bitter gourd, radish leaves are rich in this vitamin. On cooking of these vegetables a part of it is destroyed. Ripened tomatoes consumed daily in adequate quantities furnish sufficient supply of this vitamin to meet successfully the body requirements. Green chillies contain about seven times as many milligrams of ascorbic acid as the same quantity of Irish potatoes. Potatoes and sweet potatoes supply about 16% ascorbic acid of the world requirement.

Vitamin 'D'

It is a fat soluble vitamin. Its deficiency may cause rickets. It is essential for proper bone and teeth formation because it helps in calcification with proper utilization of calcium and phosphorus salts. Green leafy vegetables are rich in this vitamin.

Vitamin 'E'

It is also a fat soluble vitamin and is known as "antisterility vitamin". It is most essential for reproduction. Cabbage, lettuce, methi, spinach and vegetable oils are very rich in vitamin 'E'.

Calories and proteins

Consequences of deficiency of calories and protein in the human body are retarded growth in children, irritability, apathy and possibly retarded mental development, discoloration of skin and hair, swelling of the face and lower part of the legs and feet, fatty liver (medically known as Kwashiorkor) and extreme emaciation (marasmus). The best source of calories and proteins are immature seeds of limabean, broadbean and peas, tapioca, sweet potato, yams, colocasia, potato, garlic, Brussel's sprouts, onion etc.

Vegetables as source of roughage

Roughage is necessary to make the bulk and vegetables provide roughage in the human diet. They aid in digestion and prevent constipation. The roughage mostly contains cellulose which is hardly digested and acts as a laxative. In the daily menu the leafy vegetables like cabbage, spinach, lettuce and various Indian *sags* and most of the root crops provide roughage.

To off set protein

The tissues of the human body are alkaline in reaction and it is essential for good health that proper alkaline reserve is maintained. Proteinous foods, such as meat, eggs etc., on digestion produce acidity and this acidity is counteracted by consuming green vegetables which help to maintain the alkaline reserve of the body. Abundant use of vegetables in the daily diet is, therefore, imperative.

Economic value

i) Yield per unit area:

Vegetables are not only good in taste and rich in nutrients but also give higher total yield per unit area per unit time than cereals and other crops. The following table compares the yield per hectare of various crops:-

S. No.	Crops	Average total yield per hectare in quintals
1.	Wheat	20 to 25
2.	Paddy	25 to 30
3.	Potato	150 to 200
4.	Cauliflower	125 to 175
5.	Watermelon	200 to 225

From the above table it is clear that vegetables produce much more per unit area in terms of total yield than cereals.

ii) Net return per unit area:

Most of the vegetables are quick growing and become ready for harvest within a short time enabling the grower to practice succession and intercropping and thus providing the grower with larger profits compared with cereals. The following data obtained from G.B. Pant University of Agriculture and Technology, Pantnagar substantiates that vegetables give greater net income than cereals.

S. No.	Crop	Net return per hectare (Rs/ha)
1.	Wheat	1000 to 1200
2.	Paddy	1000 to 1500
3.	Potato	2000 to 2500
4.	Cauliflower	1600 to 2200
5.	Chillies	2500 to 3000

iii) Role in agro-forestry:

A number of vegetables are found to be most suitable for growing as intercrop along with trees. During early stage (up to 5 years) crops like potato, bhindi, tomato, brinjal, sweet potato, peas, onion etc. can be grown successfully while during later stage (from 5 to 10 years age) crops like chilli, palak and ginger can be grown effectively. Forest trees are harvested after 10th year. By this way the vegetables are much more important in forest plantation.

Vegetables are important source of farm income

Generally, during the starting of crop season the prices of fresh vegetables are much more higher than cereals and grains. However, at peak of harvest the rates are moderately lower but due to high yield they have high monetary value. Cauliflower, peas, okra, bottle gourd (*lauki*) and sponge gourd (*torai*) give very good income during early crop season. The vegetable farms situated near the market create substantial income from intensive cultivation of limited lands. By this way vegetables are an important source of farm income while this is not possible from cereals, fodder and fruit crops.

Aesthetic value of vegetables

Vegetables not only enrich man's health but also adorn the table. Immense joy and pleasure is derived in producing vegetables. The sprouting seeds reveal nature's mysteries. This interest continues up to the harvesting of glistening vegetables, especially so in kitchen gardens. This provides solace to the kitchen gardener from the stress and strain which the civilization has forced upon him and enables him to gather and consume the self-grown vegetables which acts as a tonic to the soul and mind.

Flexibility in production programme

Unlike the fruits, with vegetables, the production programme can be adjusted and changed for better profits according to need. With fruits it is difficult, time taking and also expensive to change the production programme if it turns out to be unprofitable.

More vegetables in one year

Vegetables can be grown throughout the year. A number of vegetable crops, like spinach, potato, brinjal, tomato, chillies, cucurbits, okra can be grown twice or even thrice in a year. Some of the varieties of crops like spinach, okra, radish, methi, coriander, peas, cowpea, brinjal, tomato etc., are ready for harvesting within 45 to 60 days after sowing/planting. This way we can take a number of vegetable crops one after the other throughout the year if facilities for irrigation and labour are available.

Consequences of nutrient deficiency

Nutrients	Consequences of deficiency
Calories and proteins	Retarded growth in children, irritability, apathy and possibly retarded mental development, discoloration of skin and hair, swelling of the face and lower part of the legs and feet, fatty liver etc. (medically known as Kwashiorkor) and extreme emaciation (Marasmus).
Vitamin 'A'	Inability to see in twilight, sensitivity to bright light, foamy white patches on the conjunctive (Bitot spots); softening of the cornea, eventually leading to blindness, frequent respiratory infections.

Nutrients	Consequences of deficiency
Vitamin 'B'	
i) Thiamine (B$_1$)	Causes beriberi; loss of appetite.
ii) Riboflavin (B$_2$)	Cracks at the corners of the mouth; raw-red cracked lips, glossy tongue; ulcers in the oral cavity.
iii) Nicotinic acid	Sore tongue (scarlet coloured); "Pellagra" showing skin changes in hands, feet, legs and neck; mental changes in severe conditions.
iv) Pyridoxin (B$_6$)	Ulceration of oral cavity; associated with anaemia also.
Vitamin 'C'	Scurvy, bleeding gums and mucous membranes and susceptibility to infection as common cold.
Calcium	(Important for bones and teeth, blood clotting) Osteomalacia in women after repeated pregnancies.

2

Classification of Vegetable Crops

There are more than 240 plants in the world which are used as vegetables. Hence, their classification is essential to understand the nature of vegetable crops and their commercial production. It shows mainly the relationship between the group of vegetables and helps in avoiding confusion while describing their cultural practices. The different ways of classifying vegetables are as given below:

1. Alphabetical

This classification is arranged in an alphabetical order and found to be most suitable for reference.

Alphabets	Name of the vegetable
A-	Amaranthus, asparagus.
B-	Bean, broad bean, Brussel's sprouts, bitter gourd, bottle gourd, beetroot, brinjal.
C-	Cabbage, carrot, cauliflower, celery, celeriac, Swiss chard, Chinese cabbage, chilli, clusterbean, colocasia, coriander, collard, cowpea, cress, cucumber.
D-	Dandelion, dill.
E-	Egg plant, elephant foot, endive.
F-	Fenugreek, fennel.
G-	Garlic, ginger, gram.
H-	Horse radish.
J-	Jerusalem artichoke.
K-	Kale, kholrabi, kulfa, kundru.
L-	Leek, lettuce, longmelon.
M-	Martynia, mint, muskmelon, mustard, mushroom.
N-	Newzealand spinach.
O-	Okra, onion.

Alphabets	Name of the vegetable
P-	Pak-choi, parsley, parsnip, pea, pepper, potato, pumpkin, pointed gourd.
R-	Radish, rhubarb, roselle, rutabaga.
S-	Salsify, seakale, shallot, sorrel, soyabean, spinach, summer squash, sweet potato, snake gourd, sponge gourd.
T-	Tomato, turnip, tinda, turmeric.
W-	Water cress, watermelon, winter squash.
Y-	Yam.

2. Botanical

This classification is most useful from breeder's point of view. The whole plant community may be divided into 13 divisions of which the first 11 include the plants more commonly known as the Thallophyta. The twelth (Embryophyta Siphonogama) is divided into two subdivisions (Bryophyta and Pteridophyta) while the thirteenth (Embryophyta Siphonogama) corresponds to spermatophyta.

The Pteridophytes are characterised by the presence of vascular tissue (phloem and xylem tissue of regular organisation) in the sporophyte generation with true roots present in all but a few aquatic members; alteration of a separate gametophyte generation disjunctive from the sporophyte generation clearly evident, the sporophyte generation being dominant. This division is composed of five classes; Articulatae (horsetails), Lycopodiinae (club mosses), Psilotinae, Isoetinae (quillworts), and Filicinae (true ferns). The first four are known widely by misnomer "fern allies" and more recently have been designated the lycosphens by Wherry (1949).

The seed plants are characterised by a very complex sporophytic generation and a much reduced gametophytic generation. This division has been differentiated classically from the pteridophyta and others by formation of pollen tubes and production of seeds. However, in case of certain ancient fern-like plants also seeds are produced.

It is further divided into following two sub-divisions:

Sub-division I. Gymnospermae- seeds are produced commonly from naked ovules.

Sub-division II. Angiospermae- ovules closed in an ovary.

All vegetables belong to the spermatophyta great group and sub-division II, Angiospermae. The botanical names alongwith the class and family of the common vegetable crops are given below:-

Monocotyledonae:

1. **Amaryllidaceae**

Onion	*Allium cepa* L.
Garlic	*Allium sativum* L.
Leek	*Allium porrum* L.
Welsh onion	*Allium fistulosum* L.
Shallot	*Allium ascalonicum* L.
Chive	*Allium schoenoprasum* L.

2. **Araceae**

Colocasia	*Colocasia esculenta* (L.) Schott.
Elephant foot or Zimikand	*Amorphophallus campanulatus Blume*

3. **Gramineae**

Sweet corn	*Zea mays*

4. **Liliaceae**

Asparagus	*Asparagus officinalis*

5. **Dioscoreceae**

Yam	*Dioscorea alata* L.

Dicotyledoneae

1. **Aizoaceae**

New Zealand spinach	*Tetragonia expansa*

2. **Araliaceae**

Udo	*Aralia cordata*

3. **Chenopodiaceae**

Beet	*Beta vulgaris* L.
Orach	*Atriplex hortensis*
Spinach	*Spinacia oleracea* L.
Bathua	*Chenopodium album* L.

4. Convolvulaceae

Sweet potato	*Ipomoea batatas* Lam.

5. Cruciferae

Cabbage	*Brassica oleracea* L. var. *capitata*
Cauliflower	*Brassica oleracea* L. var. *botrytis*
Brussel's sprout	*Brassica oleracea* L. var. *gemmifera*
Kale	*Brassica oleracea* var. *acephala*
Chinese cabbage	*Brassica chinensis*
Rutabag	*Brassica napus*
Turnip	*Brassica compestris* var. *rapa* L.
Mustard	*Brassica juncea*
Pitsai Chinese cabbage	*Brassica pikinensis*
Watercress	*Nasturtium officinale*
Garden cress	*Lepidium sativum*
Horse radish	*Armoracea lapathifolia*
Radish	*Raphanus sativus* L.

6. Cucurbitaceae

Pumpkin and water squash	*Cucurbita pepo; Cucurbita moschata* Duch
Watermelon	*Citrullus vulgaris* Schrad.
Tinda	*Citrullus vulgaris* var. *fistulosus*
West Indian gherkin	*Cucumis anguria*
Cucumber	*Cucumis sativus* L.
Chayote	*Sechium edule*
Netted muskmelon	*Cucumis melo.* var. *reticulatus* L.
Casaba melon	*Cucumis melo.* var. *inodorus* L.
Ridged gourd	*Luffa acutangula* Raxb.
Sponge gourd	*Luffa aegyptica* Mill.
Parwal, Pointedgourd	*Trichosanthes dioica* Roxb.
Snake gourd	*Trihcosanthes anguina* L.
Bottle gourd	*Lagenaria siceraria* Standl.

Bitter gourd	*Momordica charantia* L.
Kheksa	*Momordica cochin chinensis*
Kundru	*Coccinea cordifolia*
Kakri	*Cucumis melo.* var. *utilissimus*

7. Compositae

Glope artichoke	*Cynara scolymus*
Chicory	*Cichorium intybus*
Endive	*Cichorium endivia*
Scolymus	*Scolymus hispanicus*
Salsify	*Tragopogon porsijoliuns*
Leaf lettuce	*Lactuca sativa* var. *crispa*
Head lettuce	*Lactuca sativa* var. *capitata*
Cardoon	*Cynara cardunculus*
Jerusalem artichoke	*Helianthus* tuberosus L.

8. Euphorbiaceae

Tapioca	*Manihot esculenta* Crantz

9. Leguminosae

Edible podded pea	*Pisum sativum* var *macrocarpa*
Garden pea	*Pisum sativum* L.
Broad bean	*Vicia faba* L.
Common bean	*Phaseolus vulgaris*
Bush bean	*Phaseolus vulgaris* var *humilis* L.
Rummerbean	*Phaseolus coccineus*
Indian bean	*Dolichos lablab* L.
Cowpea	*Vigna sinensis* Savi.
Methi, Fenugreek	*Trigonella foenum graecum* L.
Gaur	*Cyamopsis tetragonoloba* Taub.

10. Labiatae

Podina	*Mentha spicata*

11. Malvaceae

Okra	*Abelmoschus esculentus* L.
Roselle	*Hibiscus sabdariffa*

12. Martyniaceae

Martynia	*Proboscidea jussieui*

13. Polygonaceae

Rhubarb	*Rheum rhabarbarum* L.
Sorrel	*Runner acetosa*

14. Umbelliferae

Carrot	*Daucus carota*
Parsley	*Petroselinum crispum*
Dill	*Foeniculum vulgare*
Coriander	*Coriandrum sativum*
Cumin	*Cuminum cyminum*
Celery	*Apium graveolens*
Parsnip	*Pastinaca sativa*
Salad chervil	*Anthriscus corefolium*
Azwain	*Carum copticum*
Sowa, Dill seed	*Anethum graveolens* L.

15. Solanaceae

Potato	*Solanum tuberosum* L.
Tomato	*Lycopersicon esculentum* var *commune*
Pepper	*Capsicum annum* L.
Pungent pepper	*Capsicum frutescens* L.
Brinjal	*Solanum melongena*
Cape gooseberry	*Physalis peruviana*
Husk tomato	*Physalis pruinosa*

16. Valerianaceae

Corn salad	*Valerianella olitoria*

17. Zingiberaceae

Turmeric	*Curcuma domestica* Val.
Ginger	*Zingiber officinale* Rosc.

3. According to cultural practices

This system is based on the similar cultural requirements. The crops having similar nature of cultural requirements are grouped together for discussion. This makes it possible to give the general practices for the group without the necessity of repetition in the discussion of individual crops. The vegetables discussed are placed in following 13 groups.

	Groups	Vegetables
1.	Perennial crops	Asparagus, rhubarb, elephant foot, parwal
2.	Potheres and greens	Spinach, New Zealand spinach, kale, chard, mustard, collards
3.	Salad crops	Celery, lettuce, endive, corn salad, cress, parsley, salad chervil
4.	Cole crops	Cabbage, cauliflower, broccoli, Brussel's sprout, kholrabi, Chinese cabbage
5.	Root crops	Beet, carrot, parsnip, turnip, rutabaga, salsify, rooted chervil, radish
6.	Bulb crops	Onion, leek, garlic, shallot, Welsh onion, chive
7.	The potato	Potato
8.	The sweet potato	Sweet potato
9.	Peas and beans	Pea, bean, broad bean, garden bean, multiflora bean, lima bean, winged bean, soyabean, cowpea
10.	Solanaceous crops	Tomato, brinjal, chilli, husk-tomato, pepper

11.	The cucurbits	Cucumber, gherkin, watermelon, pumpkin, squash, bottle gourd, bitter gourd, tinda, sponge gourd, chayote
12.	Miscellaneous	Sweet corn, okra, martynia
13.	Root crops other than potato	Colocasia, tapioca, yam

4. According to parts used

In this system of classification, the vegetable crops are grouped on the basis of plant parts used as vegetables. Based on this system, the vegetable crops are classified as follows:

	Parts	**Vegetables**
1.	Root	Beet, carrot, celeriac, chicory, horse radish, parsnip, radish rutabaga, salsify, sweet potato, turnip, colocasia
2.	Stem	Asparagus, kholrabi, white potato
3.	Leaf	Brussel's sprout, cabbage, celery, Chinese cabbage, chive, collard, endive, florence fennel, French endive, garlic, leek, lettuce, mustard, New Zealand spinach, onion, pak-choi, parsley, rhubarb, shallot, spinach, Swiss chard, water cress, coriander
4.	Immature flower part	Cauliflower, globe artichoke, roselle, spouting broccoli
5.	Immature fruit	Broad bean, chayote, cucumber, lima bean, okra, pea, snapbean, summer squash, sweet corn, bottle gourd, torai, tinda, snake gourd, pepper, bitter gourd
6.	Mature fruit	Muskmelon, pepper, pumpkin, tomato, watermelon, winter squash.

5. According to life-cycle

This classification is based on the period of life-cycle of the vegetable crops. This classification is important from growers' point of view. According to this classification, the vegetables are grouped into three groups.

1. Annual

Vegetables which complete their life-cycle in one season, eg. bottle gourd, broad bean, lima bean, watermelon, muskmelon, Indian spinach, endive, Chinese cabbage, cress, etc.

2. Biennial

Vegetables which complete their life-cycle in two seasons eg. salsify, cabbage, turnip, carrot etc.

3. Perennial

Vegetables which continue their growth for more than two seasons eg. black salsify, artichoke, cardoon, chicory, asparagus, elephant foot, parwal etc.

6. Thermo-classification

On the basis of temperature requirements, vegetable crops may be grouped into cool and warm season crops. According to thermo-classification, vegetables are grouped together according to their average monthly temperature requirements which helps in separation of cool and warm season crops. In cool season vegetable crops the edible parts are mainly root, stem, leaf and immature flower parts whereas in warm season crops the edible part is mainly fruit with the exception of pea and broad bean which are cool season crops and potato and New Zealand spinach which are warm season crops.

The cool season crops grow well when the monthly mean temperature does not exceed 21°C. They thrive best if the monthly mean temperature is 15-17°C. The average monthly maximum temperature should not go more than 27°C to 30°C nor minimum below 2-5°C. The warm season crops, on the other hand, grow best when the monthly mean and average maximum temperatures are 5°C to 6°C higher than for the cool season crops. The average monthly minimum temperature should not be below 9°C to 10°C for the warm season crops.

According to their temperature requirements, vegetable crops can be grouped as below:-

1.   Cool season crops

Group A

Vegetables preferring average monthly temperature of 15-17°C, intolerant to 21-23°C but tolerant to light freezing temperature eg., cabbage, broccoli, spinach, beet and broad bean.

Group B

These prefer monthly average temperature of 15-17°C, intolerant to 21-23°C, tolerant to freezing, eg., cauliflower, globe artichoke, lettuce, pea, potato, celery and carrot.

Group C

The plants are adopted to 13-23°C. The plants can grow under very wide temperature range, eg., onion, at the time of planting, requires low temperature but at the time of maturity requires higher temperature. Other examples are asparagus, garlic, leek etc.

2.   Warm season crops

Group D

The average monthly temperature requirement is 17-27°C eg., sweet corn, bean, tomato, pepper, squashes, cucumber and muskmelon.

Group E

These are long season crops which thrive at more than 21°C eg., watermelon, sweet potato, brinjal, chillies, okra etc.

7.   According to photoperiod

This classification is based on the light requirement for flowering. On the basis of this classification the crops can be selected for various seasons and places having different light durations.

1.   Short day vegetables

Flowering induced by periods shorter than the critical units eg., soyabean, sweet potato etc.

2. Long day vegetables

Flowering induced by period longer than the critical lower limit eg., spinach, beet, Chinese cabbage, lettuce, radish etc.

3. Day neutral vegetables

Flowering induced by period of 10-18 hours of even continuous illumination, eg., tomato, squash, pumpkin, asparagus, pepper etc.

8. According to growing season

As per climatic conditions of Indian plains, field crops are classified into three groups viz., Rabi, Kharif and Zaid. Similarly, vegetables are also classified as given below:

Rabi - Root crops, cole crops, potato, lettuce etc. which grow from October to February.

Kharif - Cucurbitaceous vegetables which complete their life-cycle from June to October.

Zaid - Melons etc. which grow from February to May.

9. According to the response to transplanting

Some of the vegetables are transplanted easily while others are not, and on this basis vegetables are classified.

1. Survive transplanting easily

Vegetables like cabbage, cauliflower, knol rabi, tomato, brinjal, chilli, lettuce are transplanted easily due to faster replacement of the roots etc.

2. Require care in transplanting

Vegetables such as onion, leek, celery, parsley require care in transplanting otherwise the percentage of survival is less.

3. Not transplanted

Vegetables such as muskmelon, cucumber, peas, turnip, beet, bhindi, gourds, radish, carrot are not transplanted and are sown directly. However, some cucurbitaceous vegetables are first sown in nursery or pots and transplanted with a ball of soil.

10. Classification on the basis of soil pH

This classification is based on the response of vegetables to soil reaction. Vegetables are classified as slightly, moderately and very tolerant to acid soils. This classification helps in the selection of vegetables for particular type of soil.

Slightly tolerant (6 to 6.8 pH)	Moderately tolerant (5.5 to 6.0 pH)	Very tolerant (5.0 to 5.5 pH)
asparagus	carrot	potato
onion	cucumber	sweet potato
broccoli	brinjal	watermelon
cabbage	garlic	chicory
spinach	pea	
cauliflower	chilli	
leek	khol rabi	
lettuce	radish	
muskmelon	pumpkin	
celery	tomato	
	turnip	
	parsley	

3

Types of Vegetable Gardening

Vegetable gardening can broadly be classified into the following types on the basis of production and utilization of the products.

1. Home or kitchen gardening

In this the vegetables are grown in areas surrounding the house for supply to kitchen for family consumption.

2. Commercial vegetable gardening

The vegetables are grown on large scale for sale in the market. These gardens are specialised and are away from the market but possess good facilities for transport. This is further divided into following four types.

  i)   Market gardening

  ii) Truck gardening

  iii) Vegetable forcing

  iv) Vegetable growing for processing

  a)   Canning

  b)   Freezing

  c)   Dehydration

  d)   Pickling and fermentation

  e)   Vegetable seed production

3. Floating gardens

In these vegetables are grown in water on a floating base like boat.

Home or kitchen gardening

The utilization of bare land around the house for the purpose of growing vegetable crops is known as home or kitchen gardening. The main objective of this gardening is to produce the required vegetables for a family regularly and it is also a way of recreation and exercise especially for ladies. A small investment of time, energy and cash in home vegetable garden does more to improve the standard of living and can reduce the family expenditure. Very often when an unexpected guest arrives, the host has to rush to the market at odd hours to bring vegetables, which, it is quite possible, may not be available all the time. This problem can very easily be avoided if a house owner is wise enough to have a small kitchen garden.

The layout of village garden will differ from a city garden. In the village garden, land is not a limiting factor while other facilities such as bullocks, water, F.Y.M. and seeds are available. Therefore, in city, due to scarcity of land, one would like to produce maximum number and quantity of vegetables from the available land by following a very intensive method of cultivation.

In cities, if land is not available, some vegetables and flowering plants are grown on the roof after putting a layer of soil on waterproof cementing floor. Other vegetables are grown in boxes, pots, containers and such other structures.

Types of kitchen garden

On the basis of cultivated plants kitchen gardens may be divided into two types as given below:

a)   Home garden having fruits and vegetables.

b)   Home garden having only vegetables. These are, however, less common in houses in urban areas. The size of kitchen gardens may vary according to the size of the residential compound.

     i)   Large size kitchen gardens.

     ii)   Medium size kitchen gardens.

     iii)   Small size kitchen gardens.

     iv)   Terrace gardens.

Selection of vegetable crops

About 350 gm of vegetables per adult are needed per day (200 gm green vegetables and 150 gm root and tuber vegetables). For a family having five adults, the total requirement of vegetables for a year will be as follows:

$$5 \times 350 \text{ gm} = 1750 \text{ gm per day}$$

$$1.75 \text{kg} \times 365 = 638.75 \text{kg per year}$$

Approximately 6.5 quintal vegetables will be required per year.

The crop that one should grow in kitchen garden depends on the region, the size of the area available and choice of the family members. Only those crops should be grown that are adopted to the region and would produce satisfactory yield. When the available area is large enough, it will be desirable to produce all kinds of vegetables that the family members like, provided that they can be grown satisfactorily in the region. If land is limited it is wise to grow those crops that are green, leafy and produce a large yield per unit of area, and time. Tomatoes, brinjals, chillies, cucurbits, beans, lettuce, spinach, coriander, methi, mint, radish, carrot, turnip, cauliflower, cabbage, onion and garlic are the main crops for an average size garden.

Selection of fruit crops

Banana, papaya, lemon, guava, plantain, strawberry are the important fruit crops for home garden.

Plan of a model kitchen garden

Rotations:

Plot No. 1	Cluster bean	July-Oct.
	Cabbage intercropped with lettuce	Nov-Mar.
	French bean in between cabbage after lettuce harvest	Jan-May
Plot No. 2	Radish (rainy season)	Aug-Sept.
	Cauliflower (late) intercropped with knol-khol	Sept-Feb.
	Cowpea (summer season)	Feb-May
Plot No. 3	Cauliflower (mid season)	July-Nov.
	Radish with carrot	Oct-Nov.
	Onion	Dec-June
Plot No. 4	Cauliflower	July-Oct.
	Pea	Oct-Feb.
	Okra	Mar-Jun
Plot No. 5	Brinjal (long)	Jul-Mar.
	Amaranthus	Mar-Jun.

Plot No. 6	Bhindi (Okra)	Mar-Jun.
	Tomato	Oct-May
Plot No. 7	Bhindi (Okra)	May-Aug.
	Chilli	Sept-Apr.
On fence	Parwal (pointed gourd)	
	Kundru (Coccinia)	
	Karela (bitter gourd)	
	Cucumber	
	Lauki (bottle gourd)	
	Torai (sponge gourd)	
Along path	Tomato	
	Garlic	
Ridge 1, 2	Turmeric	
Ridge 3, 4	Ginger	
Ridge 5	Radish-Colocasia	
Ridge 6	Carrot-Colocasia	
Fruit plants	4 plants Papaya	
	4 plants Banana	
	2 plants Karonda	
	2 plants Lemon	
Gate	Beans	

Note: Sowing or planting in bed may be done at intervals in order to get vegetables for long duration.

Advantages of kitchen garden

1. It is a source of fresh and nutritious vegetables for the family throughout the year. Sometimes during off hours, when market is closed, vegetables can be obtained.

2. It reduces the expenditure in buying vegetables, because vegetable sellers sell their vegetables to the consumers on the price fixed by them including transport charges, middlemen's share and their own profit etc.

In getting vegetables from the kitchen garden all these charges will not be included.

3.   Kitchen gardening is the best source of recreation and exercise. Ladies and retired persons can use it as an exercise by doing field operations. According to Venkataratnum (1963), "An hour or two spent either in the morning or evening in the kitchen garden provides good exercise to the body and a healthy recreation to the mind."

4.   Better utilization is done of the surrounding land, kitchen waste and kitchen water.

5.   Vegetables obtained from the kitchen garden are fresh and are not liable to infection with germs occurring in unsanitary markets, and can be consumed freely.

Monthly programme for vegetable cultivation

Month	Crop	Operations
January	Onion	Transplanting if not done earlier
	Melons	Sowing
	Garlic	Weeding, irrigation
	Pea	Spraying with kerathane and dithane M-45, Picking
	Potato	Digging etc.
	Cole crops	Weeding, irrigation, harvesting
February	Tomato	Transplanting
	Brinjal	Transplanting
	Chillies	Transplanting
	Cowpea	Sowing
	Bhindi (okra)	Sowing
	Colocasia	Planting
	Melons	Sowing if not done earlier
	Cucurbits	Sowing
	French bean	Sowing
	Cluster bean	Sowing
March	Turmeric	Planting

	Ginger	Planting
	Bhindi (okra)	Sowing
	Melons	Weeding, irrigation, spraying
	Cucurbits	Irrigation, weeding
	Colocasia	Irrigation, weeding,
	Tomato	Weeding, irrigation, spraying
	Brinjal	Weeding, irrigation, spraying
	Chillies	Weeding, irrigation, spraying
	Cowpea	Weeding, irrigation, spraying
	French bean	Weeding, irrigation, spraying
	Cluster bean	Weeding, irrigation, spraying
April	Tomato	Picking, irrigation, weeding
	Brinjal	Picking, irrigation, weeding
	Chillies	Picking, irrigation, weeding
	French bean	Picking, irrigation, weeding
	Cluster bean	Picking, irrigation, weeding
	Cowpea	Picking, irrigation, weeding
	Cucurbits	Picking, irrigation, weeding
	Melons	Picking, irrigation, weeding
	Turmeric	Weeding, irrigation
	Ginger	Weeding, irrigation
	Colocasia	Weeding, irrigation
May	Tomato	Picking, irrigation, weeding
	Brinjal	Picking, irrigation, weeding
	Chillies	Picking, irrigation, weeding
	French bean	Picking, irrigation, weeding
	Cluster bean	Picking, irrigation, weeding
	Cowpea	Picking, irrigation, weeding
	Cucurbits	Picking, irrigation, weeding
	Melons	Picking, irrigation, weeding
	Turmeric	Weeding, irrigation
	Ginger	Weeding, irrigation

	Colocasia	Weeding, irrigation
	Bhindi (okra)	Sowing

(Picking, weeding, irrigation will continue in all above vegetables)

June	Cowpea	Sowing
	Bhindi (okra)	Sowing
	Cluster bean	Sowing
	Cucurbits	Sowing
	Sem	Sowing
	Colocasia	Sowing
	Brinjal	Sowing in nursery
	Chillies	Sowing in nursery
	Cauliflower	Sowing in nursery

(Sowing will continue if not sown in June)

July	Cowpea	Weeding, irrigation
	Bhindi (okra)	Weeding, picking, spraying
	Cluster bean	Weeding, picking, spraying
	Cucurbits	Weeding, picking, spraying
	Wem	Weeding, picking, spraying
	Colocasia	Ridging, weeding, spraying
	Brinjal	Transplanting
	Chillies	Transplanting
	Cauliflower	Transplanting

(Above mentioned operations will continue as per need)

August	Cowpea	Picking
	Bhindi (okra)	Picking
	Cluster bean	Picking
	Cucurbits	Picking
	Sem	Weeding
	Colocasia	Weeding, spraying
	Brinjal	Weeding, spraying
	Chillies	Weeding, spraying
	Cauliflower	Sowing in nursery

	Cabbage	Sowing in nursery
	Knol khol	Sowing in nursery
	Palak	Sowing
	Radish	Sowing
	Carrot	Sowing
	Tomato	Sowing in nursery

(Above operations will continue if required)

September	Coriander	Sowing
	Palak	Sowing
	Radish	Sowing
	Carrot	Sowing
	Methi	Sowing
	Onion	Bulb planting (for green leaves)
	Tomato	Transplanting
	Cabbage	Transplanting
	Knol khol	Transplanting
	Cauliflower (late)	Sowing in nursery
	Broad bean	Sowing

(Picking and other above mentioned operations will continue as per need)

November	Pea	Sowing, weeding, spraying
	Potato	Ridging, spraying
	Coriander	Sowing, harvesting
	Palak	Sowing, harvesting
	Radish	Sowing, harvesting
	Methi	Sowing, harvesting
	Onion	Sowing, harvesting
	Tomato	Spraying, weeding
	Cabbage	Weeding, irrigation
	Knol khol	Weeding, irrigation
	Cauliflower	Picking, weeding

	Garlic	Weeding, irrigation
	Onion	Seed sowing in nursery
	Tomato	Seed sowing in nursery
December	Pea	Picking, spraying
	Potato	Digging, spraying
	Coriander	Weeding, harvesting
	Palak	Weeding, harvesting
	Radish	Harvesting
	Methi	Harvesting, weeding
	Onion	Planting
	Tomato	Planting, picking
	Cabbage	Weeding, irrigation
	Knol khol	Weeding, irrigation
	Cauliflower	Picking, weeding, irrigation
	Garlic	Weeding, irrigation

Planning and arrangement

Location

A good kitchen garden should be located near and in back of the house for convenience in working at odd times, working for ladies and in harvesting. The soil should preferably be loam or sandy loam. It should be well drained, not too acidic and well supplied with organic matter and nutrients. Proper exposure to light is essential for better growth and development of the plants. The location should be in the direction where the use of kitchen water can be made easily.

Size

The size of a kitchen garden depends on the number of persons to be supplied with vegetables. By close attention to succession cropping and intercropping, 250 sq metres land may be used to supply a family of five members. However, the size of village gardens may be more than that of the city garden.

Arrangement of crops

The perennials and fruit crops should be on one side or at one end of the garden, where they do not obstruct the field preparation operations. Cucurbitaceous and other vine vegetables should be grown near the fence so that it may be used as staking. Long season crops or those occupying the land throughout the growing season should be planted together. Quick maturing crops should be planted in continuous rows so that the area may be planted with a single late crop. It is desirable to plant tall growing crops together and to locate them in northern direction so that they do not shade the dwarf crops.

Soil management

Rich, well drained, friable, loamy soil is the best for growing vegetables. The surface should not have depressions where rain or irrigation water may accumulate. Most of the vegetables do best in slightly acidic soils. It should be free from deleterious salts such as $NaCl_2$, Na_2CO_3 etc. The irrigation water should also be free from these salts. Lime improves the structure of certain heavy soils, but too much of it may prove injurious to most garden crops.

The plot is divided into different beds and their size may vary according to irrigation source and crops. Each bed should be well levelled and connected with irrigation and drainage channels. Rainy season vegetable crops and root and tuber crops should be planted on ridges.

Manuring

During preparation of land manure should be thoroughly incorporated in the soil to a considerable depth. Basal dose of the fertiliser to the concerned crop may be mixed in the soil at last harrowing and top dressing done as and when recommended for the crop.

Planting/sowing

Cauliflower, cabbage, knol khol, tomato, brinjal, chillies and onion do well when transplanted. Soil should be in excellent physical condition if plants are to be set in it. Sufficient moisture should be present, and if possible, the transplanting should be done in cloudy weather, or in the evening in order that the plants may have the opportunity to recover before being exposed to strong sunshine. It is also desirable to irrigate the field and do transplanting after the soil is in working condition. Sowing of above seeds may be done right in time in the nursery and later the seedlings may be transplanted in main plots.

Vegetables like peas, beans, cucurbits, carrot, beet root, okra, cluster bean and green leafy vegetables are sown directly in the field. Distance and depth of seeds should be maintained according to crop.

Interculture

Interculture is essential to the maintenance of a loose mulch of dry soil on the entire surface of garden as long as possible in the growing season. The maintenance of this mulch is of great value in retaining moisture, in keeping the soil in good physical condition and in destroying weeds. In kitchen garden, the hand hoe and hand weeder will meet every requirement without undue labour. The operations like earthing up, blanching, staking, thinning, etc., may also be attended to whenever they are required. Earthing up consists of putting the soil around the base of the plants. Blanching is done in case of such vegetables as celery, leek, cauliflower, asparagus to make them tender and not to allow the green colouring matter to develop since it imparts certain bitterness to them. Blanching is done by earthing up in celery, leek, asparagus and by covering the curds with leaves and tying the leaves in case of cauliflower.

Irrigation

Plants should be irrigated regularly. Flow irrigation is, however, more desirable than hand watering. In small plots irrigation by rubber pipe is better. The plant should not suffer any set back in growth for want of water. When, how and what amount of irrigation water should be applied in the field will depend on the nature of crop, weather conditions and conservation of soil moisture in beds.

Control of insect pests and diseases

Vegetable crops are subject to attack by a number of diseases and insect pests. Preventive measures are best but if an attack takes place and the gardener is not familiar with the insect pests or diseases and also the proper treatment to protect his crops, he should take the advice from the plant protection department. Most of the fungal diseases can be controlled by the use of Dithane M-45, Dithane Z-78, or copper fungicides. Sevin 50 W.P. or Thiodan (endosulfan 35 E.C.) are sprayed on all leaf eating insects, like beetles and caterpillars. Metasystox can be used against aphids, white flies etc.

Harvesting

Generally, harvesting is done according to requirement. When vegetables are ready for harvest they should be harvested and only those vegetables should be harvested first which are ready to be consumed and the remaining ones should be left for later harvesting. Harvesting is done at varying intervals according to the crops. Some of the vegetables like potato, garlic, onion, turmeric, ginger, colocasia can be kept in a suitable cool and dry place for future consumption. Storage place should not be airtight and hot. Excess produce of vegetables like tomato, pea, cauliflower etc. can be used for preparation of different products or for canning.

2. Commercial vegetable gardening

i) Market gardening

It is one of the important branch of commercial vegetable gardening in which vegetables are produced for local market. At present, due to development of transport facilities, the growers are sending their produce even to distant markets where prices are more attractive and profitable. Now vegetables are brought to market from distant villages by trucks. Generally the cropping pattern in such gardens depends on the demand of the local market. Due to high prices of land, intensive methods of cultivation are followed and most skilful methods for growing vegetables for commercial purposes are adopted. In such gardens higher net returns are possible due to availability of good seeds, fertilisers, irrigation facilities, insecticides, fungicides and easy transportation facilities.

Due to high cost of land it is essential to secure large returns per unit area to realise some profit on the investment. For market gardening, crops like peas, cauliflower, cucumber, tomato, brinjal, chillies, leafy vegetables, okra etc. are produced. The main characteristics of this type of gardening are given below:

1. Prices of land and labour wages are very high.
2. Cultivation is very intensive for regular supply of vegetables to the market for earning maximum profit from the land.
3. For a long time these farms were confined to the immediate vicinity of

the cities i.e. within a radius of 5-10 miles, but now-a-days better transport facilities have increased this distance considerably.

4. A large number of vegetables are grown and the growers have to spend comparatively more time on marketing of the produce.

5. Profit is much more than in other type of gardening due to low cost of transportation and lesser share to middlemen in some instances.

ii) Truck gardening

In this type of gardening the production of few vegetable crops is taken up on a large scale for distant markets. In this gardening, in general, more extensive and less intensive method of cultivation than in market gardening is followed. The word truck when used to describe this type of vegetable farming has no relationship to motor truck. According to Webster Dictionary, it is derived from the French word "Troquer" meaning "to barter". It has come to be applied to commodities raised for sale, mainly vegetables. In recent years the development of national highways and efficient motor truck facilities have helped this gardening considerably. Truck gardening is prosperous where climate, soil and other factors of production assure better yield than average, and labour and land cost is less. The main features of this gardening are given below:

1. Such farms are located far away from the centres of consumption, preferably by the side of rail route or metalled roads, in the regions having suitable climate.

2. Price of land and labour is comparatively lower.

3. Only few crops of semi-perishable nature are grown on large area.

4. Cost of transport facilities is high.

5. Mechanisation is followed partly or wholly.

6. The cost of cultivation is less.

iii) Vegetable forcing

In this type of gardening the vegetables are grown out of their normal season in cellars, heated buildings, green houses, glass houses, cold frames and under other artificial growing conditions. The vegetables commonly grown under glass houses or glass frames are tomatoes and cucumbers. This type of cultivation is done generally in temperate regions, because crops like tomatoes and cucumbers cannot be grown outside during winter season and their prices are too high. Other vegetables such as mushroom, pea and asparagus are also grown in these structures.

In India, this type of gardening has little chance to develop because all vegetables can be grown normally throughout the year in one or other part of the country. Common people, due to their low purchasing power, cannot pay the extra cost incurred to force vegetables out of season. The following are the characteristics of this type gardening.

1. Cost of production is much more higher than in case of other methods of vegetable production.

2. Various types of structures viz., glass houses, hot beds, cold frames, etc., are required for forcing vegetables.

3. The cultivation is most intensive.

4. It requires special technical knowledge.

5. Environment is controlled artificially.

6. It is a sort of specialised demand oriented farming.

iv) Vegetable growing for processing

The main object of this type of gardening is to produce the vegetables for supply to processing factories. These gardens are situated around the factories and grow the kind and varieties required by the factories. This type of gardens in India are very limited due to lack of processing factories but the prospects of future development are quite bright as the processing industries are growing up fast. The heavier soils are considered to be better for this type of gardening in order to get higher and continuous yield rather than an early yield. The main features of this type of gardening are as given below:

1. Cultivation is less intensive with low cost of production.

2. Market is assured.

3. Vegetables are grown on contract basis.

4. Specific kinds and varieties of vegetables are cultivated.

5. Price per unit weight of produce is low.

Suitable crops for various methods of preservation

a) Canning:- Tomatoes, peas, beans, okra, pointed gourd (parwal), sweet corn, asparagus.

b) Freezing:- Peas, sweet corn, lima beans, asparagus, cauliflower, spinach.

c) Dehydration:- Onion, potato, cauliflower, peas, carrot, etc.

d) Pickling and fermentation:- Turnip, cucumber, cabbage, cauliflower, carrot, chillies, radish etc.

v) Vegetable seed production

The main object of this type of gardening is to produce quality seeds on large scale under the inspection of an organization. Climate, soil, and disease-free conditions are factors influencing the location of seed growing areas. The owner of the garden should have thorough knowledge of the crop, its growth habits, mode of pollination, isolation required and time of roguing etc. The knowledge about curing, threshing, cleaning, grading, packing and storage is also essential.

Nucleus or breeder's seed is produced by the concerned breeder of a particular organization, foundation seed is multiplied at research stations, Government farms or National Seeds Corporation's farms. The certified seeds are, however, multiplied by the farmers under the inspection of seed certification agency. This is an expanding industry in India and also profitable to the growers. Following are the main characteristics of this type of gardening:

1. Vegetables are produced mainly for seeds under strict supervision of specialists.

2. Vegetables are produced on contract basis in suitable climatic conditions.

3. More attention is paid to purity of seed by frequent roguing of off types or strains, and by giving suitable isolation distance between two varieties or strains to avoid crossing.

4. Highly skilled labour is employed.

5. More investment is made on control of insect pests and diseases.

3. Floating gardens

This is another type of gardening known as "Floating gardening" which can be seen in Dal Lake of Kashmir valley. In such areas where land is submerged in water, this type of gardening can be followed. A floating base is made from the roots of Typha grass or any other similar type of material. The floating base is kept in the water and seedlings are transplanted on leaf compost, made of the vegetation growing in the area. According to the need of the crop, intercultural operations are done. These operations can be done by sitting in boats. Most of the summer season vegetables are supplied from Dal Lake to Srinagar. This type of gardening is an art in itself and specialised too.

4

Problems and Practices of Vegetable Production in India

Vegetable growing is one of the major and important branches of Horticulture from the point of view of value of the products. Growing of vegetables is not only important for providing the protective food but also important subsidiary foods. It thus plays a significant role in the agriculture of the country. Vegetables form the most nutritive menu of man and help to tone up his energy and vigour. Nutrition and food research have conclusively shown what protective and health promoting properties vegetables offer to man. Experience has shown that many diseases commonly found in human beings, particularly in the under-developed countries, are preventible by an intelligent and fuller utilisation of vegetables. Vegetables supply some of the things in which other food materials are deficient. They supply carbohydrates, fats, proteins, vitamins and minerals, which are very essential for the body. A survey carried out in different parts of the country has shown that the chief deficiencies in our diet are calories, Vitamin A and riboflavin.

In India, vegetables constitute hardly 8 to 10 per cent of the total food intake which is distressingly low as compared to, for example, 45 per cent in Japan. Even in countries like United States of America where maximum animal and milk protein is available, the consumption per capita is almost five times than that of Indians. At present the area under vegetables is hardly 0.2 per cent of the total cropped area, out of which tubers and potatoes occupy about 50 per cent. Hence, it is very essential to increase the production of vegetables in the country to meet the actual requirement of the present population and to increase the income of the farmers by raising the per unit yield. A vegetable grower usually grows two to three crops a year in the same land because most of the vegetable crops are of short duration. However, by growing vegetables, one can employ all the members of the family to the best advantage all the year round. This way, vegetable growing communities are able to make a good living from small holdings. In our country vegetable industry is not yet well developed and many aspects of it are yet to be studied and developed.

Following are the limitations of vegetable farming in India:

1. Vegetables are highly perishable.
2. Ignorance of nutritional value of vegetables.
3. Illiteracy and lack of technical knowledge of scientific cultivation.

4.   Scarcity of literature on scientific cultivation of vegetables.
5.   Lack of adequate transport facilities.
6.   Lack of enough refrigeration and storage facilities.
7.   Non-availability of sufficient quantity of quality seed in time.
8.   Higher input requirements and cost.
9.   Malpractices in marketing.
10.   Lack of knowledge about control of insect-pests, diseases and weeds.
11.   Lack of irrigation facilities.

Vegetables are highly perishable

Fresh vegetables are like living organisms and as such undergo normal life processes. They respire, lose water through transpiration and undergo chemical changes if not sold immediately after harvest. Deterioration of vegetables is also influenced considerably by temperature, atmospheric humidity and other factors. The losses in leafy and fruit vegetables are much more than in root and tuber vegetable crops. Thus, a considerable quantity of vegetables produced in our country is wasted every year. For example, vegetables grown on hills and away from the roads take much more time to reach market, causing deterioration in quality and are thus sold at very low price. It results in 25 to 30 per cent loss to the growers. Thus, due to these reasons the growers are not cultivating vegetables on large scale.

Ignorance of nutritive value of vegetables

A majority of community is quite unaware about the nutritive value of different vegetable crops. Hence, in spite of available facilities for cultivation they are not giving much attention to vegetable gardening. In our country most of the population lives in villages and people are uneducated who do not realise the importance of vegetable crops which are an important source of vitamins and minerals. The educated ones are now realising its importance and giving more weightage to vegetables in their daily diet. If the facts are disseminated to uneducated masses, the production of vegetable crops will increase positively.

Illiteracy and lack of technical knowledge of scientific cultivation

In India, different types of soil and climatic conditions are available and almost all vegetable crops can be grown in one or other part of the country throughout the year. The literature on such aspects is very essential to the growers to provide them the information on suitable varieties for different regions for different purposes, economic methods of cultivation, including doses of nutrients, methods of controlling insect pests and diseases and the way so to get maximum return from these crops. Vegetable traders should be given information on methods of packing the produce, ways to increase the life of produce and know-how about storage for the particular vegetable crops. Similar literature should also provide information to the consumers regarding the food value of each kind of vegetable, guidance regarding the selection and adjustment of their daily requirements to suit the palate and his pocket. At present I.C.A.R, New Delhi, C.F.T.R.I., Mysore, Agriculture Universities and Extension Services in each state are publishing some literature on different vegetable crops but as yet there is inadequate supply of the same to growers. Moreover, literature should be made available in every regional language for each climatic condition so that the growers may be benefited.

Lack of adequate transport facilities

Proper transportation is very important for the success of vegetable industry in the country. Timely and speedy delivery of vegetables with minimum damage and deterioration en route at the lowest cost are important aspects of transportation. If better transportation facilities are made available the area under perishable vegetable crops can be increased. At present, because of road transportation facilities, okra, green chillies and peas are marketed from Punjab and Uttar Pradesh to Madhya Pradesh, Rajasthan and Karnataka etc. Potato is being supplied from North India to almost all parts of the country. Through railways, peas and early cauliflower are being supplied from Punjab to Uttar Pradesh and Bihar. Cauliflower is supplied from Kannauj (U.P.) to Kolkata (W.B.). Even then, in many Indian villages, though there are proper facilities for growing vegetables, yet, due to lack of proper transport facilities, the fields are left uncultivated in summer. Due to lack of proper transport facilities vegetable production is confined only to the surrounding areas of cities in our country.

Lack of enough refrigeration and storage facilities

Better returns can be obtained by the vegetable growers only when the prices are stabilised and to stabilise the prices of vegetable crops, their proper storage is very essential due to the following reasons.

1. Vegetables are available only in their respective seasons and are not available during off season. During their respective season also there is a glut in the market due to which the prices go down. Hence, by increasing the period of availability, better market price can be obtained. This is possible by cold storage facilities.

2. If better cold storage facilities are made available it is easy to supply and hold a regular trade of vegetables.

3. Consumers will not be required to pay lower prices during glut and higher prices during off season if cold storage facilities are provided.

4. Some vegetables like turmeric, ginger, potato and sweet potatoes can be stored for two to three months even at room temperature and can be made available for that period. If these vegetables are stored in proper storage the period of availability will be increased by 6 to 8 months.

At present vegetables are stored in the following ways:

A. Home storage:

Under home conditions fruit and root vegetables of winter season can be stored for a week at room temperature while leafy vegetables cannot be stored for more than 2 to 3 days.

During summer season neither fruit vegetables nor leafy vegetables can be stored for more than two days. However, during summer season, potatoes may be stored over cool and dry floor provided with a few centimetres of sand layer. Onions can be stored for three to four months by putting them in thin layers over dry floor. Garlic can be stored for 4 to 6 months by hanging in bundles in dry huts. Ginger and turmeric can be stored by putting them in moist sand. Sweet potatoes, ripened squash and ripened pumpkin can be stored for few months by putting them on shelves or slated crates. Proper precaution from rats should be taken during the storage of these vegetables. Vegetables like colocasia, jimikand and yam etc. may be stored in pits under shade in or outside the home.

B. Cold storage:

This facility is available only in cities of our country. In these storages, temperature is reduced by refrigeration up to a desired level. There is a provision for controlling temperature and humidity at the desired point irrespective of the weather conditions provided the storage building is properly insulated and equipped. In such cold storages vegetables are kept in different chambers which are to be offered for consumption or for processing in fresh condition over long periods. Sometimes, due to sweating, heating and decay there may be spoilage of vegetables. This generally happens when packages or gunny bags are crowded in the storage to accommodate more packages. Sometimes, when there is a breakdown in electricity for more time or the frequency of breakdown is more, the chances of spoilage are much more. Specially in potatoes when breakdown of electricity is very frequent there is sprouting in tuber. The availability of generators, therefore, is essential for cold storages. The following general recommendations regarding average storage temperature, humidity and duration of produce given by Knott in "Vegetable Growing" on page 155 may serve the purpose:

Vegetables	Temperature °F	Humidity %	Approximate number of months to be stored
Asparagus	32	80-90	1 to 3
Cabbage	32	90-95	5 to 6
Carrot	32	90-95	5 to 6
Cauliflower	32	85-90	1
Egg plant	50-55	85-90	1/2
Garlic	32	70-75	6 to 7
Onion	32	70-75	6 to 7
Pea	32	85-90	1/2
Potato	36-40	85-90	5 to 6
Pumpkin	50-55	70-75	5 to 6
Spinach	32	90-95	1/3
Tomato	45-50	80-85	1/3

The losses during storage may be lesser if vegetables are stored properly under regulated conditions of temperature and humidity, and are not over crowded. In India, this type of storage facility is available only in cities and at higher rent. Hence, a small grower cannot use it for small commodities. Therefore, it would be advantageous if cold storage houses are constructed near production regions for storing the produce soon after their harvest and electricity is given to such storages at lower rate so that the storage charges may be reduced.

Non-availability of sufficient quantity of quality seed in time

The success of the crop is dependent largely upon the genetic characters possessed by the seed and the environment under which it is grown. Therefore, the seed is really the foundation for the success of future crops, which is possible only by supplying good quality seed to the growers. Vegetable seed trade in this country has not yet reached the stage of efficiency as that of the Western countries. At present the position of seed supply in the country is given below.

1.   Raising of seed by the grower himself:

Growers sometimes reserve a small area for seed production or leave certain plants of vegetables for seed, as in okra, cucurbits, brinjal etc., in the field for their own planting in the next season. In this system, the quality of seed goes down and it is difficult to maintain the actual character of a particular variety. If the seeds are not properly raised and collected, they may act as carriers of diseases, insect pests, weed seeds and other foreign matters. If seeds are not properly stored, they may lose their viability and deteriorate in quality. Also, seeds of certain vegetables cannot be raised in all the regions eg. cole crops. Thus, this method is not successful.

2.   Private seed dealers:

Private seed dealers act as retailers, commission agents and petty dealers. The quality of seeds supplied by them is quite uncertain. They may adulterate the seeds with dirt, wild seeds, sterile seeds etc., to increase the bulk. Some of the seed dealers produce the seed under the supervision of a specialist. This is practised by some well established seed firms in India, e.g. Sutton and Sons, Kolkata, N. Cooper and Co., Poona, Pestonjee P. Pocha and Sons, Poona etc. Their seeds are reliable to a certain extent as they are mostly raised and stored under proper supervision and seed tests are performed before disposing them of. They also purchase seeds from outside countries.

3.   Co-operative seed stores:

There are some seeds of vegetables which are supplied by the co-operative seed stores to the vegetable growers. Mostly peas, beans, okra and cucurbit seeds are supplied. These co-operatives get the seed from Government seed agencies or from private seed firms and supply them to the vegetable growers. These seeds are not said to be very reliable because they collect the seeds from reliable as well as unreliable sources.

4. Seed corporations:

The National Seeds Corporation is a Government of India undertaking establishment to promote quality seed production in the country through modern production and processing techniques. This is the only central organisation in our country dealing in the production and distribution of certified seeds. The corporation obtains the breeder's seeds from the research institutes and produces the foundations seeds at its own farms. The foundation seeds of vegetables are supplied to the state departments, agricultural universities and progressive seed producers for further multiplication. The seed listed in the catalogue can be obtained on payment from the corporation's office at New Delhi. These may be obtained in person or by post or by railway parcel, but in all cases advance payment is necessary. In various states of India, "State Corporations" have also been started. These corporations work on similar pattern and supply the seeds to growers, particularly of their own state.

5. Government seed agencies:

These procure the seeds either from Government farms or from the farmers who have raised the seeds under strict supervision of the Government inspectors and have acted according to their instructions. They supply seeds of good quality but are unable to meet the requirements of all the growers due to lack of farms and staff. At present N.E.S. blocks are taking active part in supplying vegetable seeds to the growers in villages.

6. Seed supply from special sources:

There are some such sources which supply the seeds in limited quantity to the vegetable growers. These are:

i) Breeders and specialists:

Usually they supply breeder seeds to corporations, Government seed farms etc.

ii) Miscellaneous sources:

There are some miscellaneous sources which supply the seeds to the growers in the form of gifts or in exchange of seed. Sometimes seeds are also imported on small scale from other countries for research work. The quantity supplied by them is very small.

No doubt, the position of seed supply in the country is improving gradually. Even then steps should now be taken to improve the situation. A great number of vegetable research stations and agricultural universities are carrying on technical and time consuming work of evolving new varieties by selection and breeding and of producing pure seeds of such improved varieties. The Botany and Horticulture divisions of the I.A.R.I., New Delhi have been working on production and multiplication of virus resistant seeds of certain vegetables like okra etc. Hybrid seeds of vegetables are also produced by these agencies. The Central Potato Research Institute, Simla, has been working on production and supply of disease-free seeds of potatoes to the growers. Different agricultural universities in the country have also taken up this work.

Gardening units have been established by the Government for large cities like Lucknow, Kanpur, Allahabad, Varanasi, Delhi etc. for supplying good seeds, manures and fertilisers and for providing technical know-how in vegetable growing. It is thus, clear that much work is being done for improving the position of supply of good vegetable seeds to the growers, but still much remains to be done in future. The importance of good seed is now being fully realised in this country and it is very encouraging to find that Government departments, universities and colleges, National Seeds Corporation, seed dealers and growers are all co-operating to ensure supply of good vegetable seeds.

Higher, input requirements and cost:

The vegetable crops require higher inputs than other crops. Therefore, income should be ensured through regulated marketing.

Malpractices in marketing:

Marketing includes all the steps from the time the produce is ready for harvest till it is in the hands of the consumers. The main aim of marketing is that the producers should get a suitable price for their produce. At present, due to more middlemen and due to malpractices of *arathias*, the actual price of the produce is not received by the producer.

Control of insect pests, diseases and weeds:

Identification and control at proper time of different insect pests, diseases and weeds is very important aspect for the successful growing of vegetable crops.

Insect pests:

Due to their tenderness the insect pests' attack is more in different vegetable crops than in cereals/fruit crops/forest trees. Following are the main insect pests which are very harmful for different vegetable crops.

i)   Aphids

They are light green, deep purple or black in colour and found in big colonies. Their development is very fast. They suck the sap from the leaves and tender parts of the plant such as shoots, buds, flowers and foliage and thus check the plant's growth which may dry up ultimately causing reduction in market value.

They can be controlled by spraying the crop with 0.1% Metasystox or 0.2% Ekalux or 0.1% Nuvacron 2 to 3 times during growth period.

ii)   Stem and fruit borers

These are one of the serious insects for okra, brinjal and tomatoes. They bore the stem and fruits and the infection during early stage is very high, up to 50 per cent. Affected fruits become unmarketable and they also develop the insect population.

They can be controlled by spraying the crops with 0.2% Sevin or 0.05% Nuvacron or 0.2% Thiodan.

iii) White ants

They are found in colonies under ground and they are most serious in some places. They damage the entire underplant part by eating it up. Sometimes they even harm big fruit plants.

They can be controlled by application of Thimet 10G at the rate of 20 kg or Aldrin 5% dust at the rate of 30 kg per hectare in soil before sowing.

iv) Jassids

They are also very harmful insects as they suck the sap and devitalise the plants. In severe cases of damage the plants wilt and dry up.

They can be controlled by the application of Furadan granules (18 kg per hectare) in soil for protection during vegetative stage. Later on spray the crop with 0.5% Nuvacron or 0.05% Rogor at fortnightly intervals.

v) Epilachna beetle

They are very dangerous beetle for brinjal and cucurbits. They scrap the leaves and cause characteristic skeletonised patches. They can be controlled by spraying the crop with Ekalux 0.2% during vegetative stage of the crop or dusting the crop with carbaryl dust at the rate of 15-20 kg per hectare.

vi) Thrips

They feed on the leaves and cause white blotches. They can be controlled by spraying the crop with 0.2% Thiodan or 0.1% Metasystox or Rogor 0.05% or Nuvacron 0.05% solution.

vii) Diamond black moth

Caterpillars feed on tender parts and leaves and also the heads of cabbage and cauliflower. They can be controlled by spraying the crop with Malathion 0.2%, but do not harvest the crop just after spraying. Leave a gap of four days after application of the chemical.

viii) Fruit flies

Maggots feed on the flesh of fruit and the affected fruit starts rotting.

They can be controlled by picking up the infested fruits and destorying them alongwith insects. Apply bait sprays with 0.1% Malathion or 0.2% Sevin (40 ml of Malathion or 80 gm of Sevin 50 W.P. and 200 gm of sugar or jaggery per 20 litres of water) at weekly intervals during fruit setting period.

ix) Stem fly

Maggots of the fly bore into the outer layers of the stem at ground level. Affected young plants wilt and die.

They can be controlled by spraying the crop with Rogor 0.1% or Nuvacron 0.05%, or Sevin 0.1% twice at weekly interval starting from three weeks after germination or application of Furadon granules 20 kg per hectare at the time of sowing.

x) Cutworm

They cut the small plants at ground level. They can be controlled by applying Chlordane 5% dust at the rate of 50 kg per hectare.

DISEASES

As far as diseases of vegetable crops are concerned, they are caused by fungi, bacteria, viruses, nematodes, parasitic plants, and unfavourable environmental conditions. There are a number of diseases which attack different vegetable crops and affect yield and quality. Due to large number of diseases, farmers do not want to take more risk by growing vegetable crops. At present, due to lack of knowledge regarding type of damage, organism responsible, stage of damage and correct control measures, Indian farmers are not putting much area under vegetable crops. Some of the important diseases of different vegetable crops and their control measures are given below.

I. Damping off

It is caused by *Phytopthora, Pythium* and *Pellicularia* in young seedlings. The rotting starts below the surface of the ground, and the plants topple over suddenly and die. The seeds of some vegetables rot away below the ground level. The above mentioned organisms live in soil but sometimes they are also carried through seed. Tomato, brinjal, chillies, onion, cole crops, bottle gourd, pumpkin, melons, beans and okra are commonly affected by this disease.

Control measures

1. Make proper drainage, avoid thick sowing. This and careful irrigation keep off the disease.
2. Treat the seed with Fytolan, Thiram, Captan (2 gm per kilogram of seed).
3. Sterilize soil surface with Formalin.
4. Spray the seedlings with Dithane M-45 at the rate of 0.2% just after germination.

2. Mildews

It is caused by *Perenospora, Pseudoperenospora, Bremia* and *Erysiphe*. Cabbage, lettuce, radish, urnip, peas, beans, mustard, cucumber, gourds and okra are the crops affected by this disease. There are two types of mildews.

a. Powdery mildew
b. Downy mildew

a) Powdery mildew

It affects the foliage of plants. Leaves are coated with an ash coloured powdery substance. This causes the leaves to fall off. Young shoots wilt and die and check the growth and fruiting. Pods setted just after the attack of this disease do not develop the grain size, become brownish in colour and ultimately there is a heavy loss to the crop.

Control measures

1. Spraying the crop with Karathane at the rate of 0.1% at 15 days' interval.
2. Spray the crop with Sulfex (2 gm per litre) or Bavistin or Benlate (1 gm per litre).

b) Downy mildew

It is similar to the powdery mildew with the difference that a downy, soft film covers the affected portion of leaves making it all the more difficult for fungicides to act on them. Though the disease appears as minute dots, it spreads rapidly and extends to stems and fruits.

Control measures

1. Spray the crop with Dithane M-45 at the rate of 0.2% at 15-20 days' interval.
2. Spray the crop with Bordeux mixture or Blitox 50.

3. Rotting

Rotting of different parts is a very common problem in a number of diseases. This is due to heavy irrigation, defective drainage or heavy texture of the soil and organisms. Following types of rotting have been reported in vegetable crops.

    a.   Root and foot rot

    b.   Fruit and vegetable rot and blight

    c.   Other rots

a) Root and foot rot

This is due to *Rhizoctonia, Macrophomina* and *Fusarium.* Due to this disease seedlings start rotting and full grown plants dry up suddenly, get yellowed. It is observed in well defined patches. Dark brown marking are seen near the base of the stem. Heavy rains followed by high temperature during early stages of growth of plants are disastrous.

Control measures

1. Treat the seeds with Thiram, Captan or Arasan G.N. (2 gm per kilogram of seed).
2. Drench the plants with a solution of Dithane M-45 (0.2%).
3. Practice crop rotation with cereals and avoid seeds from infected pods of fruits.

b) Fruit and vegetable rot and blight

This is caused by *Pythium* and *Phytopthora*. During attack a cotton white growth develops and finally the whole fruit rots away. It spreads from diseased fruits to healthy ones. It appears first on water soaked areas. Mostly okra, chilli, brinjal, tomatoes, cucurbits and beans are affected.

Control measures

1. Avoid heavy irrigation, use ridge sowing/planting.
2. Drench the plants with a solution of Dithane M-45 (0.2%).

c) Other rots

These rots include black rot, soft rot, brown rot and bacterial blights caused by *Xanthomonas, Pseudomonas* and *Erwinia*. Cabbage, cauliflower, carrot, potatoes, brinjal, tomatoes and beans are affected.

i) Black rot

Leaf margins of affected plants turn yellow and the veins become dark, streaky and black. Premature leaves drop off, stem and petioles show blackening of vascular tissues. The bacteria enter through hydathodes (pores) at leaf margins and spread through splash of rain and irrigation water. Mostly cabbage, cauliflower and other crucifers are affected. In soft rot, soft and slimy decay of fleshy tissues accompanied by a foul smell are characteristic features of this disease. It is very common in a number of vegetable crops. In case of brown rot, the plants remain dwarf followed by sudden silting and the leaflets become brown. High temperature and high humidity are responsible for the development of this disease.

Bacterial blight affects leaves and fruits of several vegetable crops. It is seen in water soaked areas. Spotting and canker are common symptoms.

Control measures

1. Hot water treatment of seed (50°C for 30 minutes).
2. Seed treatment with Thirum, Captan (2 gm per kilogram of seed).
3. Spraying the crop with Paushamycin (0.1%).
4. Dithane M-45 and other thio-carbamate formulations and liquid parzate are also potent against blight diseases of a large number of vegetable crops.

4. Rusts

Rust is very common in cucurbits, peas, but other vegetables are also attacked by it. It is of many types. Generally yellow or orange or brown spots appear on stem and sometimes on leaves.

Control measures

Spray the crop with Dithane M-45 (0.2%).

5. Mosaic

Mosaic is caused by a number of viruses and is observed in a number of vegetable crops. The symptoms are mottling, distortion and puckering of leaves and ultimately stunting of plant growth. Almost all solanaceous crops, cucurbits, pea, cowpea, okra, beans and lettuce are affected by it. It spreads by contact, by piercing flies (Bemisia tabaci the white fly which is vector of yellow-vein mosaic), by biting type of insects, (beetle, grass hopper) and through the seeds of some plants (cowpea, beans, lettuce and cucurbits etc.). It is also transmitted through bulbs and tubers of affected plants of vegetatively propagated crops (onion, potato).

Control measures

1. Use disease-free seeds.
2. Rogue out affected plants immediately.

3. Use proper insecticides against the insect vectors.

4. Use resistant varieties of vegetable crops like pea (Little Marvel) and chilli (Pant C_1).

6. Wilt

It is caused by *Fusarium, Ozonium* and *Verticillium*. Cabbage, pea, beans, chillies, tomatoes, potatoes, brinjals and cucurbits are commonly affected. First collar region, underground parts and roots get affected and the plants suddenly wilt in a varied manner.

Control measures

1. . ollow crop rotation with cereals.

2. Use resistant varieties.

7. Anthracnose

It is caused by *Colletotrichum* and *Gloeosporium*. Beans, chillies, bottle gourd are commonly affected. Appearance of dark brown or black areas on the fruits and leaves are the common symptoms. Generally the spots are often sunken. During high humidity pinkish ooze comes out from these spots. The affected tissues shrivel up, break and die. In the later stage, chilli fruits fall down. The disease germs spread by splashing of rain drops, through implements and wet limbs.

Control measures

1. Follow crop rotation with cereals.

2. Do not grow fresh crop in the same plot if previous crop is affected by the same disease.

3. Spray the crop regularly by Dithane M-45 (0.2%) specially during rainy season.

8. Sclerotial disease

It is caused by *Sclerotium* and *Pellicularia*. Cluster bean, brinjal, cucurbits and other fruity vegetables are commonly affected. Yellow and sickly appearance of plant, stem and twigs, mostly blighted with cankers, collar region dark and weak and innumerable tiny mustard, like sclerotia develop at later stage. The disease germs are carried with seeds or remain in soil.

Contamination occurs through infected crop refuse. The germs spread through scattering rain drops, splash or wind.

Control measures

1.　Follow crop rotations with cereals.
2.　Avoid over-irrigation.
3.　Do not grow fresh crop in the same plot if previous crop is affected by the same disease.

9. Leaf spot

It is caused by *Alternaria, Cercospora* and other fungi. Beans, brinjal, chillies, okra, potatoes, sweet potatoes, mustard and other cruciferous are affected. Several types of spots on leaves, petioles and other aerial parts are formed. The organisms are carried by wind, rain or insects.

Control measures

1.　Spray the crop with Dithane M-45 (0.2%) at 20 days' interval.
2.　Spray the crop with Fytolon (0.3%) at 15 days' interval.

10. Root knot

It is caused by nematodes and both tap root and rootlets are affected. Root system loses all its power of absorption due to dissolution of cortical lamellae and the plant is starved of nutrients even when these are available in the soil. Tomatoes, brinjals, potatoes, chillies, okra and spinach are affected by this disease.

Control measures

1.　Follow crop rotations.
2.　Grow resistant varieties.
3.　Fumigate the soil with fumigants (DD @ 400 kg per hectare or Nemagon @ 40 kg per hectare).

Weeds

The most common weeds of vegetable crops are *Cynodon dectylon* Pers., *Cyperus rotundus, Eleusine indica* Gaertn., *Ipomoea* spp., *Eclipta alba* Hossak,

Commelina benghalensis Linn., *Corchorus* spp., *Euphorbia hirta, Digera arvensis* Forsk., *Phyllanthus niruri* L., *Celosia argentia* L., *Trianthema monogyna* L., *Solanum nigrum* L., *Chenopodium album* L., *Asphodelus tenuifolius* Caven., *Convolvulus arvansis* L., *Medicago* spp., *Melilotus* spp., *Euphorpia* spp., *Lathyrus aphaca* L., *Vicia* spp., and *Orobanchae* spp.

All above mentioned weeds are real problems in vegetable cultivation. Due to lack of labourers it is difficult to grow vegetables on a large scale though considerable attention has been paid in some countries to solve the weed problems of vegetable growers and some work is going on in India also.

11. Lack of irrigation facilities

Light and frequent irrigations are very essential for vegetable growing. During summer, it is not at all possible to grow vegetables if irrigation facilities are not available. In our country, the rainfall is seasonal and irregularly distributed. Therefore, to supplement rain water, irrigation is done either from a well or a canal. Perennial and long season vegetables should only be grown if better irrigation facilities are available. Own irrigation facilities are preferred over Government irrigation facilities.

12. Lack of research, technical guidance and sufficient capital

In our country very little attention has been given to this aspect. Before 1970, there was no coordinated scheme in the country but at present the All India Co-ordinated Improvement Project on potato, vegetables and tuber crops other than potato are running at country, level and conducting research work on important vegetable crops. All India Co-ordinated Spices Improvement Project is also running in most of the southern States of the country. With the start of these schemes in the country, significant improvements already come up and the future is even brighter. In the country, various kinds of soils and climatic conditions are available but literature for such conditions is not available to guide the vegetable growers of that locality. At present Agricultural Universities and Extension services of the State Governments are providing technical guidance to the vegetable growers.

Generally, vegetable growers in our country belong to a particular community living in villages or around the cities. This community is not well developed as yet and cannot afford heavy expenditure in vegetable growing. Due to lack of sufficient capital, they are not using better chemicals, fertilisers and labour–saving equipment. Due to these facts they are not getting better yields and quality. At present, provision of giving loans to them has been started through nationalised commercial banks.

5

Nursery Management and Transplanting

Most of the vegetable crops are raised by seeds except few such as pointed gourd, kakrol, sweet potato, coccinia, garlic, potato, turmeric, ginger and colocasi etc. These are propagated by vegetable parts. Many of the seed-propagated crops are sown directly in the field eg. cucurbits, beans, carrot, radish, turnip, peas, leafy vegetables and okra. The crops like tomato, brinjal, chillies, cauliflower, cabbage, knol khol, lettuce, onion, Brussel's sprouts are first sown in nurseries and then transplanted in the field. Management of a nursery for raising healthy seedlings and transplanting them to field are most important operations in vegetable production.

"A vegetable nursery is a place or an establishment for raising or handling of young vegetable seedlings until they are ready for more permanent planting."

Nursery can be maintained either for personal or commercial purpose, and each has its own advantages and disadvantages. Seedlings raised for own planting will be true to type, sound and healthy. Seedlings purchased from outside may not be available in adequate number, may not be true to type, vigorous and healthy and may not arrive at destination in due time. Following are the advantages of sowing the seeds in nursery.

1. Favourable conditions for germination and growth can be provided easily to small area of nursery while it is not possible if the same seed is sown directly in the field.

2. It is very easy and convenient to look after the young tender seedlings growing in a small but compact area of nursery. Suitable plant protection measures can also be made available timely and carefully.

3. Transplanting helps in getting early crops and thereby higher price for the produce.

4. There is economy of land since permanent field in this case is occupied after one to one and a half month. Thus, we can follow intensive rotations.

5. Generally, vegetable seeds are expensive, thus economy can be affected by sowing seeds in nursery beds.

Classification of vegetables according to their response to transplanting

i)   Easily survive in transplanting

      Beet

      Cabbage

      Lettuce

      Tomato

      Chard

      Broccoli

      Brussel's sprouts

ii) Require care in operation

      Celery

      Egg plant

      Onion

      Pepper

      Salsify

iii) Not successfully transplanted by usual methods

      Corn

      Cucumber

      Watermelon

      Muskmelon

      Lima bean

      Peas

      Turnip

      Bean

Selection of site and location

Following points should be considered while selecting the site and location of a nursery.

1.   The soil should be neutral in reaction, rich in organic matter and well drained and levelled.

2   The nursery should be nearer to water source to get irrigation facilities.

NURSERY AREA IN RELATION TO FIELD

Sl. No.	Crops	Field in hectare to be planted by an hectare of nursery
1.	Asparagus	8-10
2.	Cabbage	20-40
3.	Broccoli	20-40
4.	Kale	20-40
5.	Collard	20-40
6.	Cauliflower	20-25
7.	Chillies	25-50
8.	Onion	10-15
9.	Sweet potato	20-30
10.	Tomato (flat)	30-35

VEGETABLES REQUIRING NURSERY

Sl. No.	Name of the vegetables	Time of sowing for plains of northern India	Viability period of seed	Seed rate required to transplant one hectare of land
Rabi season vegetables				
1.	Cabbage	Sept-Oct	3 years	800-1000 g
2.	Cauliflower	July-Oct	3 years	800-1000 g
3.	Knol khol	Aug-Oct	3 years	1000-1200 g
4.	Onion	Oct-Dec.	1 year	5-8 kg
5.	Tomato	Sept-Oct	3 years	800-1000 g
6.	Asparagus	Sept-Oct	3 years	5-8 kg
7.	Parsley	Sept-Oct	1 year	3-5 kg
8.	Celery	Sept-Oct	3 years	600-800 g
Kharif season vegetables				
1.	Brinjal	June-July	5 years	800-1000 g
2.	Chilli	May-July	2 years	1000-1200 g
3.	Cauliflower	June-July	3 to 5 years	1000-1200 g
4.	Tomato	June-July	3 years	800-1000 g
5.	Onion	June-July	1 year	5-8 kg
Zaid season vegetables				
1.	Tomato	Nov-Dec	3 years	800-1000 g
2.	Brinjal	Nov-Dec	5 years	800-1000 g
3.	Chilli	Nov-Dec	2 years	1000-1200 g

Water should be of good quality and in adequate quantity.

3. The plot should be near the farm building so that frequent inspections may be made and it should be located on a high level for proper drainage. Nearness to vegetable growing fields is also desirable.

4. It should be located in sunny area.

NURSERY GROWING STRUCTURES

According to temperature requirement and other specifications, different types of nursery growing structures are used at different places.

1. Cold frames

Cold frames are used during summer season for growing vegetable seedlings to protect them against strong sunlight and desicating winds. Cold frames are made of boards set up in a box fashion, a few centimetres higher on the northern side than on the south. These frames are generally 200 cm wide (outside measure) from front to back, to accommodate the standard 180 cm sash (glass). Cold frames are constructed in very much the same way as hot beds except that no artificial heating is required. Permanent cold frames are commonly made of concrete. These are covered with glass sash, canvas, or cloth. When sash is used, the frames are as a rule 200 cm wide, although frames 400 cm wide are not uncommon.

2. Hot beds

Hot beds are used to protect the seedlings against low temperature. These are cold frames with provision for artificial heating. Hot beds should be located near the farm building so that management can be done properly. Availability of water is also essential for these beds. The frames may be of wood, cement, brick or stone. Where wood is used for making a permanent hot bed, 5 x 10 cm lumber is used for posts. These posts are driven into the ground at the corners of the bed and at intervals of 120 to 180 cm along the side of the bed. Boards or planks are nailed to these posts. The frames may be 30 x 45 cm above the surface of the ground on the back side and 15 to 30 cm on the front, thus affording a slope preferably to the south. At every 90 cm a cross bar or slide should be placed for electric or hot water heating.

a) Manure heated

Generally horse manure is used for this purpose. The manure preparation should begin ten to twelve days before use. If fresh horse manure is available, it can be used to advantage as a source of heat for hot beds. It should be placed into a flat pile, 10 cm high and 120 to 150 cm wide and of desired length. The dry manure should be moistened at the filling time to start fermentation. After two to three days of turning, it should be placed into the pit in 10 to 15 cm layers and trampled well. Sometimes a 10 to 15 cm layer of straw is also provided to distribute the heat equally throughout. As fermentation dies down in a few weeks, the hot bed becomes a cold frame, but by this time need for heat becomes nil.

b) Fuel heated

Hot beds are frequently heated by hot air conducted through flues from fire box located at one end of the beds. Flue heated beds are commonly used for growing sweet potato and potato plants. Wood and coal may be used for fuel in the fire box.

c) Electrically heated

In this system of heating, electricity is used for heating the beds and temperature in the beds is controlled automatically by means of a thermostat.

d) Hot water heated

Hot water provides the most satisfactory heat to hot beds as the temperature can be controlled more easily than by any other method.

3. Green houses

Green houses are convenient to work in and provide better control of temperature and moisture than the frames. In this, the plants may be grown either in beds or in containers. It can also be heated with hot water, electricity etc.

a) Flat

Generally, flat green houses are made of wood having dimension of 45 x 55 cm. The depth varies from 6 to 8 cm. Cheap wood is used for this purpose. There is provision for drainage.

b) Clay pots

These are small pots made up of clay soil and are used for small scale production. Tin containers, troughs, cans, paper pots are also used for this purpose.

Nursery soil preparation

The soil should be fine, moist and firm to provide better germination and excellent medium for seedling growth. The soil should be worked to a fine condition by repeated ploughing and spading. Stones, glass pieces etc. should be removed and the soil should be free from clods. If the seedlings are grown in pots, boxes and other containers, for filling these potting medium should consist of two parts of garden soil, one part of leaf mould and one part of sand. For beds, well decomposed organic matter @ 20 kg or two baskets for 20 sq m should be thoroughly mixed with soil. To make the soil-free from soil borne diseases it should be disinfected. This can be done by formaldehyde, steam, chloropicrin, teargas and other such soil fumigants as well as copper oxide or carbonate etc. But under Indian conditions, burning of stubbles, dried leaves etc. is practised to sterilize the soil. Dr. Mehta (1959) recommended the method for sterilizing the soil. One part of formaline mixed with 100 parts of water should be applied at the rate of 15 litres per square metre of surface soil so as to saturate it up to a depth of 15 cm. After application the soil is covered with gunny bags or thick papers for a day or two so that fumes may penetrate the soil and kill all disease producing organisms. Following two kinds of beds are prepared for the nursery.

a) Raised beds

Such beds are prepared for growing Kharif season seedlings during rainy season. The bed should be not more than 100 cm wide and its length may be as much as desired. Generally, these are made 15 cm high from the ground level and provided with 30 cm wide drainage channel around them.

b) Flat beds

These beds are prepared for growing summer and winter season seedlings while preparation of soil, manuring are similar as for raised beds.

Sowing of seeds

The sowing of seeds may be done either in lines or they may be scattered but line sowing is preferred as it facilitates proper germination and weeding, hoeing and plant protection operations. The rows are usually kept about 5 to 10 cm apart and 1/2 to 1 cm deep. Seeds are placed 1 cm apart in these rows followed by covering with fine layer of leaf mould or soil.

Generally, the cool season vegetables are sown from August to December and February to June in the hills, while warm season vegetables are sown in plains and intermediate elevation from December to February. Soaking of seeds may be done, if required, to hasten germination. Very small seeds should be mixed with a little sand and covered lightly with sand and compost. After sowing the beds, water is sprinkled with a fine rose-can (Hazara) in such a way that soil is kept moist but it is not over-watered till the seedlings emerge out in the bed.

It is wise to prepare a small wooden/aluminium label for each variety just before the seed is sown. The kind of vegetable, the variety, source of seed and date of sowing should be written on it with a hard pencil.

Watering

Before germination, watering is done with a fine spray to avoid washing away of seedlings. Every morning and evening the beds should be sprinkled with fine rose-can to keep the soil moist but not wet. The beds are neither over-watered nor under-watered. The water should be soft not alkaline or saline. After germination, the seed beds should be flooded lightly.

Weeding and hoeing

Weeding should be done frequently to reduce the competition between seedlings and weeds. When the weeding is done, a small amount of hoeing is also done side by side if space permits.

Nutrient application

Sometimes due to unavailability of proper nutrients, there may be poor growth of seedlings or the seedlings may show yellowish colour. A nutrient solution of 0.2 per cent nitrogen should be given by spraying the plants. Similarly, phosphorus and potash be made available if required.

Control of insect pests and diseases

The most common disease which is caused by fungi is damping off. It can be prevented by avoiding high soil and air moisture, disinfecting flats, work benches, green houses and frames with a solution of one part of formalin in 50 parts of water; disinfecting the soil by heating to 82°C for an hour to destroy fungi in the soil. Treatment of seed with Captan, Agrosan G.N., Thiram, Ceresan (2 g per kg) is also effective in controlling damping off. It can be controlled by spraying the seedlings with 0.2% Dithane M-45 or Dithane Z-78.

The most common insect pests causing damage to the nursery are beetles, grass hoppers, white grubs, aphids and certain bugs. These can be controlled by spraying the seedlings with Metasystox (0.1%), Thiodan (0.2%) by following crop rotation, destruction of plant refuses harbouring the insect pests and disease organisms, and growing resistant varieties.

Young seedlings are often very tender and cannot resist drying winds, strong sunlight and frost. Protection from these may be secured by using windbreakers, covering with sirki or cloth etc.

Hardening

The term "Hardening" or "hardening off" is applied to any treatment given to seedling that results in firming or hardening of the tissues of the plant thus enabling them better to withstand unfavourable environmental conditions which may be frost, freeze, chilling, drying winds, reducing water supply or temperature. Following treatments are used for hardening the seedlings.

1. Exposure to low temperature

Seedlings are exposed for a week or more to low temperature and water is withheld or irrigation frequency is reduced. These treatments can be given alone or in combination. The exposures to low temperature, however, can only be followed in green houses.

A week before transplanting watering to the seedlings may be withheld. This is accomplished by diminishing the amount of water applied and exposing the seedlings to full sunshine. The seedlings then cease their rapid growth and become more hardy. These then become more resistant to transplanting shock.

2. Blocking

This practice is not common in India but in Japan it is followed. Blocks of soil and composts are made by butcher knife, the size of block may vary from 1 x 1 cm to 5 x 5 cm. This blocking is done 8 to 10 days before transplanting. In the mean time, roots re-branch and plants become adjusted so that they may be set in the field with a minimum of disturbance.

Transplanting

Transplanting is the process of lifting living plants from one place or environment and planting them in another in order to provide better conditions for their growth and development. Crops like beet, cabbage, cauliflower, lettuce, tomato, chard, broccoli, Brussel's sprouts and brinjal give better yield when transplanted. In the above mentioned vegetables, which have very small seeds and where it is not possible to distribute them evenly on the whole surface of the field, transplanting helps to grow them at desired places successfully. Moreover, it is not possible to provide identical conditions for germination over the whole field surface. It thus becomes necessary to raise the plants in smaller beds and provide them all the essential inputs in adequate amounts so that the seeds are able to germinate and grow in a better way.

Advantages

Following are the advantages of growing seedlings and transplanting them:

1. Better germination and environmental conditions for growth can be provided to a small nursery area while this is not possible when seeds are planted on a vast scattered area.

2. It helps in intensive cultivation by reducing the cropping period.

3. It also enables to get a crop ahead of the normal season and as a result helps to fetch good price in the market.

4. It is economical in those crops where seed cost is too high, which reduces cost of production.

5. It also develops comparatively restricted and well branched root system that makes a plant liable to re-establish in the garden or field without serious check in growth.

6. Better, healthy and stocky plants are obtained, which are responsible for

higher yields and profit.

Disadvantages

Following are the disadvantages of growing seedlings and then transplanting them.

1. It requires extra labour for nursery bed preparation and transplanting the seedlings. In those areas where labour cost is too high it increases the cost of production of these vegetable crops.

2. Almost all the plants are checked in growth by transplanting.

3. Crops like cabbage and tomatoes, if transplanted when the plants are large, usually result in delayed maturity and often in reduced yield.

4. Singh *et al* (1958) reported that crops like cauliflower were very sensitive to variations in age at transplanting since with delay in transplanting yield and quality were adversely affected and at the same time early transplanting resulted in higher mortality. Results of experiments by Cranefield (1899) and Royle (1913) indicate that transplanting is a disadvantage when pots or plant bands are used. Experimental evidences indicate that the transplanting itself generally does not increase the yield or hasten maturity, but that the increase in space and better conditions usually given, do have this effect.

Operations in transplanting

The field in which transplanting has to be done is prepared thoroughly by repeated harrowing and planking. In the well levelled field, holes are made with a large sized dibbler, trowel, spade or khurpi at the proper recommended distance. In large-scale operations, use of transplanting is just before, or just after a rain, specially if the weather is cloudy. Cool cloudy evening weather is desirable because evaporation and transpiration are lesser under these conditions than in hot dry weather. Irrigating the field a few days before transplanting helps in better establishment of the seedlings. After setting the seedlings irrigation is done in order to bring the soil in close contact with roots.

Precautions during transplanting

Due to carelessness there is some mortality during transplanting. In order to get maximum success in obtaining healthy and stocky plants, following precautions must be taken:

1. Seedlings should be hardened off before lifting from the nursery. By this way seedlings become hardy and establishment is better.

2. Nursery should be irrigated before lifting the seedlings in order to give less injury to the roots.

3. Seedlings should be covered and sprayed with water during transportation from nursery to permanent field.

4. The interval between lifting and transplanting the seedlings should be minimum to protect them from excessive drying.

5. Try to select cloudy day or evening hours for transplanting.

6. Plants should be set slightly deeper than they were in the seed bed. It is advantageous to set long, slender plants quite deep as it will save them from being whipped by wind. Care must be taken in setting celery and lettuce plants as they should not go deeper in soil below the crown.

7. Pressure should be exerted towards the plant, and downward so that soil is pressed around the entire root system to prevent air pockets near the roots.

8. Plants must be irrigated just after transplanting. It has been said: "Whether dry or wet, water when you set".

9. Gap filling must be done to replace dead seedlings within a week after transplanting.

10. Details about crop, variety etc. must be written on aluminium tags and put in the permanent field.

Factors affecting transplanting

1. Stage of growth

Transplanting may be performed when the plants are at optimum physiological age as determined by experiments, since younger plants establish sooner but mortality is higher. The older plants do not perform well.

2. Weather at planting

Cool and cloudy weather is best suited for transplanting. Evenings are better suited than mornings or afternoons. Plants usually establish themselves more quickly in freshly turned soil because it contains a relatively large amount of moisture.

3. Amount of foliage

Leaves are responsible for evaporation of water from the plant. If more leaves are permitted at the time of transplanting the success will be less as compared with lesser leaves.

4. Irrigation

If the plants are irrigated just after transplanting, the percentage of success will be more, while delay in irrigation will affect adversely.

Suggestions for better success

Various kinds of protectors have been used in temperate region to protect plants for increasing success. It is claimed that by the use of protectors maturity is hastened due to increase in temperature and protection against light frosts. Protectors also protect the plants from whipping by winds and heavy dashing rains.

In France, bell jars are used for forcing plants is the field while in U.S.A. various kinds of paper protectors are used. In some other countries, polythene paper, oiled and waxed paper of various kinds are used. In addition to these, various mixtures called "starter solution" may be used at the time of transplanting to stimulate rapid growth. Gray (1957) by spraying tomato and pepper plants at transplanting time with 10 ppm gibberellic acid prevented the checking of growth that normally follows transplanting of these crops. Further, gibberellic acid (50 ppm) spray applied at transplanting time increased the yield of tomato by 40 per cent. Similarly Singh, *et al* (1958) found that seedlings treated with starter solution gave better growth and yield of cauliflower heads.

Starter solutions are most commonly made by dissolving a high analysis, readily soluble fertiliser in water and are used where they are needed by establishing close contact between roots and soil. Solution mixtures such as 15-34-14, 23-21-17, 13-26-13 or 20-20-20 N,P,K dissolving four pounds in 50 gallons of water and applying about half pint per plant give good response.

6

Solanaceous Crops
POTATO

Botanical name	:	*Solanum tuberosum* L.
Family	:	Solanaceae
Synonyms	:	Aaloo, Urulakkizhangu, Urulagadda, Urulagadde, Batata, Urala kizangu

IMPORTANCE AND UTILITY

Potato is one of the most important food crop of the world. Potato has been cultivated in Nepal for a long time and it has become one of the most popular crop for vegetable purposes. Potatoes are an economical food since they provide a source of low cost energy to the human diet. They are rich source of starch and vitamins, especially C and B_1 and minerals. They contain 20.6 per cent carbohydrates, 2.1 per cent protein, 0.3 per cent fat, 1.1. per cent crude fibre and 0.9 per cent ash on fresh weight basis. They also contain good amount of essential amino acids like leucine, tryptophane and isoleucine etc.

Potatoes are used for several industrial purposes such as production of starch and alcohol. Its starch (farina) is used in laundries and for sizing yarn in textile mills. Potatoes are also used for the production of dextrin and glucose. As a food product itself, these are converted into dried products such as 'potato chips', 'sliced' or 'shredded' potatoes.

ORIGIN AND HISTORY

The probable centre of origin of potato is in South America in the Central Andean region. Evidences indicate that potatoes were cultivated for centuries by South American Indians and the tubers were used as a common article of food. The Spaniards, during invasion, found this economic plant worthy of introduction into Europe. The Spaniards brought the potato from Peru to Spain in 1565. They were probably brought to England about 1586 by Sir Francis Drake. Following its introduction into European agriculture, the potato became an important food crop of Italy, France and Ireland. During the famine years, the potato crop became a valuable food crop in Ireland. It was introduced to India from Europe in the beginning of the seventeenth century, probably by the Portuguese, who were the first to open trade routes to the East.

CLASSIFICATION

The potato belongs to the genus *Solanum*, the family of *Solanaceae*. The commercial cultivated potato belongs to the species *Solanum tuberosum*. In addition to *S. tuberosum*, seven other cultivated species and 154 wild species of potato are important. The commercial potato generally belongs to two species.

1. *Solanum andigenum* : Plants have thin and long stem, small and narrow leaflets. Flowers are produced more profusely. It has long stolons and mostly coloured deep-eyed tubers. The tuberization takes place only under short-day conditions.

2. *Solanum tuberosum* : Plants have shorter and thicker stem, larger and wider leaflets. The tubers are generally white and oval. This species is suitable for long as well as short day conditions in respect of tuberization.

In addition to above two species, *S. demissum* and *S. stenotonum* are also of some importance as they are resistant to some forms of virus and diseases. Due to hybridization programme between many species the present varieties are only being put under *Solanum tuberosum*.

BOTANY

It is perennial but as a crop it is treated as an annual. It is vegetatively propagated by means of tubers. The tuber is an enlarged underground modified stem produced at the end of a stolon. They possess "eyes" which contain multiple buds. The tubers also contain lenticels (respiratory structures) like stems of other plants.

The upper part of the sprout develops into the aerial stem. The aerial stems are round or angular, pubescent or glabrous, green or purplish. The stem is of a branching type. It is erect when young, and spreads as the plant grows. In some varieties the sprouts are hollow whereas in others they are solid.

The leaves of the potato are alternate and compound (occasionally bi-compound). The leaves arise along the stem in a spiral arrangement, the fourth being above the first. There are 3 to 4 pairs of leaflets arising in succession along the rachis. The leaflets are more or less opposite. There is a large terminal odd leaflet which may unite with one to three leaflets.

The root of potato is adventitious, arising from the base of a sprout. The root growth is usually restricted to a depth of about 20-25 cm from soil surface. In rich soils, roots of some varieties may reach up to a depth of 90-100 cm.

The flowers of the potato plant are in terminal clusters. Each flower normally has five stamens, two-celled pistil, five sepals and five petals united for about half their length. Most varieties of potato bear infertile pollens and hence fruits or berries are not generally formed. In some of the varieties fruits or berries are formed.

CLIMATIC REQUIREMENTS

Potato is a cool season crop. It thrives best in cool regions where there is sufficient moisture and fertile soil. Satisfactory tuber growth occurs if soil temperatures are between 17-19°C. Higher soil temperatures adversely affect the tuber development. Tuber development virtually stops if temperatures rise above 30°C. At higher temperatures, the respiration rate increases, and the carbohydrates produced by photosynthesis are consumed rather than stored in the tuber. High temperatures at any part of the growing period affect the size of the leaflets, thereby reducing the tuber formation. In the growth period the temperature may be higher but during tuberization phase the temperature should be lower. This situation prevails in plains of India, causing very good yields. Some potato varieties are qualitative short-day whereas others quantitative short-day in respect of tuberization. Qualitative short-day varieties tuberize only under short-day conditions. The examples are Kufri Sindhuri, Phulwa etc. These are suitable for growing under autumn-winter period of plains of India. Under quantitative short-day group, the varieties which tuberize better under short-days but produce substantially good yields under long days are included. The examples are Kufri Chandramukhi and Kufri Jyoti.

SOIL

Potatoes can be produced on a wide range of soils, ranging from sandy loam, silt loam to loam. Soils for potato should be friable, well aerated, fairly deep and well supplied with organic matter. Well drained sandy loam and medium loam soils, rich in humus are most suitable for potato. Soil structure and texture has a marked effect on the quality of the tuber. Light soils are preferred because they tend to promote more uniform soil temperatures and make harvesting of the crop easier. Alkaline or saline soils are not suitable for potato cultivation. They are well suited to acidic soils (pH 5.0 to 6.5) as acidic conditions tend to limit scab disease.

VARIETIES

A large number of high yielding varieties of potato suited to different agro-climatic conditions have been evolved and released for cultivation on farmers' fields. The characteristics of some of the important and high yielding varieties are given below:

EARLY MATURING GROUP

Kufri Chandramukhi: This is an early maturing variety which takes 80-90 days to mature in the plains. The plants are medium tall, vigorous with lighter purple flowers. Tubers are attractive, white, oval with fleet eyes. The flesh of tuber is dull white. It has wide adaptability and can be grown in the Indo-Gangetic plains, Madhya Pradesh and the plateau region of Maharashtra. It fits very well in intensive crop rotations. The average yield is about 250-300 quintals per hectare in plains. The plants as well as tubers of this variety are highly susceptible to late blight. Thus, either this should be grown in blight-free period or sprays of fungicide should be given to protect the crop from late blight.

Kufri Bahar: This variety matures in 90-100 days. Its tubers are large, white, oval and attractive. It is not good for long distance transport purposes. It gives more yield than Kufri Chandramukhi due to its longer duration (100 days). This variety is suitable for growing in plains of northern India. However, its reaction to late blight disease is similar to Kufri Chandramukhi.

Kufri Lovkar: The plants are medium tall, vigorous, having white flowers. It is an early maturing (75-90 days) photoinsensitive variety having large, round white tubers with medium deep eyes. The flesh of tuber is white. It has slow degeneration rate. It is not suitable for hills because of heavy rotting of tubers. In plains, it gives an average yield of 250 quintals per hectare. This variety is suitable for plains of northern India as a spring crop and in tropical plateau regions both as Rabi and Kharif crops.

Kufri Alankar: It is an extra-short duration variety with tall, erect and vigorous plants with white flowers. Tubers are large, oval and white with shallow eyes. Flesh is white with floury texture on cooking. Its keeping quality is poor and, therefore, does not store well in cold storage. The maturity period in plains and hills is 75 and 130 days, respectively. It is an ideal variety for multiple cropping in plains of northern India. It yields about 200-250 quintals per hectare under average conditions in plains. This variety is more susceptible to early blight.

Kufri Jyoti: It is a short duration variety producing oval, white and shallow eyed tubers. It has all the qualities of Kufri Chandramukhi but its tubers are susceptible to cracking under long crop duration of plains. It is, therefore, advisable to harvest it within 80 days of planting in plains. It is recommended for cultivation in Himachal Pradesh, Kumaon hills of Uttaranchal, Assam and Nilgiri Hills. In the plains, it yields, on an average, 200-250 quintals whereas on hills 80-120 quintals/hectare.

MID DURATION GROUP

Kufri Badshah: It is a suitable variety for plains of India. The harvesting can start from 80 days as in case of Kufri Chandramukhi. At this time, its yield potential will be more than Kufri Chandramukhi. However, if harvesting is delayed up to 110 to 120 days, it will yield similar to Kufri Sinduri. This variety possesses resistance to late blight and frost. Its tubers are white and oval.

Kufri Sheetman: It takes about 100 to 110 days to mature in the plains. This variety possesses resistance to frost. Its tubers are oval, medium to large sized with shallow eyes. Its flesh is white and texture floury on cooking. This variety is suitable for those areas of northern India where frost is a common occurrence. However, it shows susceptibility to late blight. It yields about 250 quintals/hectare.

Kufri Lalima: This variety has been released to replace Kufri Sinduri. It is high yielding with 100 to 110 days' duration. The tubers are red, round and possess medium deep eyes. It is, however, susceptible to late blight.

Kufri Ashok: It was released in 1995. The plants are long in height. The crop matures 70-80 days after planting. This variety has features close to Kufri Chandramukhi. Tubers are large, oval type, white, smooth, having good eyes. This variety is recommended for the plains of the Ganga in U.P., Bihar and West Bengal.

Kufri Jawahar: It was released in 1997 for Plateau regions. The plant height is small. The crop matures about 80 days after planting. The size of tuber is medium, round oval type having sharp eyes, and is creamy white in colour. It is moderately tolerant against blight.

Kufri Satalaj: It is recommended for Punjab, Haryana, U.P., Rajasthan, Bihar and plains of M.P. It was released in 1997. The features are very close to Kufri Badshah and Kufri Bahar. The tubers are large, oval type, white, smooth and sharp eyed. It is very easy in cooking.

Kufri Chipsauna-1: The plant height of this variety is medium and the plant is vigorous. This variety matures in 80-90 days after planting. It is resistant against blight. This is recommended for plains of the Ganga. It is also good for making chips.

Kufri Chipsauna-2.: The plant height of this variety is medium and the plants vigorous. The crop is ready for harvest after 90-95 days of planting. Tubers are medium in size, white in colour and sharp eyed. This variety is affected by blight and is best for chips making.

Kufri Giriraj (S.M./85-45): It is found best for hills. It is resistant against blight. The yield of this variety was found to be better than Kufri Jyoti at Ranichauri, Shillong, Kufri and Utakmand. The average yield of this variety is 200-250 quintals per hectare.

Kufri Pukhraj (J.IX/C-160):- The height of this variety is medium in length, straight and vigorous. The crop is ready for harvesting about 80-90 days after planting. Tuber of this crop are medium in size, oval round, white in colour and smooth.

Kufri Anand (SS.717): The height of this variety is medium, straight and vigorous. The crop is ready for harvesting about 90-95 days after planting. Tubers are medium in size, white in colour and smooth. It is resistant against blight and is good for plains of the country.

Kufri Thanamalai (Shankar D/79-56):- This variety was released by Variety Releasing Committee of Tamil Nadu for Tamil Nadu. It is best for hills of the state of Tamil Nadu.

LATE DURATION GROUP

Kufri Dewa: It is a long duration (120-125 days) variety. It produces medium sized, oval to round shaped tubers. The skin is white except near eyes, where it is pink. The eyes are pinkish red and medium deep. The flesh is pale yellow. It combines a useful degree of frost tolerance with good keeping quality at room temperature as well as in cold storage. It is less susceptible to late blight as compared to Kufri Chandramukhi. In plains, it yields 300-400 quintals/hectare. It is suitable only for plains of India.

Kufri Sinduri: It is a late maturing (120-140 days) variety with round, light red, medium sized tubers with deep eyes. The plants are tall, erect, vigorous, medium compact with blue purple and abundant flowers. The flesh is pale yellow and texture is waxy. This variety shows wider adaptability and is suitable for cultivation as main crop in the plains of northern India. It has ability to yield about 300-350 quintals/hectare under average conditions of fertility.

FIELD PREPARATION

A well pulverised seed bed is required for good tuberization of potato crop. Where potato is taken as a Rabi crop, soon after the harvest of the Kharif crop, field should be prepared well. Enough moisture is essential at the time of planting otherwise pre-planting irrigation is necessary.

SEED AND SOWING

Selection of Seed

Select healthy and pure seeds of high yielding varieties. The tubers showing any surface-borne disease like scab, wart, nematode infection or effect of rots should be sorted out. It is advisable to use certified seeds for good yields. However, farmers can produce seed potatoes themselves provided all precautions needed for seed production are taken.

Seed Treatment

For planting the crop, the seed potatoes, after removing from the cold storage, be kept in a cool and shady place for one to two weeks to allow the emergence of sprouts. The sprouted tubers should be used as planting material. Both the whole and cut tubers should be treated with 0.25% Aretan/ Tafasan (6% mercury) solution for atleast two minutes against black scurf disease and rotting of seed potatoes. Dipping of cut seed tubers in 0.5% Dithane M-45 for ten minutes is also effective in avoiding rotting in early planting. In case plain grown seed potatoes are required for planting in March in hills, treatment of potatoes with 1 ppm Gibberellic acid is required. It involves washing of potatoes, dipping in 1 ppm Gibberellic acid solution for one hour, drying in shade and then storage in gunny bags for 3 to 4 weeks. After these steps, seed potatoes of varieties suitable for hills can be shifted to hills for planting.

PLANTING TIME

To secure high yield, it is essential to plant the potatoes at optimum time. The best time of planting is when the maximum and minimum temperatures are from 30°C to 32°C and 18°C to 20°C, respectively. Following time schedule should be followed for obtaining good yield.

i.   Early crop - 25th September to 10th October

ii. Main crop - 15th October to 25th October.

iii. Hills - February for valleys and March-April for higher altitudes.

In Deccan plateau area (Maharashtra, Andhra Pradesh and Karnataka) potatoes are grown both during Rabi (October-November) and Kharif (June-July). In Nilgiri, potatoes are planted in January, April and October.

SEED SIZE, SEED RATE AND SPACING

Tubers having 30 to 50 g weight are the most economical to use. Whole tubers should be planted for early crop. This will avoid rotting of tubers. Due to high temperature and moisture in soil, there is always more rotting of cut tubers in early plantings. Large seeds can be effectively used by increasing plant to plant spacing and smaller tubers by decreasing it. Distance between rows should be 55-60 cm and between plants 20-25 cm. About 20-25 quintals of seeds are sufficient for planting one hectare area.

For main crop, cut tubers can be planted. While cutting the tubers, care should be taken that each piece has 2-3 eyes and weighs at least 25 g. If any diseased tuber is observed, it should be discarded. For planting one hectare about 15-20 quintals of seed potatoes are required. A row to row distance of 55 to 60 cm and plant to plant distance of 15 to 20 cm should be maintained in main crop.

METHODS OF PLANTING

There are three methods of planting in India.

a.   **Planting potatoes on ridges:** After preparation of field, ridges are made at a distance of 55-60 cm with the help of spade. Planting of potato is done on the ridges with the help of '*khurpl*'.

b.   **Flat method:** Planting of potato is done of flat surface in shallow furrows. Ridges are made after emergence of shoots when plants attain 10-12 cm height. This method is suitable for light soils. Later on, 2-3 earthings are done to make the ridges thick.

c.   **Planting potatoes on flat surface followed by ridges:** In this method the field is prepared and then shallow furrows are opened on the flat surface. Potatoes are planted in furrows and immediately after planting, small ridges are made. Later on these ridges are made thicker by earthing up of the side soil.

MANURES AND FERTILISERS

Potato crop is a heavy feeder and hence needs heavy doses of fertilisers for its good growth and yield. A good crop of potato yielding about 350 quintals removes from the soil 170-180 kg nitrogen, 75 kg phosphorus and 250 kg potash. In most of our soils potash is available in sufficient amount. Phosphorus is also available in some of the soils. Therefore, application of phosphorus and potash should be based on soil test.

Nitrogen: It is the most important nutrient affecting potato production. The soil, depending upon its initial fertility, provides 20 to 60 kg nitrogen per hectare. Response of nitrogen is invariably quite high. In soils of good fertility, which are loamy in nature, the requirement of nitrogen will be about 100-120 kg per hectare. In light sandy soils with low organic matter, the requirement is high (120-200 kg/ha). Higher doses, however, may not be desirable, since these tend to delay tuber initiation and maturity of the crop. The optimum doses of nitrogen are affected by soil fertility status, agro-climatic conditions, variety, length of growing season and ultimately the yield of the crop.

Phosphorus: The phosphatic fertiliser requirements are high in acidic soils of hills because of their phosphate fixing capacity. High phosphate responses are also found in light textured alluvial soils. Application of phosphate at the rate of 80 to 150 kg per hectare is recommended in various types of soils, depending upon their available phosphorus status and their phosphate fixing capacity. In most parts of plains response has been observed up to 80 kg P_2O_5 per hectare, whereas in hills the suitable dose is about 100 kg/ha.

Potassium: Potassium requirement of potato crop is quite high. Application of potassium alongwith nitrogen and phosphorus is necessary for potato crop, especially in light textured soils which are basically low in this nutrient. The application of potassium up to 150 kg per hectare is recommended, depending upon the potassium supplying capacity of the soil and the potato variety. In plains, the dose varies from 60 to 80 kg/ha whereas in hills from 80 to 100 kg/ha. Micro-nutrients may be needed in some soils and the same may be applied as foliar spray, if needed. Such cases need specific recommendations.

The application of organic manures, particularly farm yard manure or compost, is recommended for potato crop. Organic manures not only supply nutrients to the crop but also improve physical conditions of soils, such as soil texture and its water retention capacity. If available, apply 20-30 tonnes of well-rotten farm yard manure about two weeks before planting and properly mix in soil. In case farm yard manure is applied, two-thirds of recommended doses of chemical fertilisers should be given. Recommended doses of nitrogen, phosphorus and potash per hectare are given below in Table 1.

Apply three-fourths of nitrogen and full doses of phosphorus and potash at the time of planting. The remaining one-fourth quantity of nitrogen should be given as top dressing after 35-40 days of planting when earthing is done.

WATER MANAGEMENT

Potato crop is very much responsive to good water management. Removal of excess water is essential. In no case water should reach more than 2/3rd height of the ridges. Length of the ridges should depend upon the soil type, slope and source of water. It may vary from 10 to 200 metres. The objective is to supply uniform water throughout the plot. As a rule, soils must be kept always moist but hardening or too wet conditions of soil should not be allowed. Irrigation may be moderate to heavy but water should not be allowed to reach more than 2/3rd height of the ridges. The frequency of irrigation also varies depending upon the water table and soil type. In medium to heavy soils, 3 to 4 irrigations shall be sufficient. On the other hand, in sandy soils having low water table, even 8-12 irrigations may be necessary. The available moisture in the soil should be about 75%.

EARTHING

Proper development of tubers depends upon aeration, moisture availability and proper soil temperature. Therefore, proper earthing up is necessary. Earthing should be done when the plants are 15 to 22 cm tall. Generally, earthing is done at the time of top dressing of nitrogenous fertilisers. The ridges should be broad, loose and high enough to cover up tubers. If necessary, a second earthing may be done after two weeks of the first one. A mould board plough or a ridger may be used for earthing up in large area.

Table 1. Recommended doses of nitrogen, phosphorus and potash per hectare for different potato growing regions

Regions	Doses of nutrients kg/ha		
	Nitrogen	Phosphorus (P_2O_5)	Potash (P_2O)
A. Plains			
North-eastern	100-120	60-80	100-120
North-central	100-120	60-80	100-120
North-western	80-120	80-100	80-100
Southern	80-100	80-100	100-120
B. Hills	80-110	100-120	80-100

WEED CONTROL

Weed control in potato crop is normally done by manual labour. However, in large acreage this operation sometimes may not be completed in time due to shortage of man power. Under such circumstances, weedicides may be used. In case of perennial weeds like cyperus rotundus (motha) or cynadon dactylon (doob), Gramaxone may be sprayed at the rate of 2.5 litres in 1000 litres of water per hectare. Spraying should be done at a stage when potato plants are emerging to the extent of only 5-10 per cent and weeds have germinated on the ridges. This is a contact herbicide and, therefore, should not be sprayed on well-grown potato plants. In fields where perennial weeds are not a problem, Simazine at the rate of 0.5 to 1.0 kg per hectare or Sencar 1 kg per hectare may be sprayed over the ridges just after planting of potatoes. For its effectiveness, there should be optimum moisture in the soil. Where wheat crop is to be grown after potato its application should be done cautiously and at no place excessive quantity of herbicide should be used. Lasso may also be used at the rate of 4 litres per hectare as pre-emergence spray ie., after planting of potatoes but before emergence of weeds and potatoes.

DISEASES AND THEIR CONTROL

Potato crop suffers from different pathological maladies resulting in considerable loss in yield. Symptoms of important diseases and their suitable control measures are given below.

Late blight

This disease is caused by a fungus called *Phytophthora infestans*. The disease may attack almost any time after the crop has put up fairly good foliage. Initially, the lower leaves are infected. They show water-soaked lesions, especially towards margins. The spots enlarge if proper humidity and temperature are available. In humid atmosphere, the growth of the fungus can be seen on lower side of these spots as whitish cottony growth. The spots turn black as the affected leaves start rotting. Similar symptoms may be observed on stems also. Decaying leaves often emit an offensive odour. The tubers under the ground also decay before harvest. On tubers, greenish sunken areas may be seen.

Control Measures

❖ Use potato tubers for seed from disease–free areas to ensure that the pathogen is not carried through seed tuber.

❖ The infected plant material in the field should be properly destroyed.

❖ Grow resistant varieties like Kufri Navtal.

❖ Fungicidal sprays can be effective, if given properly and timely. Sprays should start a few days before the anticipated time of occurrence of the disease or on the appearance of initial symptoms. Cool humid atmosphere favours the disease and prevalence of such weather can be an indication of disease in a short time ahead. Spraying should be done with Dithane M-45 or Dithane Z-78 (2.5 kg/1000 litres of water per hectare). Spraying should be repeated at 10-12 days' interval.

Early blight

This disease is caused by a fungus called *Alternaria solani*. Early blight is more common than late blight and can occur anywhere at any period. The spots of this disease on the leaves are brown to black with concentric rings. Their number is numerous and they are scattered all over the leaves. Heavily infected leaves fall off after drying. Spots also appear on stems.

Control Measures

❖ Crop debris should invariably be destroyed by burning after harvest.

❖ Sprays recommended in case of late blight also serve to control this disease.

Black scurf

This disease is caused by a fungus called *Rhizoctonia solani.* This disease is of common occurrence both in the hills and plains. There are two phases of the disease. In stem canker phase, the sprouts are killed before they emerge and this delays the germination resulting in loss of yield. The cankers may cause wilting of the plants also. The black scurf phase is recognised by appearance of black crust on the tubers which reduces their acceptability with the consumers.

Control Measures

❖ Plant only healthy tubers.

❖ The seed tubers should be dipped in 0.5% suspension of Aretan or Agallol for ten minutes.

❖ Soil can be treated with Brassicol at the rate of 20-30 kg per hectare. Combination of seed and soil treatment gives best control of the disease.

Bacterial wilt and brown rot

This disease is caused by bacterium *Pseudomonas solanacearum.* This dreaded disease of potato is common in mid hills, plateau region and West Bengal. The most common symptom of the disease is sudden wilting of the plant. Affected plants show droopy appearance and the branches gradually turn bronze and die. There is unusual browning of vascular bundles in the stem and tubers show a brown ring inside. Eyes of tubers are also blackened.

Control Measures

❖ Certified seed free from brown rot disease should be planted.

❖ In case cut potato tubers are being used, they should be kept at 12°C for four days so that the cut surface hardens. The tubers can also be treated with the solution of Aretan, Agallol.

❖ The crop debris should be collected and burnt.

Wart disease

This disease is caused by a fungus *Synchutrium endobioticum.* This disease is found in Darjeeling hills of West Bengal and its surrounding areas. The disease in recognised by appearance of tumours or warts on tubers, stems and stolons of the potato plant. Sometimes the whole tuber is converted into a distorted mass.

Control Measures

❖   Wart-affected tubers should not be planted.

❖   Grow wart immune varieties.

Mosaic

There are different types of mosaic diseases that attack potato. The leaves show green and dark green mosaic pattern on leaves. There may be faint yellowing in patches on the leaves. The plants remain stunted and sick. Size and number of tubers is reduced. In some mosaic diseases, the leaves may show necrosis of tissues along the vein. Diseased, small-sized tubers are main source of disease in the field. Disease is spread in the field by insects which carry the virus from sick plant to healthy one.

Control Measures

❖   Seed tubers should be healthy and certified. Do not plant very small-sized tubers since they are more likely to be from diseased plants.

❖   Inspect the field regularly and destroy the plants showing initial symptoms.

❖   Spray the crop with Metasystox or Rogor at the rate of 600-700 ml dissolved in 500-600 litres of water per hectare at 10-15 days interval to check the insects that spread this disease.

Leaf roll

This disease is very common in plains. Leaves show upward rolling of the margins progressing towards the midrib until the entire lamina is involved. The leaves assume a rigid, leathery texture having a characteristic rattle when brushed with hand. The number of tubers produced per plant and their size is greatly reduced.

Control Measures

The control measures recommended for mosaic disease are effective for leaf roll disease also.

INSECT PESTS AND THEIR CONTROL

Potato crop is attacked by a number of insect pests which either reduce the yield or spoil the quality to a great extent. The major pests, their nature of damage and measures to control them are given below.

Epilachan beetle

The grubs and adults both are the damaging stages for this insect. It is one of the serious pest of potato crop. They feed on the foliage. The grubs scrap away the chlorophyll from the leaves leaving only veins. The grubs or larvae of this beetle are very sluggish and move very slowly while feeding on leaves. They are yellowish in colour with erect spines on their body. A severe infestation may cause loss up to 70 per cent in yield.

Control Measures

❖ Spraying with 0.2% Sevin 50 WP at the rate of 1000 litres of water has been found quite effective.

❖ Dusting of 10% Sevin dust at the rate of 30 kg per hectare may also control the pest.

Cutworms

The damage is caused by the caterpillars by cutting off the growing potato plants. They may cut the twigs, leaves or entire potato plant above the soil surface. They do more harm by cutting the plants than by actual feeding. The full grown caterpillars are about 5 cm long. During day time they remain hidden in the soil and in the night damage the crop. In the later stage, they also feed on the tubers and thus reduce their market value.

Control Measures

❖ Flooding of field reduces the activity of the caterpillars.

❖ Use of Temik 10 G at the rate of 8-10 kg per hectare at the time of sowing has been found effective in controlling this insect.

❖ Use of carbafuran 3 G at the rate of 30 kg per hectare at the time of sowing has also been found very effective.

Aphids

These are small insects, either pale yellow or dark in colour. Both nymphs and adult damage the plant by sucking the cell sap from the leaves, tender shoots and stem. The leaves of attacked plants become yellowish and they lose vitality. Besides this, aphids secrete honey dew on the leaves on which black mould develops. This interferes in the photosynthesis. The winged aphids also transmit serious viral diseases in this crop.

Control Measures

❖ Spray Metasystox 25 EC or Rogor 30 EC at the rate of 600 ml in 1000 litres of water per hectare.

Leaf hoppers

The nymphs and adults of these insects have piercing and sucking type of mouth parts. They suck the cell sap due to which the leaves become yellowish and plants lose their vitality. Besides the direct loss due to their feeding, leaf hoppers transmit viral diseases in potato which reduce the yield of the crop.

Control Measures

❖ Application of Carbafuran 3G, Temik 10G or Thimet 10G at the time of sowing controls the leaf hoppers alongwith other pests.

White grub

The damage is done mainly by the grubs which remain in the soil. They damage the plant by feeding on the underground portion viz., roots, stems and tubers. The grub, in the early stage, feed on the roots with the result that the plants dry up. Later on, when tubers are developed, the grubs cut holes in the tubers. The market value of such tubers is very much reduced.

Control Measures

❖ Apply Heptachlor 5% dust or Aldrin 5% dust at the rate of 45-60 kg per hectare in soil before sowing and mix it properly.

❖ Use carbofuran 3G or Thimet 10G at the rate of 30 kg or Temik 10G at the rate of 15 kg per hectare at the time of sowing.

Potato tuber moth

This is mainly a pest of stored potato but it causes damage in the standing crop also. The caterpillars mine the leaves causing patches in them. The damage done by the caterpillars to potato in stores is much more serious. The caterpillars feed inside the pulp. The tunnels made by the caterpillars are filled with excreta. Such tubers generally become unfit for human consumption and seed purposes.

Control Measures

❖ Only healthy potatoes should be kept in the store.

❖ Potatoes should be stored in cold stores. In case they are to be kept in ordinary stores, a layer of sand about 2.5 to 5 cm thick should be spread below and above the heap of potato.

❖ Seed potato should be protected by spraying 5% BHC dust or 1% malathion on and around the heap.

HARVESTING

The crop should be harvested when haulms start yellowing and falling on the ground. At this stage, haulms should be removed at ground level. The crop should be harvested about 15 days after cutting the haulms. Digging is done with spades or khurpi in small fields. Suitable tractor–operated potato diggers are available now for digging the potatoes in big fields. There should be optimum moisture in the soil at the time of harvest. The clods hinder the efficient functioning of potato-digger. After digging the tubers may be allowed to dry on the ground for some time in shady place.

YIELD

With recommended package of practices, an yield of 300 to 400 quintals per hectare can be obtained. However, in hills, except lower valleys, the yield do not go beyond 200 quintals per hectare. In plains, under good management, an yield of 4 q/day can be easily obtained. However, to get yields higher than this much more efforts have to be made.

SEED PRODUCTION

With the help of "seed plot technique" a healthy seed crop may be raised as below:

i) Whole virus-free tubers treated with Aretan 0.25% solution should be planted from 10th October to 20th October.

ii) Sow the tuber at distance of 60 cm from row to row and 15-20 cm within the row.

iii) Apply lower dose of nitrogen i.e. 80-100 kg/ha to avoid excessive growth.

iv) The crop should be carefully examined at least thrice and all diseased plants removed and burnt.

v) Towards mid December, when the crop has tuberised well, restrict irrigations and later withhold it completely so that haulms dry up and consequently escape aphid build-up towards mid-January. Remove tops between 10th and 15th January.

vi) Leave the tuber under ground till the end of January so that they mature and the skin hardens.

vii) Take all precautions against blight and aphids.

TOMATO

Botanical name	-	*Lycopersicon esculentum* Mill
Family	-	Solanaceae
Synonymous	-	Tamatar, Vilayati baingan, Bilayati begun, Bapatala ghant, Ramamulaka, Seema Vankaya, Tambuta, Tabati, Welwangi, Takkali, Bilahi, Bhedra, Chhapperbhende, Tamattar.

Importance and Utility

In Nepal, tomato has become the most popular vegetable specially during last six decades. The crop is grown almost all round the year in one part or the other in the country and its fruits are available in the market all round the year. The fruit cost varies from Rs. 2.00 to Rs. 15.00 per kg depending upon the availability of the fruit. It is used in many ways such as cooked, salad, soup, preserves, pickles, ketchups, sauces and many other products and is served baked, fried and as a sauce on various foods. According to Chatfield (1949 and 1954) 100 g edible portion of tomato contains 94.1 g water, 1.0 g protein, 0.3 g fat, 4.0 g carbohydrates, 0.6 g fibre, Vitamin A 1100 I.U., Vitamin B 0.20 mg, nicotinic acid 0.6 mg, pantotheric acid 0.31 mg, Vitamin C 23 mg, Vitamin E 0.27 mg, Biotin 0.004 mg, mallic acid 150 mg, citric acid 390 mg, oxalic acid 3.5 mg, sodium 3 mg, potassium 268 mg, copper 0.10 mg, magnesium 11 mg, iron 0.6 mg, copper 0.10 mg, manganese 0.19 mg, phosphorus 27 mg, sulphur 11 mg, chlorine 51 mg. In Europe and America, its juice is used as substitute for orange juice for children fed on pasturized milk. It stimulates *tropid liver* and is very useful in chronic dyspepsia. Its juice contains citric acid, mallic acid and oxalate of potash. Therefore, it is not suited to those suffering from higher uric acid problems. It is very useful in bronchitis and asthma. According to Nadkarni (1927) it has good medical value, the pulp and juice of the fruit are digestible and act as mild aperient, a promotor of gastric secretion and a blood purifier. It is considered to be an intestinal antiseptic as it has a cleaning effect in the enteric portion of the alimentary canal. It is very clear that it has a very high nutritive value, therefore, it is sometimes called as 'poor man's orange'.

Origin and History

Tomato is said to be the native of Tropical America (Thompson and Kelly, 1957), its original home being probably in Peru or Mexico. Till 1695, the word tomato was not used and is said to be derived from the Aztec "Xitomate" or "Xitotomate". It is supposed to have been eaten by the wild tribes of Mexico. From Tropical America it spread to other parts of the world in the 16th century. The earliest available literature on tomato was made by Mattiolus in Italy in 1544.

Botany

It is a herbaceous annual plant with bisexual flowers. The fruit is true berry. Adventitious roots are produced from the stem if plants are planted deep at transplanting. A number of lateral branches develop from the axil of the leaves on main stem resulting in a bushy plant. Numerous hairs and oil glands are found on the stem and are ruptured when the plant is handled. Leaves are alternate and compound. On the basis of growth habit, the tomato plants have been divided into two indeterminate and determinate types. In case of indeterminate type, the varieties terminate in the vegetative bud. Generally, the flowers are borne at every third internode separated by three leaves (Dhesi and Nandpuri, 1968). In case of determinate, the varieties terminate in the flower bud. They generally have a flower cluster at every internode. Such varieties do not have adequate foliage for fruiting. The flowers are borne in clusters or internode. The anthesis starts at 6 A.M. with maximum flowers opening between 7 to 8 A.M. The dehiscence peak is between 9 to 11 A.M. Pollen grains remain viable for long period. Stigma become receptive 16 hours before anthesis and remain the same for 2 to 3 days after anthesis. The fertilization and fruit formation are maximum when pollination takes place at anthesis time. Visible sign of fruit set can be observed after about 96 hours of pollination. Maximum pollen germination and fruit setting are reported at 21°C to 23°C.

Climatic requirements

It is a moderate season crop and does not tolerate frost. High temperatures followed by low humidity and dry winds increase flower drop and there is no fruit set (Smith, 1932). Both high and low temperatures interfere with fruit setting. The best pollen grain germination takes place at 21°C to 23°C and very poor at 10°C and at 38°C. It cannot be grown successfully in high rainfall areas. The best seed germination takes place at 18°C to 30°C but at 14°C the seeds can be germinated. The fruit develops good colour and better quality when weather is warm and sunny.

Soil and its preparation

Tomato can be grown on a variety of soils ranging from sandy loam to heavy clay but better yield is obtained in a well-drained heavy loam soil free from hard layer and having better irrigation facilities. The best soil pH is 6.0 to 7.0 (Choudhury, 1967). If the soils are acidic, liming is advocated. In general, the crop does well on loams, silt loams and clay loams. Light soils are good for an early crop, while clay loam and silt loam soils are well suited for heavy yields. The soil should be prepared well by repeated harrowing and planking. During its preparation the crop resides of previous crop should be collected and burnt. The field should be well levelled and divided into different beds. Two to three weeks before planting, 250 to 300 quintals of farmyard manure per hectare should be mixed in the soil thoroughly.

Varieties

Sioux: It is a high yielding American introduced variety with indeterminate growth habit. The fruits, when immature, are yellowish green, medium large and ripen to a uniform red colour. It is good for spring-summer crop. It is good for salad purposes also.

Pant T-1: It is a high yield culture, introduced from California. It has an intermediate growth habit. The fruits are large, smooth and fleshy. It does well both in winter and summer. It is good for salad and resistant to wilt. It is unreleased culture.

Pant T-2: It is a semi-determinate culture introduced from California. The fruits are pear shaped, thick skinned having few seeds, hence it can withstand long transportation stresses. It is specially suited for summer cultivation. It is an unreleased promising culture.

AC 142: This is an extra early culture introduced from California. The fruits can be harvested first time after 50-60 days of transplanting in early winter and spring-summer. The plants are determinate in growth habit, fruits are small, nippled and are borne in clusters. The pedicel is jointed and free-necked, which makes the variety most suitable for mechanical harvesting. The variety is a good general combiner for earliness and clustered fruit habit.

Pusa Ruby: It was evolved at I.A.R.I., New Delhi from a cross between' Sioux' and 'Improved Meeruti'. The fruits are medium sized, developing deep red colour and it is good for salad. This variety is suitable for autumn-winter crop specially in the North Indian plains. The plants are indeterminate in habit.

Pusa Early Dwarf: It is an early variety selected at I.A.R.I., New Delhi from a cross between 'Improved Meeruti' and 'Red Cloud'. The fruits are medium-large and of uniform colour. It does well in both the seasons.

Pusa Red Plum: It was evolved at I.A.R.I., New Delhi from a cross of a cultivated tomato with a wild *Lycopersicon pimpinellifolium*. It is an early variety and good for kitchen gardens. The fruits are small, borne in clusters with red colour and are rich in vitamin C and sugar. Due to its small fruiting habit a good price in the market is not possible.

Co 3: It is recommended by the Agriculture Department of Tamil Nadu. The fruits are round and smooth, pale green at unripe stage while red when fully ripe. The average fruit weight is about 125 g and fruits are borne in cluster of 6 to 8 in numbers. The plants are dwarf of semi-spreading habit with dark green foliage.

Keck-Ruth Ageti: It is released by the Punjab Agricultural University, Ludhiana. It is a selection from a cross between Keckmethi and Rutgers. The fruits are medium in size, round in shape and become red at maturity. The fruits bear in clusters of 5 to 11. The plants are indeterminate in habit. The maximum yield reported by Nandpuri and Singh (1973) is 591 quintals per hectare.

Keck-Ruth: It was released by the Punjab Agricultural University, Ludhiana, from a cross between Keckmethi and Rutgers. Its fruits are large in size with green and raised shoulders which disappear at maturity. The fruits are borne in clusters of 3 to 6 in each. The plants are indeterminate in growth habit. The average yield obtained in Ludhiana condition in 641 quintals per hectare (Nandpuri and Singh, 1973).

Punjab Tropics: It was also released by Punjab Agricultural University, Ludhiana from American introductions. The fruits are borne in clusters of 4 to 6 number and at ripening they are deep red in colour. The plants are indeterminate in growth habit. It is late maturing variety than other main season varieties. The average yield in Ludhiana condition is about 690 quintals per hectare (Nandpuri and Singh, 1973).

Punjab Chhuhara: It was also released by Punjab Agricultural University, Ludhiana from a cross between EC 55055 and Punjab Tropics. Its fruits are medium in size, pear shaped, with uniform ripening having thick pericarp. The number of locules are 2 to 3 having very less seeds. The average number of fruits per plant is about 70-85. It is tolerant to blight, TMV and wilt diseases (Nandpuri *et al.*, 1977).

It is an early variety than other varieties released from this University. The plants are indeterminate with thick stout stem and luxuriant dense foliage growth. The average yield is about 608 quintals per hectare in Ludhiana conditions.

Krishnanagar S-20: This variety has been released for West Bengal (Bhan, 1966) on the basis of results obtained at Horticultural Research Station, Krishnanagar, Nadia and the Vegetable Research Station, Kalimpong, Darjeeling. The fruits are medium sized, round shaped and red coloured at ripening. It is a medium-late variety and takes about 70-80 days after transplanting for first plucking.

Angur-lata: This variety has been released from Kalyanpur, Kanpur. Fruits are oblong, borne in clusters and are deep red in colour at ripening. Plants are trailing type and can be trained on poles, and walls. This variety is most suitable for kitchen gardens.

Roma: This variety was brought from U.S.A. by the Plant Introduction Division, I.A.R.I., New Delhi. This is good for ketchup making. Plants are dwarf and bear heavily. Fruits are small, pear shaped, borne in clusters and are red in colour. Fruits start ripening at 90 to 95 days after transplanting. It is most suitable for hills. The average yield varies from 250 to 275 quintals per hectare.

Gamed: It was brought from Israel by National Seed Corporation of India. Plants are dwarf in nature and bear heavily. The fruits are small to medium in size, pear shaped, light red in colour with thick skin. This variety is good for long transport. Higher yield is obtained in summer as compared with winter season. The average yield is about 175 to 200 quintals per hectare.

S-12: It has been developed from P.A.U., Ludhiana. Plants are dwarf and bear round, medium sized fruits. They are juicy, red in colour having thick skin. This is good both for winter and summer seasons. The average yield varies from 250 to 275 quintals per hectare.

Sweet 72: This variety has been developed from Regional Agricultural Research Institute, Gwalior (Wakankar, 1977). It is a hybrid developed by the cross of Pusa Red Plum and Sioux. The fruits are round, oval and scarlet red at ripening. Fruits can be harvested after 100 to 105 days after transplanting. The average yield is about 200 quintals per hectare.

Selection 120: It was released from I.A.R.I., New Delhi. Plants are dwarf with green and broad leaves. Fruits are large, round with light ridges and start ripening after 95 to 100 days of transplanting. The average yield varies from 250 to 275 quintals per hectare.

S.L.152: It is also released from I.A.R.I., New Delhi. Plants are semi-dwarf in nature and bear small to medium sized fruits which are pear shaped with thick skin. It is good for transporting to long distances. Fruits start ripening after 90 to 95 days of transplanting. The variety is good for summer. The average yield varies from 275 to 300 quintals per hectare.

H.S. 101: It is released from H.A.U., Hissar. Plants are dwarf with dark green leaves. Fruits are round, medium in size, juicy with raised ribs. Outer skin is thick and the fruits have better keeping quality than Pusa Ruby. Fruits start ripening 75 to 90 days after transplanting. The average yield varies from 250 to 300 quintals per hectare.

H.S. 102: It is also released from H.A.U., Hissar. The plants are dwarf with green leaves. The fruits are flat round, medium in size with light ribs. The fruits are ready to harvest after 85 to 90 days of transplanting. The outer skin is thick and suited for long distance markets. This variety can be grown both in summer and winter and can tolerate high temperature. The average yield varies from 250 to 275 quintals per hectare.

Pusa Arun: It is released from H.A.U., Hissar. It is early variety. Plants are medium in height, dense bushy in nature. Fruits are round, medium in size. It is recommended for plains of the country.

Hissar Lalit: It is released from H.A.U., Hissar. It is a cross between HS-101 X and Resistant Bangalore. Fruits are medium to large in size, round and red in colour. It is resistant for nematodes.

Pusa Lalima: It is also released from H.A.U., Hissar and is a cross between Pusa Early Dwarf and HS 101. It is early variety. Fruits are large in size round, flat in shape.

Pusa Gaurav: It is released from I.A.R.I., New Delhi. Fruits are long in shape, smooth with yellowish red colour. It is good for tomato produces.

Punjab Kesari: It is a cross between EC 55055 and Punjab Tropics released from P.A.U., Ludhiana. It is early variety and tolerant to early blight and fruit borer.

Hissar Anmol: It is released from H.A.U., Hissar. It is resistant to leaf rot and viruses. Fruits are medium in size, round in shape and dark red in colour.

NDT 120: It is released from Narendra Dev University, Faizabad. Fruits are big in size, round with red colour.

Jawahar Tomato 99: It is released by Jawaharlal Nehru Agricultural University, Pune. Fruits are round, hard, medium in size and yellowish in colour.

Arka Meghali: It is released from I.I.H.R., Bangalore. It is a cross between Arka Vikas and IHR 584. Fruits are round in shape, medium in size and red coloured.

Pant Bahar:- It is released from GB Pant University, Pantnagar. Fruits are flat, round, medium in size, red in colour.

Solan Gola: It is released by Solan University. Fruits are medium in size, round, smooth and red in colour.

Seed and Sowing

Sowing time

Seed sowing in the plains is done thrice during the year.

1) For rainy-autumn crop, the seeds are sown in the months of June and July while transplanting is done in the months of July and August.

2) For autumn-winter crop, the seeds are sown in the months of September-October while transplanting is done in the months of October and November.

3) For spring-summer crop, the seeds are sown in the months of January-February and transplanting is done in the months of February and March.

In hills, the seed sowing depends upon the elevation of the place. On lower hills, the seeds are sown in February-March while on higher hills in the months of March and April.

Seed rate

The seed rate depends upon the germination percentage of seed. About 500-600 g seeds will be sufficient to plant an hectare provided it has got 80-85 germination percentage.

Seed sowing

Nursery should be at a sunny location and should have better irrigation and drainage facilities. Approximately 100-125 square metre area will be sufficient for raising the seedlings to plant one hectare. Soil should be prepared well by repeated harrowing and planking. Raised beds, one metre wide and 5 metre long, should be prepared and levelled. Ten kg of well rotten farmyard manure per bed should be mixed thoroughly. One centimetre deep furrows should be prepared at 15 cm distance and seeds sown at 1 cm distance. Cover the furrows by a mixture of farmyard manure and soil. Seeds should be treated before sowing with Thiram or Cerasan (2%). The beds are covered with a thin layer of dry grass to maintain the temperature and to reduce evaporation. Beds should be kept moist till the germination is completed. As soon as germination is complete, the layer of grass should be removed carefully without damaging the seedlings. Weeding, hoeing and irrigation should be done as per requirement. Seedlings should be sprayed with Dithane M-45 at the rate of 0.2 % and Metasystox at the rate of 0.1 % at 10 days' interval. Seedlings will be ready for transplanting after 4 to 6 weeks of seed sowing.

Transplanting

The field should be prepared and levelled well. It is divided into small beds depending upon the source of irrigation. The seedlings should be transplanted in evening hours to avoid mortality. Indeterminate varieties like Sioux, Pusa Ruby, Sweet-72 should be transplanted at a distance of 60 cm between the rows and 45 cm within the rows, while determinate varieties like S-12, H.S. 101, H.S. 102, S.L. 152 etc. should be transplanted at a distance of 45 cm between the rows and 45 cm within the rows. A light irrigation should be done immediately just after transplanting the crop.

Manures and Fertilisers

The crop responds very well to manurial and fertiliser application. The amount of plant nutrients required by the crop depends upon the variety and season of crop. A crop grown in spring-summer will require more nitrogen as compared to crop of winter season. Early maturing varieties will require less nitrogen as compared to long duration ones. Fertility status iş also one of the main factors affecting the recommendation of the nutrients. However, different recommendations made for various regions are 80 to 120 kg nitrogen, 50 to 75 kg phosphorus and 50 to 60 kg potash per hectare. In addition to above doses, 250 to 300 quintals of farmyard manure may also be added in the soil during field preparation. Half dose of nitrogen and full dose of phosphorus and potash should be applied as basal while half dose of nitrogen may be applied as top dressing after 25 to 30 days of transplanting. Sometimes the crop suffers due to boron deficiency which may cause cracking in fruits. This can be corrected by spraying the crop with Borax at the rate of 0.3 % at 15 days' interval.

Irrigation and drainage

In humid regions, the crop requires very less irrigation while under dry conditions it is impossible to get the crop without irrigation. In hot condition the crop should be irrigated at weekly or then days' interval while during winter the crop should be irrigated at 15 to 20 days' interval. During fruit ripening the interval should be increased to check fruit rotting. Fluctuations in soil moisture from complete dry to heavy moist may cause cracking of fruits. Heavy watering is also harmful to the crop because flowers do not set properly and crop is affected by fungal diseases. To avoid the situation, excess water should be drained out immediately. During rainy season, permanent drainage system should be made in the field.

Weed control

The crop should be free from weeds from very beginning till the crop is over. Hence, weeding and hoeing are very essential. If the weeds are allowed to grow in the crop, in addition to nutrients uptake by weeds the crop will also be affected by insect pests and diseases. The number of weedings and hoeings depends upon the season of crop. During winter season, the crop requires less weedings while maximum is required in rainy season crop. Since it is shallow rooted crop, weeding and hoeing should be done carefully to avoid root injury.

Chemical weedicides such as Sencor at the rate of 0.5 kg active ingradients dissolved in 1000 litre of water per hectare can be applied just after transplanting the crop. The crop will remain weed free up to 50 to 60 days after transplanting. Later on, one weeding will be sufficient.

Staking

Staking of the plants has proved to be very useful in the cultivation of tomato. In case of indeterminate varieties, the yield and quality of fruits is improved much more than in determinate varieties. Staking not only increases the yield and improve its quality but also reduces the infection by fungal diseases. Wood sticks can be used for staking the tomato plants. Pea straw can also be used for mulching in the crop which checks the crop from touching the ground. Mulching is done about one month after transplanting.

Use of growth regulators

Some of the growth regulators help in fruit setting and reduce the disease incidence in the crop. A spray of solution of 2, 4-D (5 ppm) at 30, 45 and 60 days after transplanting or dipping of seeds in 5 ppm solution of 2, 4-D for 24 hours before sowing increases the fruit set and reduces the effect of virus in the crop (Singh and Singh, 1980 and Mehta, 1983). Similarly GA 5 ppm as fruit set spray increases the percentage of fruit set in the crop (Ojha and Ranganekar, 1969). GA has been found effective in hills whereas 2, 4-D in plains.

Diseases and their control

Damping off

It is caused by *Pythium, Rhizoctonia* and *Fusarium* and *Phytophthora* sp. Emerged seedlings collapse caused by decay of stem at ground level. Sometimes the infection is much more due to high humidity.

Control Measures

❖ Seed should be treated with Ceresan, 2 to 3 g in one kg seeds.
❖ Sterilise the nursery by steam or by formaline.

Early blight

It is caused by *Alternaria solani*. Dark brown to black spots with concentric rings are formed on leaves and stems and sometimes on fruits also.

Control Measures

❖ Spray the crop with Dithane M-45 at the rate of 0.2% concentration at weekly intervals.
❖ Seed should be treated with Ceresan, 2 to 3 g in one kg seed.
❖ Proper crop rotations should be followed avoiding solanaceous crops.

Late blight

It is caused by *Phytophthora infestans*. Dark brown and black spots are formed on leaves, petioles and stems of affected plants. On the fruits, small, water soaked blotches are formed and these spread rapidly over the surface.

Control Measures

❖ Spray the crop with Dithane M-45 at the rate of 0.2 % concentration at weekly intervals.

❖ Follow crop rotations avoiding solanaceous crops.

Fusarium wilt

It is caused by *Fusarium* sp. Lower leaves start yellowing, wilt and die. Plant remains stunted and does not set any fruit.

Control Measures

❖ Grow resistant varieties like Marglobe, and Pant T1.

❖ Follow crop rotations to decrease the fungal population.

❖ Use healthy seeds.

Bacterial wilt

It is caused by *Pseudomonas* sp. It is a seed-borne disease and plants start wilting suddenly and do not recover.

Control Measures

❖ Grow resistant varieties.

❖ Treat the seed with Ceresan at the rate of 2 g per kg seed.

Fruit rot

It is caused by *Phytophthora lycopersici*. Brown spots are formed on the fruits. Fruit decays and becomes unmarketable. Fruits touching the soil are affected badly due to high moisture.

Control Measures

❖ To avoid the touching of fruits on the soil, plants should be staked.

❖ Proper drainage should be followed.

Powdery mildew

It is caused by *Olidium* sp. White powdery growth appears on the leaves and finally the leaves start falling down but it is not very common in tomato.

Control Measures

❖ The crop should be sprayed with 0.2 % wettable·sulphur.

❖ Spray the crop with 0.06 % Karathane.

Leaf curl

It is one of the most serious disease of tomato observed during summer and rainy season. Due to low temperature in winter causing reduction in white fly population the disease does not spread much. The leaves start puckering, curling and get reduced in size and ultimately the plant becomes dwarfed. It is spread by white fly.

Control Measures

❖ The crop should be sprayed with Metasystox at the rate of 0.15 % at 10 to 15 days' interval. It will reduce the white fly population.

❖ Remove the affected plants from the field.

Sun·injury

It is very common in summer·season. When the fruits are exposed to bright sunlight, they become yellow or develop brown burnt areas. It can be controlled by growing varieties having abundant foliage so as to cover the fruits with leaves.

Insect pests and their control

Cut worm

They cut the plants from the ground level in the night and remain in cracks in the day time. Sometimes the damage reaches upto 50 per cent.

Control Measures

❖ Aldrin 5 % or Heptachlor 5 % dust should be mixed in the soil before transplanting at the rate of 25 kg per hectare.

Jassids

They suck the sap from the leaves and cause curling. Their population is much more in September, October, March and April.

Control Measures

❖ The crop should be sprayed with Metasystox at the rate of 0.15 % concentration at 15 days' interval.

Epilachna beetle

Both larvae and adults feed on the leaves and the plant becomes leafless.

Control Measures

❖ The crop should be sprayed with Sevin at the rate of 0.2% concentration at 10 days' interval.

Fruit borer

It is one of the very serious pest and too much damage is observed in April and May. Fruits are bored by the borers and start rotting later on.

Control Measures

❖ The crop should be sprayed with Sevin at the rate of 0.2 % at 10 days' interval starting from flowering to fruit ripening.

❖ Remove damaged fruits and bury them in the soil.

Root-knot nematode

These are small worm-like pests affecting the roots. They check the activities and ultimately the plants become dwarf, start yellowing and finally start wilting and premature death occurs. Knot-like irregular swellings are formed on the roots of affected plants.

Control Measures

❖ Proper crop rotations should be followed avoiding solanaceous crops.

❖ Grow nematode resistant varieties like S-120.

❖ Use saw dust in the soil at the rate of 15 to 20 quintals per hectare three weeks before planting. In this case, 50 kg per hectare more nitrogen should be used.

❖ Use 6 to 7 litres Nemagon per hectare in the soil.

Harvesting

During summer season, fruits should be harvested at turning stage while during winter season, fruits at more mature stage should be harvested. For canning and processing, completely ripened fruits should be harvested to get better colour in the product.

Yield

The yield of fruits varies from 150 to 450 quintals per hectare depending upon the variety, growing season, type of soil, cultural practices followed and use of plant growth regulators. The average yield per hectare is about 200 quintals.

Preparation for market

Well developed fruits, free from insect pests and diseases and having uniform ripening stage should be selected from the harvested lot for the market. Cracked, bruised, scalded and injured fruits should be culled out. The selected fruits should be packed in baskets, using papers inside and out side the basket, and the packed fruits should be kept in a cool place before sending them to the market. A single layer of baskets should be put inside the vehicle used for transporting.

Storage

The fruits harvested at turning stage can be kept at room temperature for 3 to 6 days in summer and 6 to 10 days in winter season. The completely ripened fruits can be kept in fairly good condition for about two weeks at 10°C to 15°C temperature.

Seed production

Seed production of tomato can be undertaken in any part of the country. It is a self pollinated crop and an isolation distance of 50 and 25 metres should be maintained for foundation and certified seeds. The best time for planting the seed crop is January to mid February in plains since it is not affected by the viruses due to low temperature (Singh and Singh, 1980). All recommended cultural practices should be followed for crop cultivation. The crop should be inspected thrice during growth period. Firstly, before flowering on the basis of growth characters. Off types should be removed. Secondly, at the time of flowering on the basis of flower characters. Off types should be removed. Thirdly, at the time of fruit ripening on the basis of fruit characters. Plants affected by viruses and other diseases should be removed whenever observed in the crop.

The complete ripened fruits should be harvested and crushed under feet in wooden boxes and allowed to ferment for 24 to 48 hours. In winter, the, fermentation takes place in 72 hours. Later on the seeds are washed with water through a sieve and dried in the sun. On large scale. HCl can be used for fermentation at the rate of 1 litre per quintal of fruits but it is costly. On an average, to produce one kilogram of seed 150 to 200 kg fruits will be required depending upon the variety. Normally pear shaped varieties have less seeds than round or oval varieties. The average yield of seed varies from 110 to 200 kg per hectare. At present, seed is also being extracted in processing factories. The tomatoes of only one variety are supplied to the factory. The pulp is used by factory for preparation of various tomato products whereas seed is returned to the growers. This seed is then supplied by farmers to organisations like UPS&TDC or N.S.C.

BRINJAL

Botanical name	-	*Solanum melongena* L.
Family	-	Solanaceae
Synonymous	-	Egg plant, Baingan, Bengena, Begun, Balgan, Vange, Brinjal. Badane kayi, Vangi, Vazhuthoma, Bataun, Mulukutakali, Vayiugana, Guinea, Aubergive.

IMPORTANCE AND UTILITY

It is an annual crop cultivated all over India as one of the principal vegetables. The fruits are available practically throughout the year. The unripe fruits are used as vegetable alone or with potatoes and tomatoes or in curries. The fruits are employed as a cure for toothache. It is also an excellent remedy for those suffering from liver complaints. It's green leaves are the main source of antiscorbutic Vitamin C. According to Dr. Aykroyd (1941) 100 grams of edible fruit contains 91.5 g water, 6.4 g carbohydrates, 1.3 g protein, 0.3 g fat and 0.5 g mineral matter.

ORIGIN AND HISTORY

It is said to be the native of India where it is still found growing in wild condition and of China where it has been known for the last 1500 years. In India, more than sixteen species, many of which are closely related to brinjal, are found to grow wild in various parts of the country. It is very popular in Balkans (Southern Europe), France and Italy but minor importance is given to it in U.S.A.

BOTANY

There are four types of flowers in brinjal i.e. having long, medium, pseudo–short and short styles. Anthesis starts from 7.30 A.M. and continues up to 11 A.M. Peak time for anthesis is 8.30 A.M. to 10.30 A.M. The pollen dehiscence starts from 9.30 A.M. to 10.00 A.M. It has been observed that anthesis and dehiscence are mainly influenced by the day light, temperature and humidity. The stigma becomes receptive one day before anthesis and continues to remain receptive for two days after the anthesis. However, the maximum receptivity is at the time of anthesis. Buds with medium and long styles should be selected for emasculation and pollination.

CLIMATIC REQUIREMENTS

It is a warm season crop and is very susceptible to frost. It requires a long and warm growing season. The best mean temperature for its better growth and development is between 18.3°C to 21.1°C. Cool nights and short summers are unfavourable to its better yield. It can do well up to an altitude of 2000 metres above sea level. The varieties are also responsive to climatic conditions. For example, Pusa Purple Round variety does not fruit at all in plains if transplanting is done in February-March. On the other hand, Pant Ritu Raj and Type-3 do well in this season.

SOIL AND ITS PREPARATION

Brinjal can do well on a variety of soils ranging from sandy loam to heavy clay but for better yield and quality heavy loam soils have been found to be the best. The best pH is 5.5 to 6.0. The crop remains in the field for a number of months. Therefore, the soil should be well prepared by repeated ploughings and harrowings. The land should be well levelled. Farmyard manure at the rate of 250 to 300 quintals per hectare should be incorporated in the soil 20 to 25 days before transplanting the crop.

VARIETIES

A. LONG VARIETIES

Pusa Purple Long: It is a selection from a local variety "Batia" grown in Punjab, Delhi and Western Uttar Pradesh. It is an early fruiting variety ready to harvest after 70 to 90 days of transplanting. The fruits are purple in colour, slender, shining and 20 to 25 cm in length. The average yield varies from 200 to 250 quintals per hectare.

Pusa Kranti: The fruits are oblong and stocky with attractive dark purple colour and can be grown successfully in both spring and autumn planting under North Indian conditions. The average length of the fruit is 14 to 16 cm and the fruits are ready to harvest 90 to 100 days after transplanting. The average yield varies from 250 to 300 quintals per hectare.

Pusa Anmol: It is a new hybrid variety with attractive dark purple oblong fruits. It is an early variety and fruits are ready to harvest after 70 to 75 days of transplanting. The average yield is about 300 to 350 quintals per hectare.

Pusa Purple Cluster: It is a very early variety and is found to be most suitable for kitchen gardens. The fruits are ready to harvest after 45 to 55 days of transplanting. The leaves are purple in colour and thus the plants can be used for ornamental purposes. The fruits are small (7 to 8 cm long), dark purple in colour and bear in clusters. This variety is most suitable for "kalongi" making. The average yield varies from 175 to 200 quintals per hectare.

Krishnanagar Green Long: It is a very popular variety cultivated in South India. The fruits are long (25 to 30 cm), green, fleshy with scanty seeds. It serves best when fried. The fruits are ready to harvest 75 to 80 days after transplanting. The average yield varies from 250 to 300 quintals per hectare.

H 4: It has been released from Haryana Agriculture University, Hissar. The fruits are long (15 to 20 cm), thick with deep shining purple colour. The average fruit weight is about 125 to 150 g and it is ready to harvest in 75 to 80 days after transplanting. The average yield is about 250 quintals per hectare.

Arka sheel: It has been released from Indian Institute of Horticulture Research, Bangalore. The fruits are medium long, thick with deep shining purple colour. The yield varies from 350 to 400 quintals per hectare.

Punjab Barsati: It is released from P.A.U., Ludhiana. Fruits are 18-20 cm long and 4-6 cm in diameter. The fruits are dark purple in colour, soft and shining.

Arka Nidhi: It is released from I.I.A.R., Bangalore. Fruits are 20-25 cm long and 3-4 cm in diameter and purple in colour.

Hisar Jamuni: It is released from H.A.U., Hisar. The fruits are light purple in colour, 10-15 cm long with 3-4 cm diameter.

NDB-25: It is released from ND University, Faizabad. Fruits are 15-20 cm long and dark red in colour.

Arka Shirish: It has also been released from the Indian Institute of Horticulture Research, Bangalore. The fruits are green, extra long with very few seeds. It is an early variety and is ready to harvest after 60 to 65 days of transplanting. The average yield varies from 350 to 400 quintals per hectare.

Arka Kusumakar: It has also been released by the Indian Institute of Horticulture Research, Bangalore. The finger shaped fruits are borne in clusters. The colour of the fruits is light green. This is very commonly cultivated variety in South India. The average yield varies from 350 to 400 quintals per hectare and fruits are ready to harvest 70 to 80 days after transplanting.

Vijay hybrid: It has been released from Vegetable Research Station, Kalyanpur, Kanpur. The fruits are long, thick and deep purple in colour. They are ready to harvest in 90 to 100 days after transplanting. The average yield varies from 270 to 280 quintals per hectare.

Pant Samrat: It has been released from G.B. Pant University of Agriculture and Technology, Pantnagar. The fruits are ready to harvest in about 70 days after transplanting. The deep purple long fruits are borne in clusters. Plants are tall, erect, with dark green leaves. It has resistance to bacterial wilt and Phomopsis blight diseases and is also resistant to shoot and fruit borer and jassids. The average yield varies from 300 to 50 quintals per hectare.

ROUND VARIETIES

Pant Rituraj: It has been developed at G.B. Pant University of Agriculture and Technology, Pantnagar. The plants are semi-dwarf and semi-spreading in nature with dark green leaves having purple tinge on the margin. The fruits are round, medium in size with dark purple shining colour. They are ready to harvest after 60 to 80 days of transplanting with the average yield of about 300 quintals per hectare.

Pusa Purple Round: It is a very old variety recommended by I.A.R.I., New Delhi. Plants are very big with spreading nature. The fruits are round, big in size, purple coloured, each weighing about 400 to 500 g. It has been observed to be highly resistant to the "little leaf" virus disease. The fruits are ready to harvest in 80 to 90 days after transplanting and average yield varies from 250 to 300 quintals per hectare. In plains of India, it should not be transplanted in February-March as it does not fruit in summer season.

Manjri: It is a selection from a local material recommended by the Department of Agriculture, Maharashtra State. The fruits are medium sized, round, rosy in colour with white stripes and very tasty. It is resistant to wilt and gives about 300 to 350 quintals yield per hectare.

Surti Gola: It has been recommended by the Department of Agriculture, Maharashtra State. The fruits are medium sized, round with purple colour. They are soft but watery in taste. The average yield varies from 275 to 300 quintals per hectare.

Krishnanagar Purple Round: It was recommended from West Bengal. The fruits are large sized, round, slightly oval, dark purple, fleshy with very less seeds.

The average yield varies from 250 to 300 quintals per hectare.

IHR 22-1-2-1: It has been developed at Indian Institute of Horticultural Research, Bangalore. It is a very high yielding variety with round, shining deep purple coloured fruits. They have excellent cooking quality with more edible flesh and very less seeds. The average yield varies from 350 to 400 quintals per hectare.

Type-3: It has been developed at Vegetable Research Centre, Kalyanpur, Kanpur. The fruits are round with light purple colour. The average weight of the fruit is about 300 g to 400 g. This variety can be grown in spring–summer also. The average yield varies from 250 to 300 quintals per hectare.

Punjab-8: It has been developed by Punjab Agriculture University, Ludhiana. The fruits are round and medium in size with light purple colour. The average yield varies from 250 to 300 quintals per hectare.

Punjab Bahar: It has also been developed by Punjab Agriculture University, Ludhiana. The fruits are round with deep shining purple colour. It is earlier than Punjab-8. The fruits are fleshy with very less seeds. The average fruit weight varies from 200 to 300 g. The average yield varies from 350 to 400 quintals per hectare.

Arka Navneet: It is released from I.I.H.R., Bangalore. It is a cross between I.I.H.R., 22-1 and Suprim. Fruits are round, shining and dark purple in colour.

Hisar Shayamal: It is released from H.A.U., Hisar Fruits are round, short with dark colour.

Neelam: It is released from P.A.U., Ludhiana, It is an early variety. Fruits are round attractive and purple in colour.

Rajendra Bangan: It is released from Rajendra Krishi Vishwa vidyalaya, Sagar. Fruits are light green in colour, soft, having less seeds. This variety is recommended for South India.

S1: It has been developed at Punjab Agriculture University, Ludhiana. The fruits are round, with deep shining purple colour. The average fruit weight is about 200 to 250 g. The average yield varies from 180 to 200 quintals per hectare.

SEED AND SOWING

Seed Rate

The amount of seed required depends upon the percentage of germination. Seeds having less than 65 per cent germination should not be used. Normally 600 to 800 grams of seed will be sufficient to raise the seedlings for planting one hectare of land.

Sowing Time

The seed sowing in nursery is done in the month of December-January for spring crop and in June and July for rainy-winter crop in the plains. In hills, the seeds are sown in the month of March-April.

Method of Sowing

Raised beds should be prepared and normally twelve beds of 5 x 1 metre size are required to raise the seedlings for one hectare. The seed beds should be 15 cm high from the surroundings. The beds are prepared well and levelled and one centimetre thick layer of farmyard manure is mixed properly. One centimetre deep furrows are made at 15 cm distance and the seeds are sown one centimetre apart in these furrows. The seeds should be covered properly by a mixture of farmyard manure and soil. As soon as the sowing is completed the bed should be covered with a thin layer of dry grass and kept moist till the seeds germinate. As and when the germination is completed the grass layer should be removed and irrigation and weeding should be done as per requirement. To avoid fungal diseases, the seeds should be treated with Captan or Thiram at the rate of 2 g per kilogram of seed. For safeguarding, the seedlings should also be sprayed with Dithane M-45 at concentration of 2 g per litre of water.

TRANSPLANTING

Four to six weeks old seedlings are supposed to be the best for transplanting. The distance, however, depends upon the variety. The round varieties are transplanted at 60 x 60 cm distance while long ones at 60 x 45 cm or 45 x 45 cm distance. A light irrigation should be given immediately after transplanting. Only healthy, disease–free seedlings should be transplanted.

MANURES AND FERTILISERS

It is a heavy feeder crop and requires more nutrients for better yield and quality. As already mentioned, 250 to 300 quintals of farmyard manure should be added 25 to 30 days before transplanting. At the time of last harrowing, 50 kg nitrogen, 60 kg phosphorus and 40 kg potash per hectare should be added. Twenty–five kilograms of nitrogen should be added in the form of top dressing each time at 30 days and 60 days after transplanting.

IRRIGATION AND DRAINAGE

The amount of water to be given and interval of irrigation depends upon the soil type and crop season. During spring, the crop should be irrigated at one week interval while in rainy season the crop should only be irrigated if rains are not frequent. Normally, proper drainage facilities should be provided during this season to remove the excess water from the field.

WEED CONTROL

It is essential to keep the crop weed free by repeated hoeing and weedings specially during early stage of plant growth. Normally two to three weedings will be sufficient during spring season while three to four will be sufficient during rainy season. Lasso at the rate of 6 litres per hectare or Tok-E-25 at the rate of 4 litres per hectare are also found effective when applied just after transplanting the crop. The above quantities of herbicides are dissolved in 400 litres of water and sprayed on the soil surface.

DISEASES AND THEIR CONTROL

Damping off

It is caused by *Pythium aphanidermatum* and occurs in the nursery stage. The fungi live in the soil. The stem of the seedling decays at the soil surface and finally it collapses and the seedling dies.

Control Measures

❖ The nursery bed should be sterilised by steam of formalin.

❖ The seeds should be treated with Ceresan at the rate of 2 g per kg of seeds.

❖ The seedlings should be sprayed with Dithane M-45 at the rate of 0.2 %

solution.

Phomopsis blight

It is caused by *Phomopsis vexans.* The fungus attacks all parts of the plant above ground. Brown irregular spots appear on the leaves as well as on the fruits. Later on the fruits start dropping.

Control Measures

❖   Disease–free seeds should be used.

❖   Seed should be treated with Ceresan at the rate of 2 g per kg of seed.

❖   Crop rotations should be followed.

❖   Resistant varieties should be grown.

❖   The crop should be sprayed with Dithane M-45 at the rate of 0.2 per cent solution at 15 to 20 days' interval.

Little leaf

It is a very serious disease and affects directly the yield of the crop. The leaves become smaller and petioles get shorter considerably. In the later stage, the plants acquire bushy appearance. Due to this malady very poor fruit set takes place and ultimately there is heavy reduction in the yield.

Control Measures

❖   Remove the diseased plants in the early stage.

❖   Spray the crop with Ekalux or Folidol at the rate of 0.2 per cent at fortnightly interval till fruit set. This will check the spread of the disease which is transmitted by insects *Euletix phycitis* and *Empoasca devastans.*

Leaf spots

It is caused by *Alternaria melongenae* fungus specially during rainy season. Irregular spots are formed on the leaves and later on the leaves drop down. Sometimes the spots are also observed on the fruits and they become yellow and drop down.

Control Measures

❖   The crop should be sprayed with Dithane M-45 at the rate of 0.2 per cent solution at fortnightly interval.

Root knot

Small nodules—like structures encircling the roots are formed on the roots. The Plants become stunted and leaves show chlorotic symptoms.

Control Measures

❖ Crop rotations should be followed.

❖ Resistant varieties should be grown.

❖ Soil fumigation with some nematicides like DD or Nemagon should be done.

INSECT PESTS AND THEIR CONTROL

Brinjal fruit and shoot borer (*Leucinodes orbonalis*)

It is a very common and serious pest of this crop and attacks from early growth period till fruiting. The caterpillars bore the stem in early stage and also bore the fruit in later stage. It becomes inactive during winter.

Control Measures

❖ The infected shoots should be removed and destroyed.

❖ The crop should be sprayed with Sevin at the rate of 0.2 per cent solution at fortnightly interval till fruiting starts.

❖ Ratooning in the plot should be avoided.

Jassids (*Empoasca* sp.)

They are very small insects and suck the sap from the leaves causing curling of the leaves. In the later stage leaves show yellowness.

Control Measure

❖ Spray the crop with Metasystox at the rate of 0.15 per cent solution at fortnightly intervals.

Epilachna beetle (*Epilachna* sp.)

It is very serious during early stage of plant growth. The beetles and grubs eat the green portion of the leaves, leaving a skeleton of the veins.

Control Measure

❖ Spray the crop with Sevin at the rate of 0.2 per cent solution at weekly intervals during early stage.

Sucking insects (*Urentius sentis*)

It is one of the destructive pest of the crop and the adults and nymphs suck the sap from the leaves and cause yellowish spots.

Control Measure

❖ Spray the crop with Metasystox at the rate of 0.2 per cent solution during early stage.

HARVESTING

The fruits should be harvested at proper stage but before reaching the maturity stage. They should be allowed to attain a good size and colour. The fruits can be plucked by shears or a sharp knife or by hand. The fruits of round varieties are usually heavy and should be handled with care. Normally the plucking can be done at 7 to 10 days depending upon the variety.

YIELD

The fruit yield depends upon variety, season of cultivation and management practices followed for its cultivation. Normally, 200 to 300 quintals per hectare yield can be obtained.

PREPARATION FOR MARKET

After harvest, the fruits are kept in shade and diseased and damaged fruits are sorted out. In the early stage the quantity will be small hence the fruits can be packed in baskets and taken to the market, but during later stage or at peak of the pickings, the fruits are packed in gunny bags and taken to the market.

STORAGE

At room temperature, the fruits can be stored for two to three days but can be kept for seven to ten days at $7^{\circ}C$ to $10^{\circ}C$ with 85 to 95 per cent relative humidity.

SEED PRODUCTION

It is a normally self-pollinated crop, but cross pollination to some extent does take place through insects. To get pure seeds, an isolation distance of 100 and 200 metre in certified and foundation seed plots, respectively, should be maintained. During crop period at least three times the crop should be rogued off. First roguing is done before flowering and on the basis of foliage characters, the off types are removed. Second roguing is done at the time of flowering on the basis of flower characters and off types are removed. Final roguing is done at the time of fruiting on the basis of fruit characters and off types are removed. At all the stages, plants affected by viruses and phomopsis blight should also be removed. At ripening, the fruits become light yellow in colour and at this stage they are harvested and seeds are extracted properly. At small scale the fruits are pressed by stick or stone etc. to make the flesh loose, cut into pieces and washed in clean water. The seeds settle down in the bottom of the pan. The seeds should be dried completely and kept in cool and dry place.

CHILLI

Botanical name	-	*Capsicum annum* var. *acuminatum* Linn
Family	-	Solanaceae
Synonymous	-	Lalmirchi, Lalmirch, Mirach, Mirapakaya, Galakonda, Kempu, Mensau, Malagay, Oerangi muluk, Marichiphalam, Katuvira, Spanish pepper, Red pepper, Cayenne pepper, Filfil, Surkh Gasmiris

Importance and Utility

It is grown commercially for its fruits all over the country and constitutes the principal source of dry chilli of commerce. It is one of the important spice used mostly in cooking of all vegetables, pulses and other salty preparations. The pungency is due to the 'oleoresin capsicin', which is a volatile alkaloid, and acridity is due to a crystaline acrid substance, capsaicin. In small chillies the capsaicin ($C_{18}H_{27}O_3N$) is found more as compared to larger chillies. Capsaicin quantity present is considered to be inversely proportional to the size of fruit, being maximum in the smallest. It has a very good medicinal value. Its paste is externally used as a rubefacient and as a local stimulant for the tonsils in tonsillitis. In case of diptheria its application is said to hasten the separation of false membranes. Against cholera it is very useful when used with asafoetida and camphor. The fruit decoction with the addition of opium and fried asafoetida is also given with equal success in cholera. All its essential qualities can be preserved in vinegar. According to Mac Gillivray (1953), its 100 g edible portion contains 92.4 g water, 1.2 g protein, 29 calories energy, 11 mg calcium, 870 I.U. Vitamin A, 175 mg ascorbic acid, 0.06 mg thiamine, 0.03 mg riboflavin and 0.55 mg niacin.

Origin and History

It is reported to be the native of tropical America (Thompson and Kelly, 1957), especially Brazil where it is still found growing in a wild stage. In India, it was introduced by the Portuguese in seventeenth century. At present it is used throughout the country as a condiment and maximum area under its cultivation is in Andhra Pradesh, Tamil Nadu and Karnataka.

Botany

The fruits vary in size from 1 to 20 cm in length from thin long to conical to thick fleshed blocks shapes. In general, the anthesis takes place between 5 to 6 A.M. and dehiscence from 9 to 11 A.M. Maximum receptivity was noticed at the time of opening of flowers. Considering the time of anthesis of flowers and anther dehiscence, emasculation and pollination can be done simultaneously in chillies. At 20°C to 22°C and 50-55 per cent relative humidity pollen viability remains for 8 to 10 days.

Climatic requirements

It can do well in warm and humid climate but dry weather is also necessary during its fruit maturity. It cannot tolerate the frost during winter season. Seed germination takes place at 18°C to 20°C. High light intensities increase the yield but reduce the capsaicin content and fruit colouring is delayed considerably. It can do well up to an altitude of 2000 metres above sea level. Plants kept at 10.0°C to 15.6°C at the time of anthesis set 99.3 per cent of the flowers, but all fruits develop parthenocarpically.

Soil and its preparation

Chillies can be grown on a variety of soils ranging from sandy loam to heavy clay but for production of quality fruits a well drained heavy loam soil is found to be the best. It should be free from hard layer and provided with sufficient amount of organic matter. The best soil pH is 6.0 to 7.0. If the soil is acidic, liming is advocated. In general, light soils are well suited for earlier crop while clay loam and silty loam soils are well suited for heavy yield. The land should be prepared well by giving ploughings and harrowings to make a mellow bed. During its preparation, grass and stone pieces should be removed. Farmyard manure at the rate of 250 to 300 quintals per hectare should be incorporated in the soil 20 to 25 days before transplanting the crop.

Varieties

Pusa Jwala: It was developed at I.A.R.I., New Delhi through a cross of NP-46A and Puri Red. The plants are very similar to NP-46A but less affected by virus. The pods are light green in colour, less pungent, more curved at the end and good for salad. The length of the pod varies from 15 to 18 cm. The pods start ripening 120 to 130 days after transplanting. The average yield of green chillies varies from 70 to 80 quintals per hectare.

NP-46A: It has also been developed at I.A.R.I., New Delhi through a cross of Puri Red and Local (Delhi). The plants are susceptible to viruses. The pods are medium in pungency, curved, pointed at the end and can be used for salad. The length of the pod varies from 12 to 15 cm. The average yield varies from 50 to 60 quintals per hectare.

Pant C1: This is a new promising variety developed at Pantnagar as an advanced generation selection from a cross between NP-46A and a local variety (Kandhari) resistant to leaf curl and mosaic. First fruit set is seen after about two months and first picking can be taken up after 100 days of transplanting in plains of Northern India. Fruit colour is green when immature and bright red when ripe. The fruits are highly pungent. It is resistant to leaf curl and a better yielder than the existing popular varieties.

G3: This variety has been recommended from Chilli Research Centre, Lam (Guntoor), Andhra Pradesh. The height of the plant is about 80 to 90 cm and the spread is about 175 to 200 cm. The pods are about 5 cm long, light

Andhra Jyoti: It is released by Chilli Research Station, Lam. It is a cross between G–2 and Bihar. Fruits are 3–4 cm long with 2 cm diameter.

Bhagya Lakshmi: It is released by Chilli Research Station, Lam. Leaves are dark green in colour, fruits are 8.2 cm long and at ripening they become complete red in colour. It is tolerant to insect pest and disease.

Bhaskar: It is also released from Chilli Research Station, Lam. Fruits are 5-6 cm long, pointed and very pungent and are good for pickle.

Pusa Sada Bahar: It is released from I.A.R.I., New Delhi. It is a cross between Pusa Jwala and IC 31339. Fruits are 6-8 cm long with 3-4 cm diameter. On ripening fruits acquire sliming dark red colour.

Punjab Lal: It is released from PAU, Ludhiana. Fruits are dark green in colour in early stage and red in colour in the late stage. It is resistant to viral diseases.

Jawahar Mirch 218: It is released from Jawaharlal Krishi Vishvavidyalaya, Poalpur. It is early variety. Fruits are very pungent, 10-12 cm long with 2.5 to 3.0 cm diameter.

Jawahar Mirch 283: It is also released from Jawaharlal Krishi Vishvavidyalaya, Jawalpuri. Fruits are 5-6 cm long with 2-3 cm diameter. They are dark green in colour in early stage and dark red at ripening stage.

HC 44: It is released from HAU, Hissar. Fruits are 8-9 cm long with light green colour. It is slightly tolerant to insect pest and disease.

Solan Yellow: It is recommended from Solan University. Fruits are 4-5 cm long and dark green in colour and are very pungent.

G4: This variety also has been recommended from Chilli Research Centre Lam (Guntoor), Andhra Pradesh. The height of the plant is almost similar to G_3 plants but spread is slightly higher than this variety. The average pod length is about 7.5 cm with mild pungency. The average green chilli yield is about 70-75 quintals per hectare.

Kalyanpur Type 1: The pods are long, pungent and orange in colour at ripening.

Kalyanpur Type 2: The pods are long, pungent and red in colour at ripening.

Kalyanpur Type 5: The pods are long, thick, mildly pungent and red in colour at ripening. This variety is found to be suitable for pickles.

Seed and sowing

Seed rate

About 1000 to 1500 g seed of better quality will be sufficient to transplant one hectare of land.

Sowing and transplanting time

For spring crop of plains, seeds are sown in nursery in the months of November and December and seedlings are transplanted in February and March while for rainy season crop the seeds are sown in May and June and seedlings transplanted in June and July.

In hills (at high altitudes) seeds are sown in March-April while transplanting is done in May-June.

Raising nursery

To transplant one hectare area, 50 to 60 square metre area is required. The nursery area should be well levelled, open to sunlight and provided with better irrigation and drainage facilities. The raised beds of 5 x 1 metre should be prepared and one centimetre thick layer of farmyard manure should be spread and mixed in these beds. The small furrows are to be made 15 cm apart and seed can be sown at one centimetre distance in these furrows. These furrows are to be covered with a mixture of farmyard manure and soil. Due to low temperature, seeds take more time to germinate in beds. This problem can be overcome to some extent by perfect covering of nursery beds by polyethylene sheets. The seedlings become ready for transplanting in about eight weeks when they are 15-20 cm tall.

Method of transplanting

The distance between row and within the row varies according to the variety, season and region. Normally, the rows should be kept at 50 to 60 cm whereas plants should be transplanted at 30 to 40 cm distance. The seedlings should be transplanted in the evening hours and a light irrigation should be given immediately after transplanting. Only healthy and disease–free seedlings should be transplanted.

Manures and fertilisers

The field should be rich enough in organic matter. Green manuring can be done in the areas of assured rainfall. In general, chilli needs heavy manuring. Variety, type of soil, irrigation facilities are the governing factors for the quantity of manures and fertilisers. In general, 200 to 250 quintals of farmyard manure should be applied during field preparation and 80 kg nitrogen, 60 kg phosphorus and 60 kg potash per hectare will be required later on. Half of the nitrogen and full dose of phosphorus and potash should be applied during the field preparation and the remaining half dose of nitrogen should be given in the form of top dressing 30 days after transplanting.

Irrigation and drainage

The first irrigation is given after the transplanting and subsequent irrigations are given at the interval of 10-15 days. The interval may be increased or decreased depending on the retentiveness of moisture by the soil and frequency of rainfall during the crop season, but maintenance of uniform soil moisture is essential to prevent blossom and fruit drop. Excess water may cause certain fungal diseases, hence, to avoid this situation proper drainage should be provided during rainy season. To check blossom and fruit drop, the crop should be sprayed with Planofix at the rate of 1 ml in 4.5 litres of water. The spraying should be done at flower formation stage and followed 20 days after first spraying.

Weed control

The crop should be weed–free during early stage of plant growth. In rainy season weeds are a serious problem. To check them in time two or three shallow hoeings should be done while in spring only one or two hoeings will be sufficient. Basalin @ 2 litres per hectare can also be used before transplanting the crop to control the weeds up to 40 to 50 days after transplanting.

Diseases and their control

Leaf curl

It is spread by *Bemesia tabaci* fly. Due to this disease leaves start curling and become small, light yellow in colour. The length of internodes is reduced and ultimately the plant becomes dwarf. There is no fruit set but if there is fruit set the size of fruits is very small.

Control Measures

❖ Spray the crop with Metasystox @ 0.15 per cent to reduce the population of flies.

❖ Grow resistant varieties like Pant C_1.

Anthracnose

It is caused by *Colletotricum capsici* fungus. Visible symptoms are much more clear on ripened fruits. On fruits brown spots appear which later on turn blackish and finally fruits drop. This disease is very common in rainy season.

Control Measures

❖ Use disease–free seed material and treat the seed with Captan @ 2 g per kg of seed.

❖ Spray the crop with Blitox or Dithane M-45 or Dithane Z-78 @ 0.2 per cent at 15 days' interval.

Bacterial spot

It is caused by *Xanthomonas vesicatoria* bacteria. The raised spots appear on the leaves. In the early stage they are smooth but later on they become rough. The affected leaves become yellow and drop down.

Control Measures

❖   Use disease–free seed material and treat the seed with Captan @ 2 g per kg of seed.

❖   Follow crop rotations and maintain weed–free crop.

Mosaic

It is caused by chilli mosaic virus and is spread by chilli aphid. Green or yellow raised spots appear on the leaves and they start curling. Affected plants do not set fruits.

Control Measures

❖   Remove and burn the affected plants.

❖   Spray the crop with Metasystox @ 0.15% at 15 to 20 day's interval.

❖   Grow resistant varieties.

Insect pests and their control

Chilli thrips

The tiny sucking insects feed on leaves and lacerate tissues. They suck the cell sap at all stages of plant growth and they are more severe when plants begin to flower. They cause curling and the yield is reduced considerably.

Control Measures

❖   Spray the crop with Metasystox @ 0.15% at 15 to 20 day interval.

❖   They can also be controlled by the spray of 0.25% nicotine sulphate.

Cutworm

They cut the small plants during early stage from the soil surface.

Control Measure

❖ Apply 20 to 25 kg Aldrex dust per hectare in the soil before transplanting the crop.

Pod Borer

Sometimes, the white small caterpillars bore the pods and young shoots but the incidence is not very common.

Control Measure

❖ Spray the crop with Sevin at the rate of 0.2% at an interval of 10 to 15 days. The crop should be sprayed just after the picking.

Aphids

The tiny green yellowish insects suck the cell sap from flowers, leaves and pods and help in spreading the virus.

Control Measure

Same as for thrips control.

Harvesting

The harvesting of chillies depends upon the purpose for which the crop is grown. Green chillies, which are used fresh, are harvested when they have reached full size but before they begin to change their colour from green to red or yellow. They are picked up at frequent intervals, normally twice a week. If the crop is grown for spice then the pods should be allowed to remain on the plants till they are completely red in colour or in few varieties yellow in colour. For canning purpose, they are allowed to develop red colour before picking. Picking is done by hands but to avoid irritation, gloves can be used on the hands.

Yield

The yield depends upon the variety and cultural practices followed to grow the crop. The average yield of green chillies varies from 75 to 90 quintals, whereas that of dry chillies from 18 to 25 quintals per hectare. Twenty-five to forty per cent of dry chillies can be obtained from fresh ripe chillies depending upon the variety which differ in quantity of seeds and thickness of the inner wall.

Preparation for market

Damaged and disease affected chillies are sorted out from the harvested lot and as soon as possible they are sent to the market in baskets or in gunny bags. In case of dry chillies, they are kept in a heap for two days to get a uniform colour and they are spread on the floor for drying. Normally, complete drying takes place in 15 to 20 days in sunlight, while in drier they are kept at 55^{0}C for two to three days only. Later on they are packed in gunny bags and sent to the market.

Storage

At room temperature, green chillies can be kept for two to three days while in cold storage they can be kept for 40 days at 0°C with 85 to 98 per cent relative humidity. The dry chillies can be kept for months together in dry places, well protected from insect pests.

Seed production

Chilli is an often cross-pollinated crop and requires 200 and 400 metres isolation distance for certified and foundation seeds, respectively. The off types and disease affected plants are taken out at least thrice during the crop period. First, before flowering on the basis of external plant characters. Off types are taken out, Second, at the time of flowering on the basis of flower characters; off types are removed; and finally at the time of pod maturity. At this stage off types are removed on the basis of pod characters. At all the stages virus affected plants have to be taken out. Normal cultural practices have to be followed for the seed crop but more attention has to be paid against the control of insect pests and diseases. Complete ripe pods are harvested and dried properly for 15 to 20 days in sunlight or for two to three days in drier at 55°C. Later on the seeds can be extracted from the dry chillies.

CAULIFLOWER

Botanical name	-	*Brassica oleracea* var. *botrytis* L.
Family	-	Cruciferae
Synonymous	-	Fulgobhi, Phool kobi, Fulwar, Fulkapi, Fule kobi, Poogbi, Gospoovu, Malakobi, Kosuguddae, Fulvar, Phool Gobhi.

Importance and Utility

It is one of the most important favourite vegetable crop grown throughout the country and relished by most of the people. Its white tender head or curd are formed by the flower primordia, which are used as a vegetable in curries, soups and for prickling. It is cooked alone or mixed with potatoes when it becomes more tasty. It can be grown under wide range of climatic conditions both in plains and at different altitudes in the hills depending upon the varieties. In comparison to other vegetables, its cultivation needs more and regular care to get better quality of curds. The production of high quality curds greatly depends not only on the selection of improved varieties but also on proper nursery raising, optimum time of planting, application of manures and fertilisers and other cultural practices. Cauliflower leaves are used for feeding animals. During the peak of its harvest, the curds are dried and preserved for use in the off season. Fresh cauliflower per 100 g edible portion contains, water 91.7 g, protein 2.4 g, fat 0.2 g, carbohydrates 4.9 g, fibre 0.9 g, Vitamin A 90 I.U., B_1 0.11 mg, B_2 0.10 mg, B_6 0.2 mg, Vitamin C 69 mg, K 3.6 mg, malic acid 390 mg, citric acid 210 mg, sodium 16 mg, potassium 400 mg, calcium 22 mg, magnesium 7 mg, iron 1.1 mg, phosphorous 72 mg, sulphur 29 mg, chlorine 30 mg (Chatfield, 1949, 1954; Watt and Merrill, 1964; Aykroyd *et al.*, 1962).

Origin and History

The word cauliflower is derived from the Latin Caulis (cabbage), floris (flower), variety botrytis (meaning budding), and it is believed to have originated in Cyprus or somewhere in southern part of Europe on the Mediterranean. In India, it was introduced during the Moghul period.

Botany

The flowers are born in racemes on the main stem and its branches. The buds open under the pressure of the rapidly growing petals. This process starts in the afternoon, and usually the flower becomes fully expanded during the following morning. The anthers open a few hours later, being slightly protogynous. The anthesis of flowers starts at 8 A.M. and continues up to 11.30 A.M. under normal conditions. Maximum anthesis occurs between 8 to 9 A.M. The anthers start dehiscing at the time of opening. In general, dehiscence occurs between 8 A.M. to 12 noon. The pollen fertility is considerably high at the time of anthesis and one day before anthesis. The fertility is reduced one day after anthesis. The stigma becomes receptive two days before and remains so up to two days after anthesis.

Climatic requirements

It is a cool season crop and produces quality curds in moist and cool growing season. It requires mean monthly temperatures of 15°C to 21°C, but is less tolerant to extremes of heat and cold. A check in growth may cause the plant to form "buttons" when the curds are maturing, they become yellowish, ricey, fussy and leafy and such heads get poor price in the market. A temperature below the optimum during the growing season may delay its maturity and cause the curds to remain small. Direct sun rays on the curd produce undesirable brown pigmentation and sometimes low temperatures cause purple colouration.

Soil and its preparation

Though cauliflower can be grown on all sorts of cultivable soils except the marshy fields, but sandy loam soil is considered the best. Clay soil gives comparatively lesser yield. The soil should be fertile, well supplied with organic matter and well drained. For early cauliflower, medium to heavy soils are better as they are cool and retain enough moisture. The best soil pH is between 6.0 to 7.0. If the soil pH is below 5.5, lime at the rate of 5 to 10 quintals per hectare should be added. Field should be prepared well by repeated harrowings and levellings. During field preparation, 200 to 250 quintals of farmyard manure should be added one month before transplanting the crop.

Varieties

A. Extra Early Varieties

Note:- The time of seed sowing and maturity periods refer to plains of

Northern India.

Early Kunwari: It is an earliest variety and is ready to harvest in September. The seeds are sown in the end of May to 15th June. The heads are small, light yellow in colour and compact. Average curd weight is 300 g. Curds are ready to harvest 80 days after transplanting. Average yield varies from 80 to 100 quintals per hectare.

S-234: It is also an extra early variety developed at G.B. Pant University of Agriculture & Technology, Pantnagar. The curds are of medium size, solid, and white in colour. The seeds are sown in June and seedlings are transplanted in July. The crop becomes ready for harvest after 90-100 days of transplanting. The average yield is approximately 100 quintals per hectare.

B. Early varieties

Pusa Katki: It is an early variety and is ready to harvest in October-November. The seeds are sown from 15th June to 15th July, and seedlings are transplanted in July-August. The curds are of small size, solid and white in colour. The average yield varies from 100 to 115 quintals per hectare.

Pusa Deepali: It is also an early variety. The seeds are sown from 15th June to 15th July. The curds are of small size, compact, white in colour and ready to harvest in the month of October-November. The average yield varies from 120 to 125 quintals per hectare.

C. Mid season varieties

Pusa Aghani: The seeds of this variety are sown from end of July to mid August and heads are ready to harvest in December. The curds are of medium to big size, compact and white in colour. The average yield varies from 100 to 110 quintals per hectare.

Improved Japanese: The seeds of this variety are sown in August and the heads are ready to harvest in December. The curds are medium in size, compact and light yellow in colour. The average yield varies from 175 to 180 quintals per hectare.

Hisar-2: The seeds of this variety are sown in the second week of August and heads are ready to harvest after 130 to 150 days of transplanting. The curds are medium in size, compact and white in colour. The average yield varies from

200 to 250 quintals per hectare.

Giant Snow-ball: The seeds of this variety are sown in August-September and heads are ready to harvest after 85 to 90 days of transplanting. The curds are big in size, compact and white in colour. The average yield varies from 200 to 250 quintals per hectare.

Pusa Synthetic: The seeds are sown in August and September and heads are ready to harvest after 95 to 100 days of transplanting. The curds are medium in size, compact and white in colour. The average yield varies from 200 to 250 quintals per hectare.

Pant Subhra: It is also a mid season variety released by G.B. Pant University of Agriculture & Technology, Pantnagar in 1984. Heads are compact, white, medium sized and partially covered with leaves. Seeds are sown in mid August in the plains and in July on hills. Heads are ready to harvest after 110 days of transplanting. Average yield is about 250 to 300 quintals per hectare.

D. Late varieties

Snow-ball-16: It is a late variety and the seeds are sown from end of September to 15th October and heads are ready to harvest after 90 days of transplanting. The curds are medium in size, compact and white in colour. The average yield varies from 180 to 200 quintals per hectare.

Pusa Snow-ball-1: It is also a late variety. The seeds are sown from end of September to 15th October and heads are ready to harvest after 85 to 100 days of transplanting. The curds are medium in size, compact and complete white in colour. The storage capacity of curd is better than other varieties. The average yield varies from 200 to 300 quintals per hectare.

Pusa Snow-ball-2: It is also a late variety, sown in September and October and ready is to harvest after 90 to 120 days of transplanting. The curds are solid, medium to big in size and white in colour. The average yield varies from 200 to 350 quintals per hectare.

Seed and sowing

Seed rate

Seed rate varies depending upon the group of variety and percentage of seed germination. For early and mid season varieties, 500 to 650 g seed will be sufficient and for late varieties 400 to 500 g seed will be sufficient to plant one hectare of land.

Time of sowing

Following are the time of sowing the seed in the nursery and transplanting in the field for plains of northern India.

Group of variety	Time of seed sowing	Time of transplanting
Extra Early	May-June	June-July
Early	June-July	July-August
Mid	July-August	August-September
Late	September-October	October-November

Method of sowing

Approximately 60 square metres nursery area is required to raise the seedlings for transplanting one hectare area. The selected area should be well levelled, fertile and have better drainage facilities. The raised beds of 5 x 1 metre size should be prepared, levelled properly and one centimetre thick layer of farmyard manure be added in the beds. Grass and stone pieces etc. should be removed. Before sowing, the seeds should be treated with Thiram at the rate of 2.5 g per kg of seed. To avoid black rot the seeds should be kept in hot water (50°C) for 30 minutes. At 15 cm distance 1.5 cm deep small furrows should be made on the beds and seeds should be sown in these prepared furrows at a distance of one centimetre. Approximately 100 seeds are sown in one row. At the same time, the furrows are covered with a mixture of farmyard manure and soil. Later on the beds are covered with a thin layer of dry grass to maintain the temperature and to check evaporation. With the help of water can, light watering should be done during morning and evening hours and this practice should be followed till the seeds are germinated. As soon as the seeds germinate the grass layer should be removed and irrigations and weedings should be done as per requirement. To control insect pest and diseases spray of 0.2% Dithane M-45 and Thiodan should be done. If the seedlings are weak a light spray of 0.1% urea can be done. Approximately four weeks after sowing the seeds, the seedlings will be ready for transplanting.

Transplanting

Early varieties should be planted at a distance of 45 cm between the rows and 30 to 45 cm within the rows while mid season and late varieties should be planted at 60 cm between the rows and 45 cm within the rows. The planting should be done when the seedlings have attained three to four leaf stage. In case of early and mid season crop, it is better to transplant the seedlings on ridges to avoid any damage to seedlings due to excessive water during rainy season. Light irrigation must be given immediately after transplanting.

Manures and Fertilisers

For better yield and quality, the crop should be fertilised well during early stage of growth. Though the manure and fertiliser requirements may vary from soil to soil and from variety to variety, normally 200 to 250 quintals of farmyard manure should be mixed in the soil 3 to 4 weeks before transplanting the crop. Before transplanting, 60 kg nitrogen, 80 kg phosphorus and 80 kg potash per hectare should be added. One month after transplanting, the crop should be top dressed with urea at the rate of 60 kg nitrogen per hectare. To check boron deficiency, 10 to 15 kg borax per hectare should also be added during field preparation. Borax, at the rate of 1 kg per hectare, can also be sprayed on plants one month after transplanting.

Irrigation and drainage

The crop should be irrigated well in time to ensure continuous growth. First irrigation should be given immediately after transplanting the crop and later on the crop should be irrigated at 8 to 12 days' interval depending upon the type of soil. Sometimes during rainy season, in the early crop, excess water becomes a problem. To check it, better drainage facilities should be provided. It will be better to make ridges in the standing crop during rainy season.

Weed control

Regular shallow cultivation should be given to the soil to remove young weeds and to provide soil mulch. The roots of cauliflower are located in top 45 to 60 cm of soil, hence deep cultivation should be avoided. Normally two to three hoeings and weedings are required to keep the crop weed free. In early and mid season crops, light earthing of plants should be done about four to five weeks after transplanting. Weeds can be controlled by the application of Basalin @ 2 litres per hectare prior to transplanting the crop. The solution is sprayed on the soil and mixed into the soil surface. Later on the crop is transplanted.

Diseases and their control

Damping off

This disease commonly occurs in the nursery. Failure of plants to emerge indicates pre-emergence damping off while the post-emergence symptoms show water soaked, collapsed areas on stem below or near the soil. Later, the darkened, sunken stem fails to support the seedling which collapses and dies.

Control Measures

❖ Seeds should be treated with Thiram or Captan at the rate of 2.5 g per kg seed.

❖ Nursery soil may be treated with formalin. The chemical is diluted (one part in 50 parts of water) and the nursery beds are drenched with the solution to a depth of at least 10 cm. Approximately 10 litres of solution will be required for one square metre area. After treatment, soil should be kept covered for about 7-10 days and then soil should be worked up again and seed should be sown after about a week.

❖ Disinfection of the soil can also be achieved by sprinkling the solution of Brassicol 75 W.P. (PCNB) prepared by dissolving 3 g of chemical in 5 litres of water. This is sufficient to drench about one square metre of nursery area. This should be thoroughly worked up in the soil about a week before sowing.

❖ Post-emergence spray with Captan @ 2.5 g per litre of water should also be done.

Black rot

This disease attacks both the leaves and curds. The leaves show numerous minute brown specks which enlarge later on. The infected lower leaves wilt and drop prematurely. The veins of the affected stem and leaves are blackened. In case of severe infection, curds may not form. This is more severe in hills.

Control Measures

❖ The seeds should be treated with hot water at 50°C for 25-30 minutes but this is to be done very carefully by keeping the hot water thermos. If temperature goes high or heating is done longer than the recommended period, the viability of seed will be adversely affected.

❖ Plan at least 2-year rotation of non-cruciferous crops between cruciferous crops both in the nursery and the field.

❖ Clean and burn or plough down all crop debris after harvest.

❖ Disinfect soil with Vapam. The solution is prepared by dissolving 80 ml Vapam in 5 litres of water to drench one square metre area. This treatment should be done about three weeks before sowing the seed in the nursery.

Leaf spot and blight

This disease causes small dark coloured spots on leaves which spread rapidly to form circular lesions. In humid weather, concentric rings of dark conidiosphorous appear.

Control Measures

❖ Clean and burn or plough down all affected crop debris.

❖ Spray the crop with Dithane M-45 @ 0.2 % at 15 to 20 day's, interval.

❖ Hot water treatment of seed at 50°C for 30 minutes.

Wire stem

It is a new disease of cauliflower caused by *Rhizoctonia solani*. Due to this disease the base of the main stem becomes black like wire and later on plants die.

Control Measure

❖ The plants should be drenched with 0.2% Brassicol at 10 days' interval after transplanting.

Black leg

It is caused by *Phoma lingam* fungus. Blackish-brown spots are observed on the affected plants 10-20 days after seed sowing. If the same seedlings are used for transplanting they fall down during head formation.

Control Measures

❖ Hot water treatment to seed should be given (30 minutes at 50°C).

❖ Follow crop rotation.

Club root

It is caused by *Phasmodia phosa*. Roots enlarge to form clubs and temporary flag the leaves on bright days leading to wilt or retarding of growth.

Control Measures

❖ Avoid infected fields.

❖ Add lime in the soil at the rate of 10 to 15 quintals per hectare.

❖ Treat seedlings at transplanting time with mercuric chloride solution (0.1%).

Root knot

It is caused by nematodes of the genus *Meloidogyne*. Galls are formed on the roots of affected plants.

Control Measures

❖ Follow crop rotations with grain, cereals and legumes.

❖ Soil fumigation at 30 cm apart with Ethylene dibromide and Dichloropropane mixture.

Insect pests and their control

Mustard Saw fly (*Athalia* sp.)

The adults are minute black flies. They lay eggs inside the leaf tissues. After hatching, the caterpillars feed on the leaves of young seedlings.

Control Measures

❖ Spray the crop with Malathion at the rate of 0.1%.

❖ Collect the caterpillars by hand and destroy them.

Mustard aphids (*Brevicoryne* sp., *Myzus* sp., *Rhopalosiphum* sp.)

They are greenish or black in colour. They damage the leaves by sucking the cell sap and affected leaves get curled and plants wither away and die.

Control Measures

❖   Spray the crop with Metasystox at the rate of 0.15% at 15 day's interval.

❖   Spray the crop with Nuvan at the rate of 0.05%.

Diamond black moth

Caterpillars eat entire green leaves except veins. They are small and greenish black caterpillars found in groups. They damage the crop from August to December.

Control Measures

❖   Spray the crop with Sevin at the rate of 0.2%.

❖   Spray the crop with Endosulfan 35 EC at the rate of 0.2%.

Cabbage butterfly (*Pieris* sp.)

The caterpillars feed on the leaves and skeletonise them. In case of heavy infestation they feed on leaves, tender shoots, flowers and pods.

Control Measures

❖   Spray the crop with Metasystox at the rate of 0.15%.

❖   Spray the crop with Malathion at the rate of 0.2%.

Semilooper (*Plusia* sp.)

The green caterpillars which are identified by the characteristic loop while moving, attack cruciferous crop and cause serious damage to the crop. The nature of damage is similar to that of cabbage butterfly.

Control Measures

❖   Spray the crop with Sevin at the rate of 0.2% at 15 to 20 day's interval.

❖   Spray the crop with Malathion at the rate of 0.2%.

Harvesting

Harvesting should be done when the curds have attained proper size and are white and compact. Delay in harvesting will result in loose, yellow and poor quality curds. While harvesting, the inner two whorls of leaves should be retained alongwith the curd to provide them adequate protection against injuries during handling, packing and transport.

Yield

The yield generally varies from 100 to 250 quintals per hectare. In early varieties the yield varies from 100 to 125 quintals, in mid season varieties 150 to 200 quintals and in late varieties, 200 to 250 quintals per hectare.

Preparation for market

After harvesting, the curds should be kept in shade at a clean place and all diseased and damaged ones should be removed. The curds are then graded and kept in baskets according to size of the curd. These baskets should be sent to market early in the morning.

Storage

Cauliflower curds can be kept for two to three days at room temperature and can be kept in cold storage at 0°C with 85 to 90 per cent relative humidity for about a month.

Seed production

Cauliflower is a cross-pollinated crop and pollination takes place by honey bees. The pollen from another flower during pollination is needed otherwise there is no seed set. To get genetically pure seed and to maintain varietal purity, it is essential that isolation distances of 1600 metre and 1000 metre are maintained from variety to variety and from the crops like cabbage and knol-khol.

The seed production of early and mid season varieties can be done successfully in the plains of the country while the seed production of late varieties is only possible on high hills where temperatures are suitable for flowering and seed formation. Following are the two recommended methods for cauliflower seed production.

1. Curds to seed

In this method, the selected curds from the normal crop are transplanted at 75 x 50 cm distance. This method is known as "transplant" method. If the curds are very compact then they should be scooped in middle portion. When temperature rises the curds start bolting, new shoots come up in the month of February and March. Flowering takes place in the month of March-April and podding in April. The pods are ready to harvest in May. This is a costly method and only small quantity of seeds can be produced.

2. In situ method

In this method, no transplanting is done and the entire normal crop, after roguing, is left as such for seed production. After curd formation, normal cultural practices are done regularly. As mentioned above, bolting, flowering and podding takes place in a similar way. By this method the seed production can be done on a large scale with lesser cost of cultivation.

For getting genetically pure seed, the off types should be removed at the following times.

1) Before curd formation

At that time on the basis of external characters of the plant the off types are removed. At the same time diseased plants are also removed.

2) At the time of curd formation

At the time of curd formation on the basis of curd characters all the off types and diseased plants are removed.

3) At the time of flowering

At the time of flowering, on the basis of flower character, off types and diseased plants are removed.

Physiological disorders

Following physiological disorders are recorded in cauliflower.

1) Whip tail

This results due to the deficiency of Molybdenum and occurs in acidic soils where soil pH is low. The leaf blades do not develop properly and become strap-like. The growing point is deformed and there is no formation of marketable heads. It can be controlled by using lime at the rate of 10 to 15 quintals per hectare or by the application of 1.2 kg sodium molybdate or ammonium molybdate per hectare.

2) Browning

This results due to the deficiency of boron. Commonly, the stem becomes hollow and the curd becomes brown. Later the edges of older leaves develop purple colour. It can be controlled by application of sodium tetraborate at the rate of 5 to 7 kg per hectare. The spray of 1 kg Borax after 30 days of transplanting shall also serve the same purpose.

3) Buttoning

This is due to the deficiency of nitrogen and causes small curds called "Buttons". Normally the plants are small and consequently the curd gets open. The older seedlings show less vegetative growth and produce buttons. This can be controlled by application of proper nitrogen doses.

4) Ricyness

If the harvesting is not done at right stage the curds become granular and loose. Harvesting at proper stage may control this abnormality.

5) Blindness

If the plant does not bear curd the state is known as blindness. In few cases the terminal bud does not develop or gets broken or eaten up by insects and there is no curd formation on a particular plant. Such plants should be removed.

CABBAGE

Botanical name	-	*Brassica oleracea* var. *Capitata*
Family	-	Cruciferae
Synonymous	-	Band gobhi, Karam Kalla, Kobee, Patgobhy, Muttai Kose, Patta Kob, Bandha Kobi, Bandha Kapi, Gobee, Yelekosu, Cabbage, Aku gobhi.

Importance and Utility

Cabbage is grown in Rabi season as cauliflower and is one of the important vegetables under extensive cultivation in India and other countries. It is generally grown by market gardeners, specially vegetable growers and general farmers in the vicinity of large and small cities in India. Cabbage is mostly used for culinary and dietic purposes. In advanced countries, it is used for feeding livestock and chicken as well. Sometimes it is also used for pickles. The taste in cabbage is due to "Sinigrin glucoside" which is pergative. Cabbage is useful in urine disorders. It is very rich in minerals, vitamin A, B, B_2 and C_1. Young and tender leaves are rich in Vitamin A as compared with old leaves. A 100 g edible cabbage contains 91.9 per cent water, 4.6 per cent carbohydrates, 1.8 per cent protein, 0.1 per cent fat, 1.0 per cent fibre and 0.6 per cent minerals.

Origin and History

It is believed that cabbage originated from wild type and occurs on the chalk cliffs of eastern England and along the coast of Denmark and north-western France. The wild plant does not form head and is very similar to collared, hence it is consumed by the surrounding population. In India, cabbage was introduced in 15th century from Portugal and for the first time it was cultivated on the banks of Malabar and later it spread in whole country.

Botany

It is a herbaceous annual for vegetable, whereas for seed production it is biennial. It has bisexual flowers and has four sepals and petals. The fruit is long, slender pod called a silique, but when short and broad is referred to as siligue. The flowers are pollinated by insects, so it is possible to have both self and cross pollination. However, it tends to be cross pollinated because most of the plants carry self incompatibility factors. The edible portion which is made up of numerous thick overlapping smooth leaves covering a terminal bud is known as 'head'. The cabbage varieties differ in size, shape and colour of the head.

Climatic requirements

It is a cool season crop and thrives best in a cool moist climate with an average monthly temperature of 13° to 16°C but it can tolerate freezing weather. Growth is slow at 12° to 13°C and also above 16°C. At warmer temperature the quality is poor. Frost is believed to improve the quality of cabbage. The seed germination takes place at soil temperature of 12°C to 13°C. The plants are affected by yellow disease when temperature goes above 17°C.

Soil and its preparation

It can be grown on a wide range of soils ranging from light sandy loams to heavy clay loams. It is moderately tolerant to pH as low as 5.5 but where club root is prevalent, reaction should be brought to about pH 7.2 using hydrated lime. The land should be prepared well by repeated harrowings and levellings. During field preparation, 200 to 250 quintals farmyard manure should be added one month before transplanting the crop.

Varieties

A. Early varieties

Golden Acre: It is an early variety with uniform solid and round heads. The leaves are cup shaped around the head. Stem is small and average weight per head is 700 g to 750 g. The yield varies from 200 to 250 quintals per hectare. The best time of its seed sowing in nursery is from second week of August to end of September.

Pride of India: It is also an early variety with solid and medium sized heads. Heads are ready to harvest after 60 to 70 days of transplanting. The average yield is about 200 quintals per hectare.

Early Drum Head: The heads are solid, flat and big sized. The stem is small and colour of the head is light green. Heads are ready to harvest after 80 to 90 days of transplanting. The yield varies from 150 to 250 quintals per hectare.

Copenhagen market: It is an early variety having round, compact and solid head. Stem is small and leaves are light green. The yield varies from 180 to 200 quintals per hectare.

B. Late varieties

Late Drum Head: It is a late variety with solid, flat and big sized heads. The heads are light green in colour and ready to harvest after 110 to 120 days of transplanting. The yield varies from 250 to 300 quintals per hectare.

Pusa Drum Head: It is a new but late variety selected from EC 6774 (Japan) and evolved at Katrain (IARI). The heads are uniform, flat, solid with small stems. The head weight varies from 1.5 to 2.0 kilogram. It is resistant to black leg or dry rot (*Phoma lingam*). The yield varies from 250 to 300 quintals per hectare.

Drum Head Savoy: It is a late variety with dark green foliage, which is blistered or wrinkled. The heads are big in size, solid and dark green in colour but the variety is not commercially acceptable in our country.

Red cabbage: It is a late variety with deep purplish leaves which are of great attraction in the kitchen garden. The yield is low and due to poor taste it is not acceptable in our country.

Late K1: It is new variety. Heads are solid, medium in size and snow white in colour. It is resistant to black rot. The yield varies from 300 to 325 quintals per hectare.

Seed and sowing

The seed rate depends upon the percentage of seed germination. About 500 to 750 gram seed is sufficient to plant one hectare area.

Time of sowing

Early varieties are sown in nursery from August to September while late varieties in September to October in the plains. In hills, seeds are sown from March to June depending upon altitudes.

Method of sowing

Approximately 60 square metre nursery area is sufficient to raise the seedlings for transplanting one hectare. The selected area should be free from soil–borne diseases, well levelled, fertile and provided with better irrigation and drainage facilities. The raised beds of 15 cm height, of 5 x 1 metre size should be prepared, levelled and covered with one centimetre well rotten farmyard manure. It should be mixed well in the upper surface of the soil. To avoid seed–borne diseases, the seeds should be treated with hot water at 50°C for 30 minutes and also treated with Thiram at the rate of 2.5 g per kg of seeds. The seeds should be sown in furrows made 15 cm apart and 1.5 cm deep. Approximately 100 seeds are sown in one row and the furrows are covered with a mixture of farmyard manure and soil. Just after sowing, the beds should be covered with a thin layer of dry grass to check evaporation and to maintain temperature. Watering should be done in morning and evening to maintain the moisture required for proper germination. As soon as the seeds germinate the upper grass layer should be removed carefully and later on cultural operations should be followed as per requirement. To control insect pests and diseases, a combined spray of Dithane M-45 (0.25%) and Endosulfan 35 EC (0.1%) should be done. If the seedlings are poor in growth a spray of 0.1 per cent urea can also be given. Normally four weeks after seed sowing .he seedlings are ready for transplanting.

Transplanting

The seedlings to be transplanted should be 4 to 6 weeks old, having 4 to 5 leaves. The transplanting may be done from mid September to mid November depending upon the variety. The early varieties should be planted at 45 x 45 cm distance while late maturing varieties at 60 x 45 cm distance. Only healthy and disease-free seedlings should be planted and immediately after transplanting a light irrigation should be given.

Manures and fertilisers

Cabbage being a heavy feeder, it requires heavy doses of organic matter and crop nutrients. However, the fertilisers should be added on the basis of nutrient status of the soil. Normally, as already indicated, 200 to 250 quintals of well rotten farmyard manure should be mixed in the soil one month before transplanting the crop. Later on, one week before transplanting, 60 kg nitrogen, 80 kg phosphorus and 80 kg potash per hectare should be added. One month after transplanting, the crop should be top dressed with urea at the rate of 60 kg nitrogen per hectare. The doses of fertilisers will vary as per soil fertility status.

Irrigation and drainage

The optimum moisture content should be maintained by regular irrigations. The number of irrigations and amount of water depends upon the nature of variety, soil type and climatic conditions. However, the crop should be irrigated at 10 to 15 day's interval. When the heads are fully developed and firm enough, the irrigation should be stopped otherwise many of the heads will split resulting in loss of marketable quality. Whenever there is excess water, it should be drained out properly.

Weed control

For better yield and quality the field should be kept free from weeds etc. Regular shallow cultivations should be given to remove weeds and to provide soil mulch. After 5 to 6 weeks of transplanting, earthing of plants should be done. In order to produce solid heads, the inter-culture may be done carefully to avoid injury to the developing plants and their roots. Basalin can also be used at the rate of 2 litres in 1000 litres of water per hectare before transplanting.

Diseases and their control

Similar to cauliflower.

Insect pests and their control

Similar to cauliflower.

Harvesting

The cabbage heads should be harvested when they attain full size and are solid. The heads may be cut with sickle or long knife and two or three outer leaves should be left as such. The best time of harvesting is in the afternoon or early in the morning. If the harvesting is not done at correct maturity time then the heads burst or split and lose their market value. The early crop may require 2-3 cuttings whereas the late crop should be harvested only in one operation. Due to low market price or for any other reason if harvesting is not possible in that situation the growth can be checked by deep cultivation and by twisting, loosening or slightly pulling the plants without actually digging them out. This way, roots are broken and the intake of soil water is reduced and loss from bursting is lessened.

Yield

The yield of cabbage heads varies from soil to soil, variety to variety and from locality to locality. Generally all varieties of cabbage yield higher in northern India as compared to southern India. Similarly, early varieties yield low as compared to late varieties. Normally the yield of early varieties varies from 150 to 250 quintals whereas of late varieties from 250 to 350 quintals per hectare.

Preparation for market

The heads should be kept in shade at clean place and all diseased and damaged ones should be removed. At the same time, the outside leaves of each head should be peeled down to the solid head for convenience in handling and for giving a better appearance. The heads are arranged in shallow baskets according to size.

Storage

Only mature and solid heads should be stored since over-matured and loose heads do not keep well in storage. At room temperature the heads can be stored for 3 to 4 days while at $0°C$ with 90 to 95 per cent relative humidity for about 40 to 50 days.

Seed Production

Like cauliflower it is a cross-pollinated crop and requires 1600 and 1000 metres isolation distance for foundation and certified seeds, respectively. The seed production can only be done on hills where temperature remains $0°C$ for two to three months. Following are the two recommended methods of its seed production.

1. In situ method

In this method the original plants are allowed to produce the seed. For largescale seed production this method is very successful and also higher yields are obtained by this method. Sometimes due to compactness of the heads the bursting is delayed. To avoid the situation a cross cut on the heads is given. Generally bolting takes place in February-March, flowering in March and April, and podding in April. The pods are ready to harvest in May. During this stage all cultural practices as required by the crop should be followed.

2. Head to seed method

In this method the selected heads are transplanted at 75 x 50 cm distance. This method is also known as "transplant method". As per former method, the cross is made on the heads to hasten bolting. All other cultural practices should be followed according to the crop need.

For getting genetically pure seed the off types should be removed at the following times.

1. Before head formation

At that time, on the basis of external characters, off types and diseased plants should be removed.

2. At the time of head formation

At the time of head formation, on the basis of head characters, all the off types and diseased plants should be removed.

3. At the time of flowering

At the time of flowering, on the basis of flower characters, off types and diseased plants are removed.

KNOL KHOL

Botanical name	-	*Brassica oleracea* var. *Caulorapa*
Family	-	Cruciferae
Synonymous	-	Ganth gobhi, Nool khol, Oalkabi, Old kapi, Navilu kosu, Gaddagobhi, Nawal kol, Knol khol.

Importance and Utility

Knol khol is not cultivated on largescale as cauliflower and cabbage. The swollen stem is used for cooking. Mainly it is cultivated in Maharashtra, Assam, Uttar Pradesh, Madhya Pradesh, Himachal Pradesh, Punjab, Haryana, and Jammu and Kashmir. It is very much liked by Kashmiri people. At some places it is used as cattle feed. Its 100 g edible portion contains 90.1 g water, 2.1 g protein, 6.7 g carbohydrate, 1.1 g fibre, 0.1 g fat, 292 mg potash, 57 mg chlorine, 50 mg phosphorus, 40 mg calcium and 55 mg Vitamin C.

Origin and History

It is reported to have originated in the coastal countries of northern Europe. According to some scientists, it originated from wild cabbage whereas others are of the view that it came by the cross of cabbage and turnip. In France, it was being cultivated earlier than that period. In England, it was cultivated from 1850 and during 1938 the total area under its cultivation was 2000 hectare. It was introduced in India from England.

Botany

It is a herbaceous plant of which swollen stem just above the ground is the edible portion. It is a temperate crop which produces edible vegetable as an annual in the plains as well as in the hills. Flowers are borne in recemes on the main stem and its branches. The buds open under the pressure of the rapidly growing petals. The process starts in the afternoon and usually the flowers become fully expanded the following morning and the anthers open a few hours later. The flowers are slightly protogynous. The formation of flowers depends on the temperature and not on the day length.

Climatic requirements

The climatic requirements are almost same as for cauliflower and cabbage, but it can tolerate slightly higher temperature than those crops. It can do well in humid and cool climates. In North India, it is cultivated in Rabi season while in Maharashtra and at very high altitudes, it is cultivated in Kharif/summers when temperature is not very high. Better growth takes place during winter.

Soil and its preparation

It can do well in a variety of soils but loam or clay loam is found better for quality production. The best soil pH for its cultivation is between 6.0-7.5. The soil should be fertile, provided with organic matter and should have adequate drainage facilities. The field should be prepared well by repeated harrowings and levellings. During its preparation, 200 to 250 quintals of farmyard manure should be added one month before transplanting the crop.

Varieties

White Vienna: It is an early variety. Bulbs are globular, light green and very smooth. The flesh is tender with delicate flavour and is creamy white in colour. The stem and leaves are light green in colour and medium in size. Average yield is about 150 quintals per hectare.

Purple Vienna: It is a late variety and bulbs are globular, thick skinned with purple colour. The flesh is tender and light green in colour. The number of leaves are much more than in White Vienna variety. The average yield is about 150 quintals per hectare.

Yellow Vienna: It is also a late variety. The bulbs are globular, small in size and golden yellow in colour. The flesh is creamy white. The average yield is about 125 quintals per hectare.

Seed and sowing

Seed rate

The knol khol seed is slightly bold than that of cauliflower and cabbage but similar in colour. On an average 1000 to 1500 g seed will be sufficient to transplant an hectare of land.

Time of sowing

The seed can be sown in nursery from August to October end. Normally, early varieties are sown in August and September while late varieties are sown in September and October. In hills, at very high altitude (8000 ft above sea level) the seeds are sown from February to March.

Method of sowing

Approximately 75 square metre area is sufficient to raise the seedlings for transplanting one hectare. The raised beds of 5 x 1 metre size should be used for sowing the seed. The seeds should be treated with Thiram at the rate of 2.5 g per kg of seeds. To control black rot the seeds are kept in hot water (50°C) for 30 minutes. The furrows are made at 15 cm distance and seeds are sown in these furrows at one centimetre distance. The furrows are covered with a mixture of farmyard manure and soil. Later on the beds are covered with dry grass to maintain the temperature and to check evaporation. Watering should be done in evening and morning hours till seeds germinate. As soon as the seeds germinate, the grass should be removed and later on watering, weeding and hoeing should be done according to need.

Transplanting

The plants should be planted at 30 cm distance between the rows and 20 cm within the rows. The plants should be healthy and free from insect pests and diseases. The crop should be irrigated immediately after transplanting.

Manures and Fertilizers

For better yield and quality, the crop should be well fertilised. Though the quantity of manures and fertilisers may vary from soil to soil and from variety to variety, normally 200 to 250 quintal farmyard manure should be mixed in the soil one month before transplanting. Later on 80 to 100 kg nitrogen, 50 to 60 kg phosphorus and 80 to 100 kg potash per hectare should be applied. Half dose of nitrogen and full dose of phosphorus and potash should be added one week before transplanting and the remaining half dose of nitrogen should be given as top dressing 4 to 6 weeks after transplanting.

Irrigation and drainage

The crop should be irrigated well in time to ensure better growth during early stage. The first irrigation should be given immediately after transplanting the crop and later on the crop should be irrigated at an interval of 10 to 15 days. Light irrigation should be given each time. To avoid excess water proper drainage system should be provided.

Weed control

The crop should be maintained weed-free to get better yield and quality. Regular shallow cultivation should be given to check the weed growth and to provide natural mulch. The earthing up may also be beneficial if done after 5 to 6 weeks of transplanting. Basalin can also be used at the ate of 2 litres per hectare as pre-planting.

Diseases and their control

Similar to cauliflower.

Insect pests and their control

Similar to cauliflower

Harvesting

For getting better quality, the crop should be harvested well in time. The bulbs should be soft and of proper size at the time of harvesting. If they are not harvested at the right stage they may become fibrous and unfit for market. The harvesting should be done twice or thrice a week.

Yield

The yield depends upon the variety and region of production. The average yield varies from 200 to 250 quintal per hectare.

Preparation for market

After harvest, the roots are cut off and the enlarged stems alongwith the leaves tied up. The bundles are put in shallow baskets and sent to market.

Storage

Under ordinary room conditions it can be stored for 2 to 3 days but in cold storage the bulbs can be stored for 30 to 40 days at $0^{\circ}C$ with 90 to 95 per cent relative humidity.

Seed production

It is also a highly cross pollinated crop and requires 1600 and 1000 metres isolation distance for foundation and certified seeds, respectively. Seed production can only be done on high hills where temperature remains $0^{\circ}C$

for two to three months. Following are the two methods for its seed production.

1. In situ method

In this method plants are left as such in the field and they are allowed to flower. This is a commercial method of its seed production. From time to time off types and diseased plants are taken out.

2. Transplanting method

In this method selected plants are further transplanted in an isolated place. This method is used for nucleus seed production. From time to time off types and diseased plants are taken out.

RADISH

Botanical name	:	*Raphanus sativus* L.
Family	:	*Cruciferae*
Synonymous	:	Mula, Mullangi, Mulo, Mullanki, Mullamgi, Mooli, Muli, Radish.

Importance and utility

It is one of the most common root crop grown all over the country for its enlarged roots. It is commonly used raw for salad with salt, pickles, morabba as vegetable curry and for parathas and rayata making. Its green tops are used as salad and for making vegetable. It is one of the favourite crop of the kitchen garden as it is easily grown and is ready for use in 3 to 6 weeks from the time of sowing. It has cooling effect, prevents constipation, and increases appetite. It is considered good for patients suffering from piles, liver trouble, enlarged spleen and jaundice. It is not easily digested if taken alone. Therefore, it should be taken with gur (raw sugar). According to Chatfield (1949 and 1954), Walt and Merrill (1964) 100 grams of edible roots contain 93.7 per cent water, 4.2 per cent carbohydrate, 1.1 per cent protein, 0.1 per cent fat, 0.7 per cent fibre, 30 I.U. Vitamin A, 24 mg Vitamin C, 37 mg calcium, 31 mg phosphorus, 260 mg potassium, 15 mg magnesium, 37 mg sulphur, 37mg chlorine and 1 mg iron.

According to Aykroyd (1941) its 100 grams leaves contain 89.1 per cent water, 3.9 per cent protein, 0.6 per cent fat, 4.1 per cent carbohydrates, 31 mg calcium, 6 mg phosphorus, 8 mg iron, Vitamin A 8 I.U., Vitamin B 21 mg, Vitamin C 21 mg, nicotinic acid 1.4 mg and riboflavin 2.7 mg.

Origin and history

It is native of Europe or Asia (Thompson and Kelly, 1957), perhaps of China. In India, it is cultivated since ancient times. It is still found in wild condition in Mediterranean region, therefore, many scientists, believe that it originated from southwestern Europe. It was introduced in England in about 1548 and in America in 1629.

Botany

It is a quick growing herbaceous annual. Its enlarged edible roots are fusiform, which are different in colour from white to red. There are two genetical groups in radish, the first group consists of Asiatic varieties which produce edible roots in tropical/sub-tropical climate in first season and seed in the second season as a biennial crop, whereas the second group is of European variety producing roots in the plains of tropical and sub-tropical regions and seeds in the temperate climate on hills. Their seed production is possible only in Kashmir and Kulu valleys and in Nilgiri hills. Generally, Asiatic varieties are more pungent than the European ones.

Climatic requirements

Though it is a cool season crop but Asiatic varieties can resist more heat as compared to European varieties. Best root size, flavour, texture and earliness is obtained at temperatures ranging from 10.0°C to 15.6°C during growing season. Long day followed by high temperature induces bolting without adequate root formation. During hot weather, roots become more pungent and hard before reaching its edible quality. Short day alongwith low temperature conditions are best for quality roots.

Soil and its preparation

It can be grown on all kinds of soils, but better results are obtained in well drained, deep, loose sandy loam soils, having high amount of humus. In clay soils, rough, ill-shaped roots with a number of small fibrous laterals are formed. The summer crop should be grown in cool, moist soils such as silt loam. The soil should be deeply ploughed and harrowed to make it friable and free from clods. The organic manures are very useful to make the soil fit for development of roots. Well rotten 200-250 quintals of farmyard manure or compost per hectare should be applied during land preparation about 20 to 25 days before sowing. This amount may vary according to the availability of nitrogen, phosphorus and potash in the soil.

VARIETIES

Pusa Desi: It should be planted in August-September. Roots are tapering, about 20-30 cm long and highly pungent. Skin is white with green colour at shoulder point. It is tropical and subtropical type. It is pungent and heavy yielder.

The crop matures in 50-55 days.

Pusa Rashmi: It can be sown from September to November. It is also tropical and subtropical type, tapering with green shoulder at the end, mildly pungent and long type. The crop matures in 55 to 60 days after sowing.

Japanese White: Its optimum planting time is October to December. Roots are pure white with blunt end, 25-30 cm long, heavy yielder, less pungent and maturing 60-65 days after sowing. Roots grow better when temperature is low.

White Icle: A pure white, thin and tender variety. The roots become ready in about 30 days after sowing. It is a temperate type. It is suitable for salad.

Rapid Red White topped or French Breakfast: This is a globular variety which becomes ready in 26 days after sowing. This variety is most suitable for kitchen garden. The globular portion is red and tip is white. It is temperate type and is good for winter season sowing.

Pusa Himani: It is long, heavy yielder, maturing in 60-65 days after sowing. This variety is suitable for growing in spring-summer in the hills but most suitable for plains for planting from mid December to mid January, when no other variety except table varieties can successfully be grown due to bolting without root formation.

Pusa Chetaki: Roots are pure white, mildly pungent, tender, smooth, medium long, thick in size, maturing in 40-45 days. This variety sets seed profusely in the plains because bolting starts very early in late November or early December. It has tolerance to high temperature and thus is suitable for sowing from mid March to mid August. During summer, the yield will be comparatively low but due to high rates in the market, the farmers fetch good profits from this variety.

Punjab Safed: Roots are pure white, mildlly pungent, 30-40 cm long and ready to harvest after 50-55 days of sowing. It is more popular in Punjab. It has been developed at P.A.U., Ludhiana.

Hisar Muli No. 1: It is developed at H.A.U., Hisar and is more popular in Haryana. Its roots are straight, white and ready to harvest after 50-55 days of sowing. It is sown from September to October.

Jaunpur White: It is more popular in Jaunpur district of Uttar Pradesh. Roots are sometimes 1 to 1.5metre long, 15 to 20 cm in diameter, 15-20 kg in weight, white in colour, soft and mildly pungent. It is more suitable for vegetable and pickles. The roots are ready to harvest at 75-85 days after sowing.

Seed and Sowing

Sowing time

It can be grown almost throughout the year if the varieties are planted at their recommended time and at definite intervals. The main crop sowing starts from August and continues up to March-April. Asiatic types are sown in August-October while European types in November-January. On high altitudes in hills it is sown from March to August.

Seed rate

Larger seeds germinate better and grow more vigorously and mature earlier than the small seeds. About 8 to 10 kg seeds are required to plant one hectare of land.

Method of sowing

Sowing can be done either in the flat or on the ridges. Rows are prepared at 30 cm distance and sowing of the seed is done at 10 cm distance. At one place generally two seeds are sown, if both germinate then one seedling can be removed after 10-12 days of sowing. The depth of the seed should not be more than 4 cm. On large scale, the seeds can be sown by seed drill. Ridge sowing gives better yield and better root shape and size. Close planting delays maturity and produces ill-shaped roots.

Manures and fertilisers

A radish crop yielding 200 quintals removes 120 kg nitrogen, 65 kg phosphorus and 100 kg of potash as reported by Choudhury (1976). It is quick growing root crop, therefore, the soil should be highly fertilised to make nutrients available to the plant in sufficient quantity. Farmyard manure at the rate of 200-250 quintals per hectare is mixed in the soild during soil preparation 20-25 days before sowing. Thirty kg nitrogen, 50 kg phosphorus and 50 kg potash is also applied as basal dressing. After 25-30 days of sowing, in late varieties and 10-15 days in early varieties, another dose of 30 kg nitrogen per hectare should be applied in standing crop in the form of top dressing.

Irrigation and drainage

If the moisture is not sufficient in the soil, a light irrigation is given immediately after sowing. Later on, irrigations at interval of 10-15 days should be given regularly. For better growth and development of roots, sufficient moisture should be available during its growth period. The field should not be irrigated very frequently, but at the same time care should be taken that the field does not become dry and compact and the root development is not checked. In this case it is always safer if the sowing is done when already enough soil moisture is available for germination in heavy soils. In such soils, irrigation just after sowing may adversely affect germination. Excess water should also be drained off after rains.

Weed control

Weeding should be done regularly to keep down the seasonal weeds. Generally two to three weedings are sufficient. Shallow hoeing may be necessary to facilitate better root growth. At the time of second weeding, thinning in thick sown fields should be done to maintain proper spacing and plant population. Earthing should be done for enlarged root production at the time when roots start growing, otherwise the growing roots may grow above the soil surface.

Diseases and their control

White rust

It is caused by *Albugo candida* fungus and in some areas it is very serious. It produces a white powdery substance in patches on the under surface of the leaves. It commonly appears on the leaves and flowering shoots causing malformed flowers.

Control Measures

❖ Remove the affected plants.

❖ Spray the crop with Dithane Z-78 having a concentration of 0.2 to 0.3%.

Insect pests and their control

Aphids (*Brevicoryne* sp Myzus)

It is a common pest of cruciferous crops and persists on the alternate host throughout the year. Young seedlings get infested and from them it spreads to the whole field. The cloudy and humid conditions are most favourable for the multiplication of this insect. In case of heavy attack the leaves and shoots curl up, get yellowed and finally die.

Control Measure

❖ Spray the crop with systemic insecticides e.g. 0.1% Metasystox, Rogor etc.

Mustard Saw fly (*Athalia* sp.)

It is one of the most common insect of radish and appears during flowering and vegetative stage. Its grub damages the leaves and fruits by biting the leaves and fruits and making holes.

Control Measure

❖ Spray the crop with 0.2% Sevin (50 W.P.).

❖ Spray the crop with 0.2% Endosulfan 35 EC.

Flea beetle (*Phyllotreta* sp.)

In some areas it is very common pest and damages the crop during vegetative stage by biting the leaves.

Control Measure

❖ Spraying the crop with 0.15% Malathion or 0.4 per cent Sevin at 10 to 15 day's interval.

Harvesting

Early varieties generally become ready to harvest after 25 to 30 days of sowing. If they are not harvested in time they become spongy and hollow from inside. Other late varieties should be harvested, according to the time required for maturity by the specific variety but root should be tender and crisp. The roots of whole field should not be harvested at one time but should be harvested as and when they reach full size for the market or home consumption. They are pulled out with the tops by hand and washed in fresh water before sending to the market.

Yield

Yield varies from variety to variety and from soil to soil. Generally Indian varieties give more yield as compared to European varieties. The average yield of Indian varieties varies from 150 to 200 quintals per hectare and that of European varieties from 75 to 100 quintal per hectare.

Preparation for Market

Roots are taken out from the field by hand and washed in fresh water to remove the soil and to give good appearance. Before sending the roots to market' old leaves and hairs present on the roots are removed to make them attractive. They are then sent to the market loose in the basket or tied in bunches of 3-6 roots. During transportation, water may be sprayed on the roots to avoid their drying up.

Storage

Radish roots can be stored at room temperature for 3-4 days without impairing their quality as reported by Purewal (1957). Roots can also be stored under cold storage conditions for over two months at $0°C$ and 90 to 95 per cent relative humidity.

Seed Production

It is a cross pollinated crop, the pollination being done through the insects mainly, and hence requires 1600 and 1000 metres as isolation distance to produce foundation and certified seeds. This way the contamination from other varieties can be avoided. Only the Asian varieties produce seeds in the plains while European varieties do not produce seed in the plains. Hence, their seed production is restricted to the hills only.

The true to the type roots of a particular variety are picked up at the normal stage from the nursery grown for this purpose. The selected roots are prepared for planting by cutting two-thirds tops and one-third roots. These prepared roots are transplanted in the well prepared field at the distance of 75 x 60 cm. Some growers leave the plants with the roots in the field and allow them to produce seed stalks. This method is not recommended because the selection of true to the type roots is not done and off type plants cannot be removed. Also, the seed quality and yield is affected adversely. On an average 4 to 6 quintal per hectare seed yield can be obtained.

TURNIP

Botanical name	-	*Brassica campestris* var. Rapa
Family	-	Cruciferae
Synonymous	-	Salgom, Shalghum, Shalgam, Salgum, Gonglu, Shaljum, Thipperseema, Mullanki, Turnip, Turnip-kannad

IMPORTANCE AND UTILITY

It is a very common vegetable in northern India and is grown commercially in Uttar Pradesh, Bihar, Punjab, Delhi, Jammu and Kashmir etc. Its roots are used as vegetables, salad and for making pickles and leaves are used for vegetables, and as green fodder for feeding cattle. European varieties are much more sweeter and more palatable than Asian types. It's 100 gram edible roots contain 91.1 per cent water, 7.6 per cent carbohydrates, 0.5 per cent protein, 0.6 per cent mineral matters. Turnip leaves are a good source of minerals such as calcium and iron. Vitamin A, B, C are also found in them in appreciable quantities.

ORIGIN AND HISTORY

It is not known where the turnip originated but is said to be found growing wild in Russia and Siberia. As per Purewal (1957), there are three centres of its origin i.e., Central and Western China, Middle Asia, Punjab and Kashmir and the Mediterranean region.

BOTANY

Flowers are hermaphrodite and highly cross pollinated. It is a herbaceous annual grown for the root production but biennial for the seed production. Its enlarged roots are napiform consisting of the hypocotyl which swells and becomes spherical. As in case of radish and carrot, this crop also has two distinct groups known as Asian and European types. The Asian types set seeds freely in the plains, whereas other types fail to do so.

CLIMATIC REQUIREMENTS

Though it is a cool season crop but the Asian varieties can resist heat more than European varieties. Better growth, flavour, texture and size of roots can be obtained at 10°C to 15°C temperature. Long day with high temperature may induce bolting without proper development of root. At high temperature roots become tough and pungent before its edible stage while at low temperature roots are sweet, soft with proper shape and size.

SOIL AND ITS PREPARATION

It can be grown on a variety of soils but the best results are obtained on sandy loam soils which are friable and contain higher amount of humus. In clay soils, roots are rough and ill–shaped with a number of small fibrous laterals. The best soil, pH for this crop is 6.5 to 7.5. Soil should be prepared well by repeated harrowings and planking. Crop resides of previous crops and stone pieces should also be removed. Farmyard manure at the rate of 150 to 200 quintals per hectare should be added during the land preparation.

VARIETIES

A. European varieties

Purple Top White Globe: It is a large-rooted and heavy yielding variety released from I.A.R.I., New Delhi. The roots are almost round, smooth and bright purplish red in the upper part whereas creamy in the lower part. The flesh is white, firm, crisp and mildly sweet flavoured. Roots are ready to harvest after 60 to 65 days of seed sowing. Its tops are dark green, erect with deeply lobed leaves.

Golden Ball: The roots are globe in shape, medium in size with smooth surface and bright creamy yellow skin. The colour of flesh is pale amber with fine texture. Roots are ready to harvest after 70 to 75 days of seed sowing. The leaves are small, erect with deeply lobed margins. It was released from I.A.R.I., New Delhi.

Snowball: The roots are round in shape, medium in size with smooth and white skinned surface. The flesh is white, finely grained, sweet and tender. Roots are ready to harvest after 60 to 65 days of seed sowing. Its leaves are small erect with medium yellow green colour. It was released from I.A.R.I., New Delhi.

Pusa Chandrima: It was also developed at I.A.R.I., New Delhi by crossing Japanese White and Snowball. Roots are round in shape, big in size with white smooth surface. The flesh is white, soft and sweet. Roots are ready to harvest after 55 to 60 days of seed sowing.

Pusa Swarnima: The roots are round in shape, medium in size with light yellow smooth surface. The flesh is creamy in colour, soft and sweet. Roots are ready to harvest after 65 to 70 days of seed sowing. It was developed at I.A.R.I., New Delhi.

Early Milian Red Top: It is a very early variety and becomes ready to harvest after 45 days of seed sowing. The roots are deep flat with purplish red tops and are white underneath. The flesh is white, crisp, fine grained and mildly pungent. The tops are very small with 4 to 6 sessile leaves.

B. Asian varieties

Pusa Kanchan: It was released from I.A.R.I., New Delhi. Roots are round in shape with light red colour and can stay in field without getting spongy. The flesh is creamy yellow with mild pungency. Roots are ready to harvest after 50 to 55 days of seed sowing.

Pusa Sweti: The roots are round and flat in shape with white colour. The flesh is white, sweet with mild flavour. Roots are ready to harvest after 45 to 50 days of seed sowing. It was developed at I.A.R.I., New Delhi.

White-4: It is an early local variety having round and white roots. Roots are ready to harvest after 60 to 65 days of seed sowing. The average yield is about 200 quintals per hectare. It was released by the Department of Agriculture, Punjab.

Red-4: It is also an early local variety having medium-sized red roots. The roots are ready to harvest after 55 to 60 days of seed sowing. The average yield is also about 200 quintals per hectare. It was also released by Department of Agriculture, Punjab.

SEED AND SOWING

Sowing time

Asian varieties are sown in plains from July to September and in hills from March to the end of May. European varieties are sown in plains from October to December and in hills from March to end of May.

Seed rate

In better storage condition, the turnip seeds remain viable for four years. The seeds having 90 to 95 per cent germination will be required to the extent of 3 kg per hectare.

Method of sowing

Sowing can be done in flat beds or on ridges. Ridge sowing gives better yield and superior roots. In flat beds, lines are made at the distance of 45 cm and seeds are sown in these lines. After germination, plants are thinned at 10 to 15 cm distance. Same thing is followed for ridge sowing except ridges are made at 45 cm distance and on the top of ridges small furrows are prepared and seeds are sown in them. If the crop is grown for fodder purpose it is sown relatively thick.

MANURES AND FERTILISERS

The quantity of manures and fertilisers depends upon the fertility status of the soil. Normally 150 to 200 quintals of farmyard manure should be added during field preparation. Besides this, 60 kg nitrogen, 50 kg phosphorus and 40 kg potash per hectare will be required. Half dose of nitrogen and full dose of phosphorus and potash should be given as basal and the remaining half dose of nitrogen as top dressing after 25 to 30 days of seed sowing.

IRRIGATION AND DRAINAGE

The interval and amount of irrigation depends upon the soil type. The first irrigation should be given just after the germination. The subsequent irrigations are given every 5th to 8th day during growth period. At the time of maturity the interval of irrigation can be increased to 10-12 days. Excess water adversely affects the root development and therefore it should be drained out immediately.

WEED CONTROL

One or two weedings should be done between the rows to remove the weeds and to conserve the moisture and for better growth. At this time, excess plants should be thinned out to avoid competition.

DISEASES AND THEIR CONTROL

White rust (*Albugo Candida*)

In some areas, it is a very common disease and produces a white powdery substance in patches on the undersurface of the leaves. The patches mostly appear on leaves and flowering shoots, which get deformed and bear only malformed flowers.

Control Measure

❖ Spray the crop with Dithane Z-78 or Dithane M-45 with a concentration of 0.2 to 0.25% (2 kg/ha).

INSECT PESTS AND THEIR CONTROL

Aphids (*Brevicoryne sp. Myzus sp.*)

This is the most common insect of cruciferous crops and persists on the alternate hosts throughout the year. The cloudy and humid conditions are most favourable for increasing their population. Due to damage by this insect, the leaves and shoots curl up, get yellowed and finally die.

Control Measures

❖ Spray the crop with 0.15% solution of Metasystox.

❖ Nicotine sulphate (1:800) may also prove to be effective at higher temperature of about 21°C.

Mustard Saw Fly (*Athalia* sp.)

It is also a common insect pest damaging the cruciferous crops. During flowering stage, the damage is more. Grubs make holes in the leaves and fruits.

Control Measure

❖ Spray the crop with 0.2% solution of Sevin (50 W.P.).

Flea beetle (*Phyllotreta* sp.)

Sometimes leaves are eaten by this beetle and heavy damage is observed.

Control Measures

❖ Spray the crop with Malathion at the concentration of 0.15%.

❖ Spray the crop with 0.2% solution of Sevin (50 W.P.).

HARVESTING

The roots can be harvested when they are 7 to 10 cm in diameter. If they are allowed to grow to bigger size, the quality will go down. Harvesting should be done in evening hours and the soil should be slightly dry so that roots can be lifted clean out of the soil.

YIELD

The root yield varies from variety to variety and from soil to soil. Normally, late varieties grown in sandy loam soil give better yield than early maturing varieties. The root yield varies from 200 to 450 quintals per hectare while average yield is about 225 quintals per hectare.

PREPARATION FOR MARKET

After harvesting, the roots should be prepared for market by washing in running water, removing the side roots and grading them properly. The tops should be cut off near the surface of the crown. The selected roots can be packed in baskets for market.

STORAGE

At normal room temperature the roots can be kept only for two to three days while at 5°C to 10°C the roots can be stored for 10 to 15 days.

SEED PRODUCTION

On the basis of seed production, turnip has two distinct types viz., temperate and Asiatic. The first type produces seeds only in temperate regions while the latter can produce seeds in plains. Like radish, isolation distance of 1000 metres and 1600 metres should be maintained for certified and foundation seeds. Inspect the crop thrice for off-types at root selection, bolting and flowering stages. Roguing of off-type plants should be done as and when noticed in the field. For early and late bolters also roguing should be done. Seed crop should be harvested when the pods start turning yellow. Timely harvesting leads to high seed yields because shattering is a problem in this crop. Harvesting should be completed in 2-3 lots. The harvested crop should be put in a pile and covered with tarpauline for 2-3 days. Give one turning and again cover for proper curing. Dry the crop and thresh it with the help of wooden sticks. Clean the seed in the seeds cleaning-cum-grading machine. Get the seeds tested for germination, purity etc. The graded and dried seeds should be packed in moisture proof containers.

CARROT

Botanical name	-	*Daucus carota* L.
Family	-	U mbelliferae
Synonymous	-	Gajar, Gajor, Gajjar, Gajargadda, Kaaret, Kempu, Mulangi, Mormuj, Bulmuj, Carottee, Cullive, Gemeiner, Mohre, Karoth, Jazar, Zardak, Garijara.

IMPORTANCE AND UTILITY

Carrot is being grown in India for a very long time for forage and human consumption. It is used in both the forms, raw as well as in curries. It is generally used for halwa, pickles, gajar pak, sweet meals, preserves, rayata, salad and carrot pudding (gajrela). Its deshi varieties are also used for consumption, by animals used for heavy work. It is an excellent source of Vitamin A and iron and contains good quantities of vitamins B and C and is rich in sugar. It has a useful effect on the kidney and acts as a preventive for brick dust sediments sometimes found in urine. Its seeds are used for abortion and its decoction is a popular remedy for jaundice. According to Aykroyd (1941), Chatfield (1949 and 1954) Walt and Merrill (1964) fresh edible carrot contains 88.6 per cent water, 1.1 per cent protein, 0.2 per cent fat, 9.1 per cent carbohydrates, 1.0 per cent fibre, Vitamin A 12000 I.U., Vitamin B_1, B_2 and C and minerals in traces.

ORIGIN AND HISTORY

It is said to be a native of Europe, Asia and North Africa and possibly North and South America (Thompson and Kelly, 1957). It was cultivated by the ancients but was not used in their common food.

BOTANY

The carrot (*Daucus carota* L.) belongs to the family Umbelliferae and has got fleshy edible conical root. Carrot has two types which are categorised as Asian and European types. The first one produces roots and seeds freely in the plains while the second one produces roots in plains during winter but fails to produce seeds. The root end in the case of first one is conical while blunt or stump in the case of second one. It is a cross pollinated crop with bisexual flowers.

CLIMATIC REQUIREMENTS

It is tolerant to high temperature but it thrives best in cool climate. The optimum temperature for its germination is 7°C to 29°C and for root growth is 18°C to 24°C. At higher temperatures foliage growth is more with poor root development and if grown at low temperature the roots are comparatively longer and slender. Barnes (1936) reported that greenhouse-grown carrots produced the longest root between 10°C to 15.5°C with poor colour and between 15.5°C to 17°C with good colour. Sufficient soil moisture is very essential for proper germination. Abundance of sunlight is conducive to high quality roots.

SOIL AND ITS PREPARATION

It can be grown on a variety of soils but best results are recorded in well drained, deep loose sandy loam soils having high amount of humus and free from hard layer. Loose soils help in the production of good round shaped roots and the yield is also high. The crop does not flourish in highly acidic soils and the best yield is expected at soil pH 6.5 as reported by Choudhry (1962). In clayey soils, rough, ill shaped roots with a number of small fibrous laterals are formed. The soil should be deeply ploughed and harrowed to make it friable and free from clods. The soil surface should be loose and smooth otherwise root development will be poor. Organic manures are very essential to make the loose soil for the proper development of roots. Well rotten 200-250 quintals of farmyard manure or compost per hectare should be applied during land preparation, about 20-25 days before planting. This amount may vary from soil to soil.

VARIETIES

Nantes: It is a fine quality European variety which cannot be used for seed production in plains but can be used for its root production. The seed can be produced under temperate conditions in the hills. Its roots are medium sized, orange red, smooth, well shaped with blunt tips. The flesh colour is uniform orange red, fine textured with small core which is not prominent. Good quality roots are produced in the plains.

Chantaney: It is also an European type carrot having attractive deep reddish orange coloured roots. The roots are half long, smooth, thick shouldered and gradually tapering. Its seed is also produced under temperate conditions in the hills but well developed good quality roots can be obtained in the plains. The roots are tender, sweet and fine textured. The flesh is beautiful rich orange coloured with indistinct core.

Pusa Kesar: Bred at I.A.R.I., New Delhi as a selection from a cross between Local Red and Nantes (Singh, 1963). The leaf top is markedly shorter than that of Local Red. The root develops a narrow central sufficiently red coloured core. It is Asian type and seeds can be produced freely in plains. It has more carotene than Local Red. A notable feature of this variety is that the roots stay a month longer in field without any sign of bolting.

Selection No. 233: Though it is an Asian type but roots are similar to Nantes. Roots are orange in colour, 15 to 18 cm long, sweet and having pleasant flavour. They are ready to harvest after 60 days of sowing and do not become harder up to 90 days of sowing. Yield varies from 200 to 300 quintals per hectare.

Gajar No. 29: In is an early Asian type. Its roots are long and light red in colour. Yield varies from 250 to 300 quintals per hectare and its seed can be produced very easily in the plains of country.

SEED AND SOWING

Sowing time

In plains of the country, Asiatic type are sown in the month of August and September and European types from October to mid-December. On very high hills, carrot is sown from March to June. For regular supply, it should be sown at 15 days' interval starting from August to mid-December in plains and similarly from March to June in the hills. At lower altitudes, the sowing is done as in plains.

Seed rate

When seed is stored at room temperature its germination percentage goes down, therefore, germination percentage of seed must be tested before sowing. Bold seeds germinate better and produce better roots than the small ones. About 6 to 8 kg seeds having 90 or above germination percentage is sufficient to sow one hectare of land.

Method of sowing

Carrot can be sown either in flat beds or on ridges. For better germination the field should be pre-irrigated. Rows are prepared by hand hoes at 30 cm distance and sowing of seed is done át 10 cm distance. Similarly the ridges are prepared by spade or hand hoes and seeds are sown at 10 cm distance. The depth of the seed should not be more than 2 cm. On largescale, the seeds can be sown by the seed drill. Ridge sowing gives better and early yield than the flat bed sowing. Thick sowing delays its maturity and produces ill–shaped roots.

MANURES AND FERTILISERS

A carrot crop yielding 280-300 quintals of roots per hectare removes about 32 kg of nitrogen, 18 kg of phosphorus and 100 kg of potash as reported by Thompson and Kelley (1957). For better yield and better root development the land should be sufficiently manured. Well decomposed, 200 to 250 quintals per hectare farmyard manure should be applied 20 to 25 days before sowing. Twenty-five, kg nitrogen, 50 kg phosphorus and 80-100 kg potash should be given as basal dose at the last harrowing and 25 kg nitrogen should be applied as top dressing 30-40 days after sowing the crop. For better development of roots, farmyard manure is very essential as it improves the physical condition of the soil.

IRRIGATION AND DRAINAGE

There should be sufficient moisture in soil at the time of seed sowing. This helps in proper seed germination. First irrigation should be given 10-12 days after seed sowing when the seed germination is complete. Later on light irrigations should be given at 10-12 days' interval. Never irrigate the crop heavily otherwise it will result in excessive foliage growth with poor root formation and the maturity will be delayed. Excess water should be drained out after irrigation.

WEED CONTROL

Carrot seeds germinate in 10-12 days and at the same time a light hoeing or weeding should be done carefully. It also facilitates soil aeration and better root development. Lasso, at the rate of 4 litre per hectare dissolved in 800 litre of water may be used as pre-emergence. If chemical is not used three to four weedings will be required during the crop season.

DISEASES AND THEIR CONTROL

Damping off

It is caused by *Pythium aphinidermatum*. Plants are affected during early stage of growth. Affected plants start rotting in the collar region of seedlings. It is generally observed when the drainage of the soil is poor.

Control Measures

❖ Light irrigations should be given to the crop.

❖ The seed should be treated with Thiram or Captan at the rate of 3 g per kg of seed.

Bacterial soft rot

It is caused by *Erwinia carotovora* and fully matured roots are affected. They start rotting after infection and become unfit for consumption. In poor drained soils the infection is more than in well drained soils.

Control Measures

❖ Top dressing of nitrogenous fertiliser should be stopped.

❖ Excess water should be drained off.

Carrot yellow

It is a viral disease transmitted by the six-spotted leaf hopper. Affected foliage becomes yellowish.

Control Measures

❖ Affected plants should be removed carefully without touching the other plants.

❖ Crop should be sprayed with 0.2 per cent solution of Rogor or Thiodan to check the spread of the disease.

INSECT PESTS AND THEIR CONTROL

Cut worm, White worm and White grub

They eat and bore the roots and reduce their market value. At some places white grubs commonly damage the roots.

Control Measures

❖ Heptachlor dust at the rate of 25 kg per hectare should be applied in the soil before sowing the seeds.

HARVESTING

The crop can be adjusted for harvesting at the marketable stage depending on the size of root. One should take care that it should not be allowed to stand in the field beyond the marketable stage as otherwise roots become fluffy and unfit for consumption. Normally, Asiatic types can be harvested when their diameter is 2.5 to 5 cm at the upper end. They can be harvested by spade or pulling them out by hand if sufficient moisture is available. A light irrigation before harvesting will facilitate harvesting.

YIELD

The Asian varieties generally produce more yield per unit area than the European varieties. Average yield varies from 100 to 200 quintals per hectare.

PREPARATION FOR MARKET

As and when the roots are dug out or pulled out by hand, they are washed in running fresh water to remove the adhering soil. Side roots and foliage is completely removed. Generally Asian varieties are sold in loose while European varieties are bunched in a fixed number, say half a dozen, or one dozen, together and sold in the market.

Damaged and illshaped roots are sorted out and the betters ones packed in baskets or in gunny bags before sending them to the market.

STORAGE

Before storage, diseased, damaged and mis-shaped roots are removed from the lot. These are kept in baskets or in wooden trays. They can be stored at room temperature for 3 to 4 days and at 0-4.4°C with 93 to 98 per cent relative humidity they can be kept for three to four months (Wright *et al.*, 1954).

SEED PRODUCTION

Only the Asiatic types can produce seeds in the plains of the country while in European types seed can be produced only in hills. It is a cross pollinated crop hence every care should be taken to keep the two varieties away from each other. About 1000 metre and 800 metre isolation distance should be maintained for foundation and certified seeds, respectively.

True to the type roots are selected when they are at marketable stage. The selected roots are prepared for planting by cutting two-thirds of the tops and one-third lower root portion. These roots are transplanted in the well prepared field at the distance of 60 x 60 cm. Some growers leave the plants in the field and allow them to produce the seeds. This method is not successful because the seeds produced by this method produce poor quality roots and result in early bolting. Off types are removed at the time of root selection and at the time of flowering. A yield of 300 to 500 kg of seed per hectare is obtained.

ONION

Botanical name	:	*Allium cepa*
Family	:	Alliaceae
Synonymus	:	Piyaz, Piaj, Palandu, Payaz, Kyet-th-woni-ni, Earulli, Kanda, Dungli, Ganda, Ulli, Vengagam, Erangayam.

IMPORTANCE AND UTILITY

Onion is one of the most important vegetable crop cultivated extensively throughout the country under a wide range of climatic conditions. It is used both in green and mature stage for salad and spice in a variety of flavour dishes and soups. It is very important in cookery, hence it is called the "queen of kitchen" by Germans. It is also a useful food for cattle and poultry. The pungency is due to a volatile oil known as allyl-propyl-disulphide ($C_6H_{12}S_2$) which varies from variety to variety, stage of maturity, type of soil, and other cultural practices. The yellow colouring material found in outer skin of bulb is called quercetin. It has several medicinal uses as reported by Nadkarni (1927). Its bulbs with common salt are used as a domestic remedy for colic and scurvy. Onion is applied as poultice to indolent boils, bruises and wounds. During summer it reduces the body heat and is also useful in dysentery. Bulb juice is very useful in faintness, infantile convulsions, headache, epileptic and hysterial fits. Its hot juice is also dropped into the ear to relieve ear pain. It is applied in eyes in dimness of vision, to allay irritation of insect bites, scorpion stings and also in skin diseases. It can also be a good antidote for tobacco poisoning. Roasted bulbs mixed with cumin sugar candy and cow's ghee, give relief in piles. If cooked onion is used with vinegar it helps in jaundice, spleenic enlargement and dyspepsia. It is useful in sore throat cases when used with vinegar without cooking. If mixed with mustard oil in equal amount, it is good for application in rheumatic pain and other inflammatory swellings.

According to Rao and Purewal (1954) onion contains 86.84 per cent moisture, 1.2 per cent protein, 0.1 per cent fat, 11.6 per cent carbohydrates, 0.4 per cent mineral matters, 0.18 per cent calcium, 0.05 per cent phosphorus, 0.7 per cent iron, calories 51, Vitamin B, 120 I.U., Vitamin C, 0.4 per cent nicotinic acid.

ORIGIN AND HISTORY

It originated from the region comprising north West India, Afghanistan, the Soviet Republic of Tajik and Uzbek and western Tien Shan. Western Asia and areas around the Mediterranean are the secondary centres of development (Choudhury, 1965). Hippocrates speaks of onions being eaten commonly in 430 B.C. Onions were grown in America as early as 1629 and in 1806 some varieties were listed by seedsmen.

BOTANY

The food stored in the mature bulb consists primarily of sucrose and the leaves are hollow and tubular structures. Each leaf emerges from inside the previously formed leaf through a hole on the side. The stem remains as a plate-like structure during the vegetative stage. The leaf bases (petioles) form a slender cylinder during the early stages of development. Under proper environmental stimulus, the inner leaf bases swell forming the bulb. The outer leaf bases remain thin. An umbel of flowers born at the tip. The stigma of an individual flower does not become receptive until after the anthers have stopped shedding pollen. Thus, stigma is pollinated from the flowers in the umbel which open later. The pollen is spread primarily by insects.

CLIMATIC REQUIREMENTS

It can be grown under a wide range of climatic conditions but it does well in a mild season, without great extremes of heat or cold or excessive rainfall. It is successfully cultivated as rain-fed crop even at elevations of 1500 to 2300 metres between April and August. The plants are quite hardy and can withstand freezing temperature. Bolting is initiated by exposure to cold temperature at early seedling growth stage. It has been observed that transplanting from November till December 15 in plains of northern India causes bolting in a greater percentage of plants due to exposure of seedlings to low temperatures. On the other hand, transplanting after January does not allow the vegetative growth phase to prolong more causing poorer growth. It ultimately causes poor sized bulbs. The main reason is bulb growth at a rapid rsate under long day conditions of March-April. Thus, transplanting in proper period is very essential for reduced bolting and proper yield. the temperatures for different stages are as shown in the table.

Stages	Temperature °C		
	Minimum	Optimum	Maximum
Germination	2	10-30	35
Growth and quality	7	11-24	30

Twenty per cent available moisture or more is needed for better germination. The root system of onion is shallow and hence crop responds well to irrigations. Temporary retardation of growth due to dry weather followed by rapid resumption of growth may result in double bulb, splits or resumption of growth after the bulb has started to mature. Hot-dry conditions following a period favourable for rapid growth cause a die-back of the tips of the leaves. This is called blast. Dry conditions are preferred during maturation for proper curing. Bulbing occurs only under long–day conditions. Optimum day length for bulb formation is 12 to 14 hours.

SOIL AND ITS PREPARATION

Onion can be grown on a variety of soils ranging from sandy loam to heavy clays, but sandy loam, silty loam and deep friable soil, having better retention of moisture are best suited for its cultivation. The soil should not be low lying, marshy and heavy clay. The most favourable soil pH range is 5.8 to 6.8. In light sandy soils, onion matures earlier than in heavier soils. The field should be prepared in a fine tilth by ploughings, harrowings and planking etc. During its preparation residue of previous crops should be collected and burnt. The field should be well levelled. About 200 to 250 quintals of farmyard manure per hectare should be mixed in the soil thoroughly about 20-25 days before transplanting.

VARIETIES

Pusa Red: It is one of the earliest variety grown over a wide area in the hills and plains of North India. It is a selection from the local red varieties. It has medium sized, bronze-red coloured globular bulbs. It is less pungent than other local red varieties. On an average, 12 bulbs weigh about 1 kg. Bulbs mature in about 130 days after transplanting. The average yield ranages from 200 to 300 quintals per hectare. It is released from I.A.R.I., New Delhi.

Pusa Ratnar: It is a new variety recently released by the I.A.R.I., New Delhi. It has large, slightly oblate, globular and flatish globular bulbs with attractive red colour. It is good for salad because of mild pungency. The crop matures in 145 to 150 days after sowing. It has good storage quality under ordinary conditions. The average yield is higher than Pusa Red.

Early Grano: It is an American variety but cultivated in India since long back. It has globular bulb of yellow colour and mild pungency and is most suitable for salad purposes. The crop matures in about 95 days after transplanting. The green onion can be used after 80 days of transplanting. It does not have a good keeping quality. This variety is very good for dehydration. It is released from I.A.R.I., New Delhi.

Niphad-53: It is an improved strain of onion which has a bright red colour. It has well shaped thin necked bulbs of red colour. It has good keeping quality had has been found suitable for growing in Kharif season in those areas which have moderate rainfall. The average yield during Rabi season is about 200 to 250 quintals and in Kharif season about 150 to 200 quintals per hectare. It is released from Onion Research Station, Nasik.

Punjab Selection: It has red coloured globular bulbs of medium size having moderate pungency. The crop matures 130-140 days after transplanting. The average yield is about 300 quintals per hectare. It is released from P.A.U., Ludhiana.

VI-67: It is a hybrid having large sized, red coloured bulbs. The crop matures in about 130-140 days after transplanting. The average yield is about 350 quintals per hectare.

Hisar-2: Bulbs are bronze red coloured like Pusa Red. They are flatish, globular and slightly more pungent. The bulbs mature in about 135 days after transplanting. The average yield is about 300 quintals per hectare. It is released from H.A.U., Hisar.

Punjab-48: It is released from P.A.U., Ludhiana. The bulbs are of medium size, flatish round and attractive white. They are good for dehydration. The T.S.S. are about 12-13 and the average yield is about 250 to 300 quintals per hectare.

Udaipur 102: It is released from Agricultural University, Udaipur. It has white coloured, medium to large sized bulbs. The average T.S.S. are 11.5 per cent. The average yield is about 200 to 250 quintals per hectare.

Patna Red: It is released from Department of Horticulture, Agriculture College, Sabour, Bihar. The bulbs are medium in size, globular in shape with red colour.

Kalyanpur Red Round: It is released by Vegetable Breeding Station, Kalyanpur, Kanpur. The bulbs are medium in size with red colour.

In addition to the above varieties, seven new varieties of onion namely Brown Spanish, Cream Gold, White Spanish, Early Locker Brown, N-5, N-7 and N-123-7 have been reported recently.

CHARACTERISTICS OF A VARIETY

A variety should have following characteristics for dehydration purposes (Mital and Srivastava, 1975).

1. The bulb should be white in colour without any green patches so that the final product should not be discoloured.

2. T.S.S. of the variety should range from $15°$ to $20°$ brix. The ratio of reducing to non-reducing sugar is desired to be low to avoid any discolouration.

3. The variety should have good storage quality, high yield and resistance to insect pests and diseases.

4. Moisture percentage should be around 80.

SEED AND SOWING

Seed rate

The seed rate depends upon the germination percentage of seed. Six to eight kilogram seed of the lot with 80-85% germination will be required for planting one hectare. The seed remains viable only for one year at room temperature, therefore, old seed should not be used. On an average one kilogram seed contains about 2,00,000 seeds.

Sowing time

The seed sowing varies from region to region. As per Rao and Purewal (1957) the following recommendations are available.

Region	Sowing time	Transplanting time
North India	October to middle of November	Middle of December to January
Maharashtra, Andhra Pradesh & M.P.	October	Middle of November to end of November
West Bengal	September to November	October to December
Hills	October and November	December to March

In some parts of the country where rainfall is moderate the seeds can be sown in June-July and transplanting can be done in July and August. During this season only few varieties can do well. In Andhra Pradesh and Tamil Nadu, two crops in a year are taken viz. June to October and October to January and also sometimes a third crop during summer is also raised from January to June.

Sowing

The land selected for the nursery should be fertile, well drained, free from weeds and should have proper sunlight during day time. Sandy loam soils are, therefore, preferred for this purpose. The nursery area should be prepared well by repeated ploughing and harrowings. The roots and weeds should be collected, removed and burnt. One metre wide, 5 metre long and 15 cm raised beds are made with interspaces of 30 cm between the beds. This space is used for watering, weeding and other field operations. One centimetre thick layer of well rotten farmyard manure should be put on the beds and mixed properly. Finally, the beds are levelled well. The seeds should be sown in lines 15 cm apart and covered thoroughly with about one centimetre thick fine soil. Care should be taken to distribute the seeds evenly to produce uniform seedlings. Later on, the beds are covered by dry grass and water is then applied with a sprinkling can soaking the soil well. This sprinkling should be repeated every day till the seeds germinate. Covering material is removed carefully after the seeds have germinated. Irrigation, weeding and other operations should be done as per requirement. The seedlings are generally ready for transplanting in six to eight weeks after sowing the seed, when they are about 15 cm tall.

Transplanting

As and when the land has been brought to a fine tilth, the field should be divided into small plots of convenient size for irrigation. Transplanting should be done in rows 20 cm apart, with a distance of 6-8 cm between plants. Though a lot of work has been done on this aspect at different centres in the country but this spacing was found to be the most economical. Large-sized seedlings should be preferred over small ones for transplanting. In some of the areas the tops of seedlings are generally cut but as per findings this operation does not have any significant difference in yield and quality. Seedlings should be set about 1 to 2 cm deep and irrigation should be given immediately after transplanting.

Sowing of seed directly in the field

In some parts of the country, the onion seed is directly scattered during August to November in the plains and it is mixed in the soil by stirring with hand hoes so that the seeds reach to a depth of 2 to 3 cm. Hand watering or light irrigation is given immediately after sowing. The seeds germinate a week after sowing. Weeding should be done at an interval of 10 to 12 days in early stage to avoid weed competition. Sometimes to maintain proper distance, thinning is also required and thinned plants can be used in some other places where the population is thin.

Manures and fertilisers

Onion crop appears to be a heavy feeder of nitrogen and potash. Amount of manures and fertilisers needed by it depends upon the variety and season. Two hundred to 500 quintals of farmyard manure should be applied three to four weeks before transplanting. Besides this, 80-100 kg nitrogen, 50-60 kg phosphorus and 80-100 kg potash per hectare is required. Half dose of nitrogen and full dose of phosphorus and potash should be added as basal and rest half nitrogen should be given in two split doses as top dressing, 30-40 and 70 days after transplanting.

Irrigation and drainage

The quantity of water and interval of irrigations depend upon the time of planting, rainfall during the season, type of soil etc. The crop planted between June to October requires very less number of irrigations only during dry periods. October planted crop requires more number of irrigations and the crop planted in February requires maximum number of irrigations. First irrigation should be given immediately after transplanting. Later on, 10 to 15 days' interval between irrigations should be maintained. During bulb formation, irrigation is very essential. In sandy soils the number of irrigations will be twice than that of heavy soils. The irrigation should be stopped 20 days before harvesting.

Weed control

Removal of weeds, especially in the first two months, is very essential for better yield and quality. The weeding should be shallow to avoid injury to roots. Because it is a shallow rooted crop, deep tillage is likely to injure the roots and thus decrease the yield. Generally three to four weedings are sufficient to get a normal yield. Basalin (1 kg active ingredient in 1000 litres of water) can be sprayed before transplanting to make the crop weed free. With the help of the above chemical only one weeding will be required after 55 to 60 days of transplanting.

Diseases and their control

Purple blotch

It is caused by *Alternaria parri* fungus. In this disease, black spots are seen on the leaves as well as on the flowering stalks. Later on the leaves drop down and plants die. In the *Taria,* due to attack of this disease seed production is not possible. If the attack is mild the plants may survive, but the bulbs will be ill-developed.

Control Measures

❖ Seed should be treated with Thiram @ 2 g per kg of seed.
❖ Crop rotations should be followed and in the plot where disease occurs the onion crop should not be grown for at least three years.
❖ Crop should be sprayed with 0.2% solution of Dithane M-45 at an interval of 10 to 12 days regularly.

Downy mildew

It is caused by *Peronospora destructor* fungus. This disease is commonly seen in low lying areas and in heavy soils, when the crop is subjected to excessive moisture and humid atmosphere. In this disease oval spots are seen on the leaves and later on, the spot size increases and finally leaves become dry. Small bulbs are formed in the affected plants.

Control Measures

❖   Arrangement of proper drainage should be made.

❖   Spray the crop with 0.2% solution of Dithane M-45 at an interval of 10-15 days.

Bacterial soft rot

It is caused by *Erwinia carotovora* bacteria. This disease is observed in storage. In this disease the water-soaked and soft inner scales emitting a foul odour are commonly noted.

Control Measures

❖   Bulbs should be cured well before keeping them in store.

❖   All the diseased bulbs should be removed by periodical inspection.

❖   Store should be properly ventilated.

Neck rot

It is caused by *Botrytis* fungus. In this disease the rot usually begins at the neck of the bulb and later on the bulb loses its firmness.

Control Measures

❖   Spray the crop with 0.2% solution of Dithane M-45 at 15 days' interval.

❖   Completely cured bulbs should be kept in store.

Onion smut

It is caused by *Urocystis cepulae* fungus. It is a soil-borne disease. At the time of seed germination the smut appears as elongated, dark, slightly thickened areas at the base of seedlings. During early growth, as new leaves are formed, they become infected, swollen and bent downward. The fungus becomes inactive in the soil at soil temperature of 26.7°C and above.

Control Measures

❖   Seed should be treated with Thiram at the rate of 2 g per kg seed.

❖ Nursery bed should be treated with Formaldehyde solution (0.5 litre of 40% formaldehyde in 30 litres of water).

Insect pests and their control

Onion thrips (*Thrips* sp.)

It is a very common insect pest of the crop. It is a small yellow sucking insect which damages the leaves by sucking the juice, resulting in the browning of the tips. The damage is very severe during rainy season.

Control Measures

❖ Keep the crop weed free.

❖ Spray the crop with Parathion or Toxophene or Heptachlor or Dieldrin (0.2 to 0.3%) but insecticide should not be applied to the crop which is to be eaten as green.

❖ Grow resistant varieties such as Early Grano, Sweet Spanish, White Persian etc.

Onion Maggot (*Hylemya* sp.)

They feed upon the onion leaves and bulbs both of all the ages from young seedlings to mature bulbs. They make holes in the onion bulbs permitting bulb rotting organisms to enter. In field, sometimes heavy damage takes place due to its attack.

Control Measures

❖ Affected bulbs should be sorted out and dumped at an isolated place and covered with at least 30 cm of soil in early spring before the adults emerge out.

❖ Use Thimet 10-G at the rate of 15 kg per hectare before transplanting the crop.

❖ Crop should be sprayed with Malathion (0.2% solution) at an interval of 15 days.

Leaf eating caterpillar (*Laphygma eriqua*)

Occasionally, this insect pest is found eating the leaves and feeding inside the leaves.

Control Measure

❖   Spray the crop with Lindane (0.3%) or Malathion (0.2 per cent).

Harvesting

Green onions may be harvested as soon as the bulbs and leaves attain edible size. For mature bulbs, the crop can be harvested three to five months after transplanting, depending upon the variety. Maturity can be judged by the tops falling over while the leaves are still green. The bulbs should be pulled out when the tops have fallen over and the leaves have turned yellow. In case harvesting is not done at proper time the bulbs may become soft due to sun injury. Rain at the time of maturity of bulbs causes development of roots which impair the market quality of bulbs. After harvesting, the bulbs should be spread in thin layers under shade for curing. During this period, the outer skin of bulbs would be well dried to make it hard. This way the keeping quality in storage is improved.

Yield

Onion yields depend upon several factors such as the time of sowing, seed material used, variety, amount of manures and fertilisers and type of soil. The average yield may vary from 150 to 350 quintals per hectare in irrigated conditions, and 70 to 100 quintals per hectare in rain-fed conditions.

Preparation for market

After curing, the leaves are removed and diseased, damaged and forked bulbs are sorted out. The selected bulbs are again spread for two to three days in shade and well ventilated place. Care should be taken that during this period the bulbs are not exposed to sun heat. Completely dried bulbs are packed in thin gunny bags and loaded in truck or cart for market.

Storage

At room temperature the bulbs can be stored for several weeks whereas under cold storage conditions the bulbs can be stored at $0^{\circ}C$ to $1.7^{\circ}C$ with 80 to 85 per cent relative humidity for four months and at 60 per cent relative humidity it is possible to store them even for 6 to 7 months. If the Maleic Hydrazide at 1500-2000 ppm is sprayed 15 days before harvesting, sprouting in the storage may be checked and the bulbs remain healthy for about eight months.

The dried bulbs are spread on damp-proof floor or on racks in well-ventilated shady place. Periodical turning of the bulbs and removal of rotten and sprouted bulbs is highly essential. At ordinary condition there may be 20 to 25 per cent loss in weight due to removal of rotten bulbs and due to loss of moisture.

Seed Production

It is biennial in seed production hence it requires two seasons to complete its life cycle. During first year the bulbs are produced, in the second year the bulbs are planted for seed production. Bulb size in terms of diameter, spacing and soil fertility are the main factors affecting the seed production. In the second fortnight of October, the true to the type bulbs are planted at 30 x 30 cm distance. At this time the bulbs should be inspected carefully. Normal cultural operations should be followed. Three months after planting the flowering stalks are produced. Off types and diseased plants should be removed at this stage. Early umbels produce heavier seeds with a better germination capacity than late umbels. Within six to eight weeks the seeds ripen and become black at this stage. Ripened individual umbels are cut and dried in a well ventilated and shaded place. Later on, these umbels can be threshed. The seeds so collected are dried in the sun for a day or two and stored in bins. In normal condition, 8 to 10 quintals of seed can be obtained from one hectare.

GARLIC

Botanical name	-	*Allium sativum* L.
Family	-	Alliaceae
Synonymous	-	Lahsoon, Poodu, Lassan, Veluthull, Lasun, Rashun, Nohoyo, Vellulli, Lasan, Shumandha, Bhutagna, Mahasuda, Sir.

IMPORTANCE AND UTILITY

Like onion it is cultivated throughout the country and is an important spice or condiment used for flavouring and seasoning vegetables and meat dishes. The main growing states are Tamil Nadu, Uttar Pradesh, Gujarat, Punjab and Andhra Pradesh. In ancient period, it was used in the food of soldiers of West Germany to stimulate their power and also to encourage them. Garlic oil, which is brown or yellow in colour, contains Allyl propyl disulphide and another sulphur compound Allin. The oil is used in paralytic and rheumatic infections and also in several food preparations such as chutneys, pickles, curries, vegetables and tomato ketchup. Its powder can be used for the above mentioned things but as yet it is not prepared on large scale. Green fresh leaves are also used for seasoning purpose as well as in chutney and salad dishes. Garlic has many medicinal uses also. Antibiotics have been prepared from its extracts. It is used in stomach troubles, headache, tooth-ache, ear-ache, sore eyes and numerous other diseases. It is applied to the nose, like onion, in cases of fainting. It is very useful in infantile convulsions and other nervous and spasmodic infections. During winter, if it is eaten it wards off attacks of rheumatism and neuralgia. The oil in which garlic has been fried proves excellent for application against scabbies and maggots infesting ulcers. Its rubbing over ringworm gives relief to the patient. By regular use of garlic harmful bacteria are killed in digestive system. According to the investigations at C.F.T.R.I., Mysore (1962), in natural condition it does not exhibit any flavour, but as soon as it is bruised, peeled or macerated, an enzymatic action of allinase enzyme occurs, transforming allin to allicin resulting in the strong characteristic odour. Allicin has antibacterial activity which is approximately 15 Oxford units of penicillin. According to Dr. Aykroyd (1941), and Rao and Purewal (1957) its edible portion contains 62.8 per cent moisture, 6.3 per cent protein, 0.7 per cent fat, 1.0 per cent mineral matters, 0.8 per cent fibre, 29.0 per cent carbohydrates, 0.03 per cent calcium, 0.31 per cent phosphorus, 0.0013 per cent iron.

ORIGIN AND HISTORY

It is supposed to have originated from Central Asia and Mediterranean regions. At present it is grown in all countries where onion is cultivated.

BOTANY

It is a herbaceous annual for bulb production. Leaves are narrow and flat. The edible underground stem (bulb) its made of smaller bulblets known as "cloves". Cloves vary from 6 to 15 in numbers in one bulb and they are enclosed in a thin sheath of white or light pink colour. Generally, cloves of garlic do not produce flower stalks or the inflorescence may be partial or not at all. But its bulbils form a swelling within the false stem.

CLIMATIC REQUIREMENTS

Garlic can do well under same conditions as required for onion bulbs and it prefers a low temperature in winter but higher temperature in March and April. The cultivation can be done up to the elevation of 1000 to 1200 metres. It is a cool season crop and hardy to frost. The crop requires low temperature for the vegetative phase as well as for bulb formation. When temperature goes above 30°C the crop does not form better-sized bulb. Therefore, the crop is normally planted in winter and harvested when hot season sets in.

VARIETIES

Very less information is available regarding the varieties of garlic. Two types of varieties are available depending on their colour i.e., red and white. The white coloured varieties are more popular as they are less pungent. Red coloured varieties are mostly used for medicinal purposes. They are more pungent as compared to white varieties. Amongst white varieties some produce small-sized bulbs while some of them produce big-sized bulbs. The different varieties of these groups are as below:

(A) Small-sized varieties : T 56-4, Creole, Italian and Tahiti.

(B) Big-sized varieties: Solan, Phawari, Rajali gaddi.

T 56-4 and Solan are popular in North India whereas Phawari and Rajali gaddi in South India.

SOIL AND ITS PREPARATION

It can be grown on a variety of soils ranging from sandy loams to heavy clays, but sandy loam, deep and friable soils having better moisture retention capacity are best. If soil is clayey it can be improved by adding well rotten farmyard manure. High acidic and low lying soils are not suitable for its cultivation. The optimum soil pH for this crop is between 5.8 to 6.5. The soil should be well levelled and drained. The land should be prepared to a fine tilth by ploughings and harrowings. During its preparation, resides of previous crop should be collected and burnt. Two to three weeks before planting, farmyard manure at the rate of 250-300 quintals per hectare should be applied in the soil.

SEED AND PLANTING

Seed rate

Individual cloves are used as seed material which are carefully detached from the composite bulbs. The seed rate depends upon the size of the bulbs. However, 3.5 to 5.0 quintals of bulbs are required for planting of one hectare field.

Planting time

In South India, it is planted in August-September while in North in October-November in the plains. In some localities the planting may be done twice, in May and October if the climatic conditions are favourable. On hills it is planted in March-April.

Planting

The cloves are planted in rows made at a distance of 15 cm. Clove to clove distance should be 7.5 cm in the row. The planting can be done by dibbling or dropping cloves in furrows. The former method would be useful for small scale planting while the latter would be more applicable for large-scale cultivation. It has been seen that the position of the cloves—whether they are vertically placed or slanted or flat does not affect the emergence, but completely inverted position is not desirable.

MANURES AND FERTILISERS

As already mentioned, about 200 to 250 quintal farmyard manure should be mixed in the soil 20-25 days before planting. In addition to this, 100 kg nitrogen, 60 kg phosphorus and 60 kg potash per hectare should be applied. Half dose of nitrogen and full dose of phosphorous and potash should be given as basal at the time of sowing while the remaining half dose of nitrogen should be top dressed about 45 days after planting.

IRRIGATION AND DRAINAGE

At the time of planting sufficient moisture should be available in the soil so that emergence does not pose any problem. However, because of lack of moisture one should not wait long and apply irrigation to enhance the emergence. Initially, during winter months, in medium type of soils, irrigations at fortnightly intervals would be enough but as the weather warms up, the interval between two irrigations should be gradually reduced, finally coming to about one week. Light irrigation 2-3 days before harvesting makes the bulb-harvest easy. Excessive moisture before harvesting may result in poor quality bulbs. Whenever there is excess water in the soil, it should be drained out immediately.

WEED CONTROL

Shallow cultivation should be given between the rows in order to keep the soil around the plants to check the weeds. Usually within first 60 days of planting two weedings are required to control the weeds satisfactorily. If first weeding is done in time there may not be any need for second weeding in some areas. Care should be taken not to injure the roots while weeding or hoeing is done.

DISEASES AND THEIR CONTROL

Downy mildew

It is caused by *Peronospora destructor* fungus. The fungus develops very fast in low lying areas and in heavy soils when the crop is subjected to excessive moisture and humid atmosphere and oval spots are seen on the leaves. Later on the spot size increases and finally leaves become dry. Small bulbs are formed in the affected plants.

Control Measures

❖ Proper drainage should be arranged.

❖ Spraying of crop with 0.2% solution of Dithane M-45 at an interval of 10-15 days should be done.

Bacterial soft rot

It is caused by *Erwinia carotovora* bacteria. Water-soaked areas and soft inner scales emitting a foul odour are generally noted.

Control Measures

❖ Use of disease-free cloves for planting should be done.

❖ Arrangement of proper drainage should be made.

INSECT PESTS AND THEIR CONTROL

Thrips (*Thrips* sp.)

It is a small yellow sucking insect which damages the leaves by sucking the juice resulting in the browning of the tips.

Control Measures

❖ Keep the crop weed free.

❖ Spray the crop with 0.1% Metasystox.

Maggot (*Hylemya* sp.)

The insects feed upon leaves and bulbs of all ages, from young plants to mature bulbs.

Control Measures

❖ Use Thimet 10-G at the rate of 15 kg per hectare in soil before planting the crop.

❖ Spray the crop with 0.2% solution of Malathion (50 W.P.)

HARVESTING

The crop is ready to harvest 170 to 180 days after planting. It can be harvested when the top of the leaves become yellowish and fall down after drying. At the time of harvesting, bulbs with leaves should be collected and small bundles should be made. These bundles should be kept in shady place for 5-7 days and then the bulbs should be stored in a cool place.

YIELD

The yield depends upon the variety and management practices followed. However, the average yield varies from 80 to 100 quintals per hectare.

PREPARATION FOR MARKET

After curing in shade for 5 to 7 days after harvesting, the leaves are removed and diseased and damaged bulbs are sorted out. The selected bulbs are packed in thin gunny bags for market.

STORAGE

Completely dried bulbs can be kept fairly well in an ordinary well ventilated room for 5 to 6 months. The weight loss is of about 20 to 25 per cent during storage of five months. It can be kept in cold storage at temperature from 0°C to 3°C at 60 per cent relative humidity.

SEED PRODUCTION

It is propagated vegetatively, hence pure bulbs, free from insect pests and diseases, are selected for further multiplication. Selected bulbs are planted in the field and all possible care is taken to get disease–free material. Recommended cultural practices should be adopted. After harvesting, the seed material should be stored in cold storage.

FRENCH BEAN

Botanical name	-	*Phaseolus vulgaris*
Family	-	Leguminosae
Synonymous	-	Pharash bin, Farasi Simba, Bangalore beans, Avarai, Hurali kayi, Phanasi, Frans bean, Kidney bean, Hariket bean, Bush bean, Rajma, Garden bean, Dry bean, Field bean, Navy bean

IMPORTANCE AND UTILITY

It is an excellent vegetable crop grown for pods as well as for seeds. Its major area is confined to hills, where it is grown for green pods. Punjab, Jammu and Kashmir, Gujarat, Karnataka, Tamil Nadu, Uttar Pradesh and Himachal Pradesh are the main states where it is being cultivated on large scale. Dry grains are an excellent source of cheap protein and many varieties contain about 22-23 per cent protein. According to Chatfield (1949 and 1954) its 100 g edible fresh pods contain 91.4 per cent water, 1.7 per cent protein, 0.1 per cent fat, 0.5 per cent mineral matters, 4.5 per cent carbohydrates, 50 mg calcium, 28 mg phosphorus and 1.7 mg iron. Its 100 g dry seeds contain 9.6 per cent water, 24.9 per cent protein, 0.8 per cent fat, 3.2 per cent mineral matters, 60.1 per cent carbohydrates, 60 mg calcium, 433 mg phosphorus and 2.7 mg iron.

ORIGIN AND HISTORY

It is a native of South America and is grown there on a large scale. It was introduced in India in 19th century by Europeans and at present it is grown commercially in some parts of the country for its dry seeds and green pods.

BOTANY

The flower opens between 9 to 17 hours, the peak period being 14 to 16 hours while anther dehiscence occurs prior to opening and requires 5 to 25 hours, the peak period being 10 to 14 hours.

CLIMATIC REQUIREMENTS

It is a day-neutral crop, that is, the length of day does not materially affect the reproductive habit except of few semi-pole type varieties which are short-day crop. It is sensitive to frost and very high temperatures. There is heavy blossom or pod drop in very hot weather. The best seed germination takes place at 18°C to 24°C while maximum yield can be obtained at 16°C to 21°C. During continuous rains, flowers do not set properly.

SOIL AND ITS PREPARATION

It can be grown on a variety of soils ranging from clay to loam. Sandy loam to loam soils are good for early varieties while clay loam to clay soils are good for late varieties. The optimum soil pH for its cultivation is between 5.3 to 6.0. The soil should be rich in organic matter and should have better irrigation and drainage facilities. The soil should be prepared well before sowing.

VARIETIES

Pant Anupma: This variety has been developed by Pantnagar University through selection in germplasm and is recommended for hills of Uttaranchal and plains of Uttar Pradesh. The pods are smooth, soft, straight, long with attractive green colour. It is less affected by virus. Pods are ready to harvest after 55-65 days of sowing. The average yield of this variety is about 100 quintals per hectare.

Pusa Parwati: It has been developed at I.A.R.I., New Delhi through X-ray irradiation of the American variety, Wax pod. The pods are attractive round, meaty, light green in colour which are ready to harvest in about 45 to 50 days after sowing.

Contender: It is an introduction from U.S.A. This variety is resistant to mosaic. It is a bushy type variety with light green fleshy and thick pods. The average yield of this variety is about 60 quintals per hectare.

Jampa: It is a Mexican variety, reported to be outstanding in performance in Maharashtra. The plants are shy in tillering habit. The first picking of pods can be done after 60 days of seed sowing. The pods are flat, smooth, non-stringy and pale green in colour. The seeds are black, smooth, small and flat.

Kentucky Wonder: It was introduced in India from outside. The plants are trailing type and late in fruiting. The pods are green, fleshy and large, curved, round, thick and meaty which become stringy at the later stage. The seeds are light brown in colour.

Giant stringless: It is also an introduction to India from outside. The plants are dwarf in nature with early fruiting. The pods are green, medium large, long, slightly curved, tender, meaty and stringless. Seeds are glossy and yellowish brown.

V.L. Bauni Bean-I: This variety has been developed by Vivekanand Parvatiya Krishi Anusandhanshala, Almora, Uttaranchal. It is a bushy type variety which produces non-stringy, long, fleshy green pods. The pods are medium round. It does well in the hills but suffers badly from mosaic in the plains.

SEED AND SOWING

Time of sowing

In the plains, where rainfall is low, the crop is sown from August to September for winter season harvest and from 15th January to 15th February for spring-summer season crop. In hills, the crop is sown from March to August.

Seed rate

The seed rate varies considerably depending upon variety, soil and climatic conditions. However, seed rate varies from 80 to 100 kg per hectare.

Method of sowing

Sowing is done in lines 40 to 50 cm apart in the plains while it can be reduced to 30 to 45 cm in hills. Within the lines, the seeds should be sown at 10 to 12 cm distance. The depth of sowing shall be 2-4 cm. To avoid fungal infection, treat the seed with Thiram at the rate of 2-4 g per kg seed.

MANURES AND FERTILISERS

Though it is a leguminous crop but it does not form nodules properly, therefore, for obtaining better yields, nitrogen at the rate of 60 kg per hectare along with 80 kg phosphorus and 40 kg potash should be mixed in the soil at the time of sowing. About 20 kg nitrogen per hectare should be applied as top dressing 30 to 35 days after sowing.

IRRIGATION AND DRAINAGE

Interval of irrigation and amount of water to be applied depends upon the season. In spring season, the crop should be irrigated at an interval of one week and 6 to 8 irrigations are sufficient. In winter season, the crop should be irrigated at an interval of 15 to 20 days and 3 to 5 irrigations are sufficient. Excess water reduces nodule formation and ultimately the growth of plants. Therefore, proper drainage is must.

WEED CONTROL

The roots of French bean mostly go down in the soil up to the depth of 15 to 20 cm, hence shallow cultivation is advisable. Deep cultivation is likely to cause injury to the plants by destroying the roots near the surface. The weeds should be removed as and when they appear. Two to three weedings followed by one hoeing are sufficient to check the growth of weeds.

DISEASES AND THEIR CONTROL

Anthracnose

It is caused by *Colletotrichum lindemuthianum*. The disease is more serious when the weather is moderately cool, humid or rainy during growing period. Elongated dark brown or black sunken spots with reddish or yellowish margins appear on veins, petioles, stem and pods.

Control Measures

❖ The seed should be treated with Thiram at the rate of 2 to 4 g per kg seed.
❖ Sow disease-free seeds obtained from disease-free localities.
❖ Follow the crop rotations.
❖ Spray the crop with 0.25% solution of Dithane Z-78.

Powdery mildew

It is caused by *Erysiphe polygoni*. White powdery patches are formed on the upper side of the leaves and later on, on the lower sides also. These spots also appear on stem and pods. Due to the attack of the fungus, photosynthetic activities go down and ultimately this reduces the yield and quality.

Control Measures

❖ The crop should be sprayed with 0.06% solution of Karathane.
❖ Thiovit, Sulfex or any other sulphur compound can also be applied to check the incidence of disease.

Mosaic

It is a very common disease which causes stunting of the plants and mottling of leaves. Due to the attack of this disease, size of pods are reduced and it reduces the yield to a great extent.

Control Measures

❖ Spray the crop with 0.15 per cent solution of Metasystox to check the vector.

❖ Grow resistant varieties.

INSECT PESTS AND THEIR CONTROL

Aphids

These are very small insects and are found in large number in clusters under the leaves or on the tender parts, flowers and fruits. They suck the cell sap from the affected parts causing curling, thickening, yellowing and finally drying.

Control Measure

❖ Spray the crop with 0.15 per cent solution of Metasystox or Endosulfan (35 EC) at the interval of 15 days.

Pod borer

The young caterpillars first feed on the surface of the pods and later on bore into them and feed on the seeds. It is very common in spring-summer crop.

Control Measure

❖ Spray the crop with 0.2% solution of Sevin (50 W.P.) at 10 days interval starting from flowering to one week before pod harvest.

Leaf minor

They are also smallinsects found in large numbers. They suck the sap from the leaves causing curling and ultimately reduction in yield and quality.

Control Measure

❖ Spray the crop with 0.15 per cent solution of Metasystox during its attack.

HARVESTING

The pods should be harvested before they are fully grown and seeds are small. The period of first picking varies from 40 to 65 days after sowing, depending upon the variety and season of crop. If the pods are not harvested at right stage they become tough and stringy. Picking is done by hand and normally the interval is about 6 to 10 days depending upon the variety. Dry beans are harvested as soon as a large percentage of the pods are fully matured and have turned yellow.

YIELD

The yield of the green pods depends upon the variety, season, soil and climatic conditions. Normally, 60 to 100 quintals of green pods or 15 to 20 quintals of grain can be obtained per hectare.

PREPARATION FOR MARKET

After harvesting, the pods should be kept in shade to avoid evaporation and water should be sprinkled on the pods. Over-matured, diseased and damaged pods should be sorted out. Selected pods may be packed in gunny bages or in baskets depending upon the quantity.

STORAGE

The pods can be stored for 2 to 3 days in summer season and 4 to 6 days in winter season at room temperature. In cold storage, the pods can be stored at 2°C to 4°C with 60 to 70 per cent relative humidity for about 15 to 20 days.

SEED PRODUCTION

It is a self-pollinated crop, even then an isolation distance of 50 and 25 metres should be maintained for foundation and certified seeds, respectively. All agronomic practices are to be followed as for green pods production. One roguing before pod set should be done and on the basis of foliage and flower characters, off types and diseased plants should be removed.

Second roguing should be done at the time of pod formation and on the basis of pod characters, off types and diseased plants should be removed. Completely dried pods are harvested and kept in sunlight for drying. Threshing and cleaning can be done by hand or by thresher.. The average yield of seeds is about 15 to 20 quintals per hectare.

PEAS

Botanical name	-	*Pisum Sativum* L.
Family	-	Leguminoceae
Synonymous	-	Mattar, Bataneelu, Mattri, Motor, Mah, Bara, Pathani, Watana, Muttar, Batani

IMPORTANCE AND UTILITY

Pea is a popular vegetable and pulse crop of India. It provides varieties of vegetarian dishes and hence it is liked throughout the world. There are two types of cultivated peas, the garden pea and the field pea. Garden peas are harvested in an immature condition to be cooked as green to provide a delicious dish, or to be canned or frozen for subsequent use. Field peas are grown as a forage crop for cattle or as a green manure crop for soil improvement or as a cover crop to reduce soil erosion or as a mature seed. The mature seed may be used as whole or split into 'dal' and prepared in various ways for human consumption. It is highly nutritive and contains high proportion of digestible protein, carbohydrates, minerals and vitamins. The idea of nutritive value of pea can be had from the following figures. Values have been drawn up on the basis of 100 g of dried edible portion.

Moisture	11 g	Calcium	64 mg
Protein	22.5 g	Iron	4.8 mg
Fat	1.8 g	Riboflavin	0.15 mg
Carbohydrates	62.1 g	Thiamin	0.72 mg
		Niacin	2.4 mg

The grains of edible mature pods contain 72.1 per cent water, 19.8 per cent carbohydrates, 7.2 per cent protein, 0.1 per cent fat and 0.8 per cent mineral matters.

ORIGIN AND HISTORY

The cultivation of pea is very ancient. Cultivation of pea can be traced to Swiss lake dwellers of the Bronze Age (about 3000-1100 B.C.). The pea is native to the Mediterranean region of southern Europe and to western Asia. It is probably indigenous to the region comprising Italy and south-western Asia eastwards to the Himalayas, including northern India.

CLASSIFICATION

Two types of peas are generally cultivated all over the globe. One is the garden pea and the other is field pea.

1. Garden pea (*Pisum sativum* var. *hortense*)

It is also called table pea. In this type, young, green seeds are used mostly in vegetables and also for canning purposes. Seeds are bold and wrinkled. The plants are generally white flowered. Leaf axils are generally green. Seeds are yellowish, whitish or bluish green.

2. Field pea (*Pisum sativum* var. *arvense*)

In this type, the ripe, mature seeds are used as pulse (dal). They are also grown as forage or green manure crop. Field peas are hardy plants and grown on a large scale without irrigation. These plants are also able to withstand frost. Seeds are round and little angular. Generally they have coloured flowers. Leaf axils are often pigmented. Seeds are greyish green, greyish brown or greyish yellow.

BOTANY

Pea belongs to the family Leguminosae. It is an annual herbaceous plant. The plant is semi-erect, but when a support is available, it has a tendency to climb. The plants grow to a height of about 30-200 cm. Peas germinate in a hypogeal fashion; the cotyledons remaining below the ground surface. Plants develop a tap root system. Stems are slender, hollow and succulent. Leaves are typically pinnately compound. Each leaf has one to three pairs of leaflets and terminal branched tendrils. A large pair of stipules, or leaf-life bract, is found at the base of the petiole of each leaf and these bracts are so large that they can be mistaken for sessible leaves. The inflorescence is an axillar raceme. It is a typical legume flower. The flowers of field peas are smaller than those of garden pea and are coloured, the colour of the standard being pale lilac, the wings purplish and the keel yellowish white. The flowers of garden pea are white in colour. The fruit is a typical pod containing 4 to 9 seeds. The length of the pod is 5-9 cm and shape is inflated or almost cylindrical. Seeds vary in shape from round to angular to very rough and in colour from green-yellow to grey and brown. Peas are generally self-fertilised, but cross fertilisation may also occur.

CLIMATIC REQUIREMENTS

Peas require a cool growing season and moderate temperatures are essential throughout the growing season. For germination, about 22^0C temperature is considered favourable. High temperatures are more injurious to pea crop than frost. Frost can damage the plants during flowering stage. Peas can be produced successfully in temperate, semi-arid zones. Peas are most sensitive to moisture stress at flowering stage. High humidity is harmful to pea crop as it favours incidence of diseases. The optimum monthly temperature suitable for its growth is $13-18^0$C.

SOIL AND ITS PREPARATION

A well drained soil is essential for successful production of peas. Pea is highly sensitive to waterlogging conditions, hence, a well-drained loam soil is considered best for pea cultivation. It tolerates a moderate soil pH range (6.0 to 7.5). The optimum pH is 6.5.

Field is prepared as in the case of other Rabi crops. After harvest of Kharif crops, the field should be ploughed with disc or mould board plough. Where tractor is available, one deep ploughing followed by 2-3 harrowings and plankings should be given to prepare a well pulverized seed bed. Where bullocks are the source of power, deep ploughing followed by 2-3 harrowings or 3-4 cross ploughings with *desi* plough should be done. Avoid powdery seed bed. Field should be well levelled and should be prepared after pre-sowing irrigation to ensure adequate moisture at the time of sowing.

VARIETIES

Pea varieties may be divided into two groups according to seed shape, that is (a) smooth seeded and (b) wrinkled seeded. The wrinkled seeded varieties are generally sweeter in comparison to smooth seeded ones. The description of some of the important varieties of garden pea is given below:

Type-19: It is a selection from a sample of Varanasi district of Uttar Pradesh. It matures in 120 days. It has dark green foliage and white flowers. Seeds are wrinkled and greenish white. Pods are ready for picking in about 75 days. It yields about 70-100 quintal green pods per hectare. It is recommended for growing in all the tracts of Uttar Pradesh.

Punjab 87: Its plants are medium dwarf, vigorous, erect and dark green. The first picking takes place 100 days after sowing. Pods are dark green, 9-10 cm long and slightly curved at the end. The grains are bold and sweet. Shelling out-turn is 49 per cent. The yield of green pods is about 150 quintal per hectare.

Early Badger: It is an introduction from U.S.A. It is wrinkle seeded, early and dwarf variety. Pods are of light green colour and about 7 cm long. Pods are ready for picking after 60-65 days of sowing. The average yield of green pods is 80-85 quintal per hectare.

Early December: It has been developed from a cross of T-19 and Early Badger. It is wrinkle–seeded short duration variety. Its pods get ready for picking after 55 days of sowing. Pods are about 7 cm long and of dark green colour. Average yield of green pods is about 75 quintal per hectare.

Arkel: It is a wrinkle–seeded dwarf variety. Pods are ready for picking after 60 days of sowing. Long, bent at the stigmatic end, pods look very sound at full maturity. Average yield of green pods is 80-90 quintal per hectare.

Meteor: It is smooth seeded, early and dwarf variety. Its pods get ready for picking after 60 days of sowing. Average yield of green pods is 80-90 quintal per hectare.

G.C. 141: It is a wrinkle–seeded variety. It takes about 95 days for producing marketable pods. Average yield of green pods is about 100 quintals per hectare.

Asauji: It is a very early variety and pods are ready to harvest after 45 to 60 days of sowing. The seeds are round and green.

G.C. 195: It has been developed from a cross of T 19 and Little Marvel. It is a wrinkle–seeded early maturing variety. Its plants are of medium size. Pods are ready for picking in 75-80 days. Pods are about 7 cm long. The average yield of green pods is about 90 quintal per hectare.

Bonnvelle: It is an introduction from U.S.A. It is wrinkle–seeded double podded variety. It is tall (100-120 cm) in height. It gets ready for picking in about 95 days. On an average, it yields about 100-120 quintals of green pods per hectare. It is susceptible to powdery mildew.

Sylvia: It is an introduction from outside and is most suitable for kitchen garden. The pods are edible as such, curved, yellowish green without parchment.

Swarna Rekha: It is an early maturing selection from local material of Bihar. It matures in about 120 days. Plants are semi-spreading type with white flowers. Seeds are round, smooth and creamy in colour with black hilum. It is suitable for green pods and dry seeds as well. Its average yield is 80-100 quintal of green pods and 15-20 quintal of dry grains per hectare.

Khaperkheda: It is a local selection from Maharashtra state. Pods are small and seeds are wrinkled. Average yield of green pods is about 50-60 quintals and grains yield about 10-12 quintal per hectare.

Pant Matar-2: It is recommended from Pantnagar University. It is cross between Early Badger and Pant Uphar. Pods are ready to harvest 60 days after sowing. The average yield is 100 quintals per hectare.

Pant Sabzi Matar-3: It is a cross between Arkel and GC 141 and recommended from Pantnagar University. It is tolerant to powdery mildew. Pods are ready to harvest 60-65 days after sowing.

N.P. 29: It is developed from I.A.R.I., New Delhi. It is a wrinkle–seeded variety, very tasty and pods are ready to harvest after 100 to 110 days of sowing. It has been reported to be highly suitable for dehydration.

SEED AND SOWING

Before sowing the seeds should be treated with Thiram at the rate of 0.25 per cent. Time of sowing is more critical in case of garden peas. The optimum time for sowing of garden peas (vegetable purpose) is from 25th October to 15th November in northern India. In case of early sowing, special care should be taken against stem fly. Seed rate and spacing vary according to the periods of maturity of different varieties. The early maturing varieties like Arkel, Early Badger etc. are given closer spacing and higher seed rate and the late varieties are given wider spacing and lower seed rate. In case of early maturing dwarf varieties, crop should be sown in rows 20 cm apart and about 100-125 kg seed per hectare should be sown. In late maturing and taller varieties a row spacing of about 30 cm seems to be optimum. The seed rate should be reduced to 75-80 kg per hectare.

Sowing of pea should be done according to prevailing temperature in a particular area. It should be sown when daily maximum temperature is below 30^0 C and the daily minimum temperature comes down to 20^0 C. If pea is sown above this temperature range then crop will have more incidence of stem fly.

MANURES AND FERTILISERS

Being a leguminous crop, the pea does not require high doses of nitrogen. If available, about 200 quintals of farmyard manure should be incorporated in the soil at the time of land preparation. This should be supplemented with 20-30 kg nitrogen as a starter dose per hectare as a basal dressing at the time of sowing which can meet plant requirement before the formation of nodules. For good nodulation, seed should be treated with proper strain of bacterial culture before sowing. However, in plots where peas are being regularly grown there is no necessity of bacterial culture.

Phosphorus and potassium are the other two important major nutrients required for better growth and yield. These should be applied as a basal dose based on soil test. If soil is deficient in these nutrients, apply 60-70 kg phosphorus and 30-40 kg potash per hectare. Mixture of all the fertilisers should be given 4-5 cm away from the rows and 4-5 cm deeper from seed. Where placement is not possible, scattes the fertiliser on the soils before the last harrowing.

In case of zinc deficiency, 0.5% zinc sulphate and 0.25% lime should be sprayed after the appearance of disease symptoms characterised by chlorosis, stunted growth etc.

IRRIGATION AND DRAINAGE

Pea crop can tolerate drought condition to some extent. By providing one or two irrigations higher yields can be obtained. First irrigation should be given at 45 days and second, if needed, at pod filling stage. The irrigation may bring 100 to 150 per cent increase in the yield depending upon the soil type, winter rains and depth of water table. Special precaution should be taken while irrigating a pea crop. Light and uniform irrigation should be given. Waterlogging condition in pea field, even for a day, causes considerable loss in the yield since this crop is highly sensitive to poor drainage conditions. Poor drainage leads to reduction in the number of branches and pods per plant.

WEED CONTROL

The pea field should be free from weeds for a period of 40-50 days after sowing. Later on the crop itself checks the growth of weeds by covering the ground surface. The major weeds found in pea crop are *Chenopodium album* (bathua), *Fumaria Parviflora* (gajri), *Lathyrus* spp. (chatrimatri), *Melilotus alba* (senji),

Vicia sativa (ankari). There is drastic reduction in yield under heavy infestation of weeds. Therefore, the field should be kept free from weeds by giving two weedings and hoeings after three and six weeks of germination. Weedicides like Basalin and Tribunil can be used safely for weed control. Basalin at the rate of 0.75 kg (a.i.) in 800-1000 litres of water as pre-planting spray may be used as effective herbicide. It should be well incorporated in the soil before sowing. In case Basalin is not available, use 2.5 kg Tribunil in 800-1000 litres of water per hectare as pre-emergence spray.

DISEASES AND THEIR CONTROL

The important diseases of pea are wilt, root rot, powdery mildew and rust.

Wilt and root rot

These diseases are caused by *Fusarium oxysporum* and *Rhizoctonia solani* fungi. The symptoms may be seen in seedling stage. The roots rot and plants show yellowing of the lower-most leaves, followed by wilting. These diseases cause considerable damage when the crop is sown early.

Control Measures

❖ Treat the seed with 2.5 g of Ceresan or Brassicol or 2 g of Captan per kg of seed before sowing.

❖ Avoid early sowing in badly infested areas.

Powdery mildew

This disease is caused by the fungus *Erysiphe polygoni*. It is a serious disease of pea crop. The symptoms first appear on the leaves and then on other green parts of the plant. They are characterised by white powdery, patchy growth on both the surfaces of the leaf and also on the tendrils, pods, and stem. In advanced stage, entire plant's surface may be covered with white powder which consists of mycelium and spores of the fungus. The number and weight of the pods are reduced. In case of severe infection the plant dies prematurely.

Control Measures

❖ Avoid late planting.

❖ After harvest, collect the plants left in the field and burn them.

❖ The disease can be controlled by two to three sprays of any of the wettable Sulphur compounds like Sulfex, Elosal or Hexasual at the rate of 3 kg per hectare in 1000 litres of water. Give the first spray after appearance of the disease in the crop. The second spray should be done 14 days after the first spray and the third spray only if there is a need for it.

Rust

The disease is caused by the fungus *Uromyces fabae.* This disease is serious in northern India. The stem of the plant becomes malformed and the affected plant dies. All the green parts of the plants are affected. The earliest symptoms are the yellow spots having aecia in round or elongated clusters. Then the unredo pustules develop which are powdery and light brown in appearance.

Control Measures

❖ After harvest, the affected plant trash should be burnt.

❖ Spray the crop with Dithane M-45 at the rate of 2 kg per hectare in 1000 litres of water. Two to three sprays are sufficient.

INSECT PESTS AND THEIR CONTROL

The crop is infested by a number of pests which are described below.

Pea stem fly

The adult fly layseggs in the plant tissues and the maggots damage the internal tissues of the stem and ultimately the entire plant dies. Damage is more severe in early plantings.

Control Measures

❖ Mix 30 kg Furadon or 10 kg Thimet granules in the soil before sowing the crop.

❖ When plants attain 10-15 cm height, spraying with 0.04 per cent Thiodan should be done.

Leaf Miner

Larvae feed by making tunnels in the leaves. They cause serious damage during December-March.

Control Measure

❖ Spray 250 ml of Dimecron 100 EC or 1 litre of Metasystox 20 EC in 1000 litres of water per hectare when the attack begins and repeat at 15 days' interval.

Pea Aphids

They suck the sap of the cells, owing to which the leaves turn pale and yellow. In case of server infestation the plant growth is checked.

Control Measure

❖ Spray 250 ml Dimecron 100 EC or 1 litre of Metasystox 25 EC in 1000 litres of water per hectare.

Pod borer

They bore into the pods and feed on the grains inside. Generally late sown crop is damaged more by this insect pest.

Control Measure

❖ Spray crop with 1.25 litres of Thiodan 35 EC (Endosulfan) in 1000 litres of water per hectare or 1.5 litre of Diazinon 20 EC or 400 ml of Phosphamidon in 1000 litres of water per hectare. Picking of green pods should be done 15 days after spraying.

HARVESTING AND THRESHING

As stated above, different varieties of garden pea have varying maturity periods. The picking of green pods should be done by giving a simple jerk to the pedicel with minimum possible disturbance to the plant. Crop for seed should be harvested when it is fully ripe and threshed after sufficient drying in the sun.

YIELD

With improved package of practices, one may expect about 100-125 quintals of green pods per hectare and about 15-20 quintals of grain and about same quantity of straw from one hectare of land.

PREPARATION FOR MARKET

The pods deteriorate rapidly after harvest. Therefore, they should be kept in shade and at a cool place. The over-mature, diseased and damaged pods should be removed before sending to the market. The pods can be packed in gunny bags and can be sent to market.

STORAGE

Unshelled pea pods can be kept better than shelled pea. At room temperature the pods can be kept for two to three days provided they are frequently sprayed with fresh water, but in cold storage they can be kept for 15 to 20 days at 0^0C with 85 to 90 per cent relative humidity.

SEED PRODUCTION

It is a self-pollinated crop and requires 25 and 50 metres isolation distance for certified and foundation seed production, respectively. During its crop period, the crop should be inspected thrice. First, before flowering, and on the basis of external characters, off types and diseased plants should be removed. Secondly, at the time of flowering, and on the basis of flower characters, off types and diseased plants should be removed. Finally, at the time of pod ripening and off types and diseased ones should be removed. Complete dry pods alongwith the plants are harvested and kept for 6 to 8 days for drying. Later on threshing is completed.

COWPEA

Botanical name - *Vigna sinensis* L.

Family - Leguminoceae

Synonymous - Lobia, Karamani, Alasandulu, Baragudi, Avadai, Kottapayaru, Barbati, Bobbarlu, Chola, Thatapayaru, Mambayar, Chavli.

IMPORTANCE AND UTILITY

From nutritional point of view it is one of the important vegetables grown in our country and a large number of dishes can be prepared from the pods as well as from developed grains. The green pods are used for vegetables and soup while green and dried rains are used for vegetables like peas, and for different types of delicious dishes (chat). It is drought resistant and can grow well on dry farms up to some extent but under very dry conditions the size of pod and grains become small. It is a short duration crop and can be fitted in any crop rotation. It can also be grown as intercrop in the orchards. On dry weight basis the cowpea grains contain 23.4 per cent protein, 1.8 per cent fat and 60.3 per cent carbohydrates. The crop produces heavy vegetative growth and covers the ground so well that it checks soil erosion as well as growth of weeds .

ORIGIN AND HISTORY

Cowpea is probably a native of Central Africa where almost all the wild forms are found. It has been cultivated since very ancient time in the Mediterranean region by the Greeks, Romans and Spaniards. It has now been introduced in many countries throughout the world. It is also claimed to be indigenous to India.

BOTANY

Cowpea belongs to family Leguminosae. The common cowpea is a twining annual herbaceous plant. The root system consists of a well developed tap root with considerable number of lateral roots. Most of the roots are located in the upper 40 centimetre of soil. The stem is slightly ridged and almost glabrous. The leaves are trifoliate, alternate and with scattered short hairs. The flowers are white, yellow or pink in colour and are usually self-pollinated. Pods are long, cylindrical and constricted between the seeds. The seeds are bean-shaped and many times spotted with different colours such as brown, green yellow, white and mottled.

CLIMATIC REQUIREMENTS

Cowpea can be grown in all tropical and subtropical climates. Being a warm weather crop it can withstand a considerable degree of drought. But under very dry conditions the plants produce a poor crop. Crop thrives best between 27-35^{0}C temperatures. It can also grow under shade of trees but cannot tolerate cold or frost.

SOIL AND ITS PREPARATION

The stubbles and other residues of previous crop should be picked up as far as possible to have clean and smooth seedbed. Field should be prepared by giving two or three cross harrowings followed by planting. For summer season crop, give a pre-irrigation immediately after harvesting of Rabi crop. When the field comes in condition, prepare it by giving two or three harrowings.

VARIETIES

According to use, there are different varieties. However, the same variety may be raised for more than one purpose. For instance, variety meant for grain may be used for vegetable and fodder purposes. Similarly, fodder varieties may be used for green manuring purpose. Several cowpea varieties are grown in various parts of our country. The promising ones are as below:

Type 2: It is a late maturing (125-130 days) variety suitable for growing in plains of Uttar Pradesh. Plants are spreading type with dark green leaves. Flowers are bluish purple. Seeds are grey mottled and bold. Its yield potential is 12-18 quintals of grain or 300-325 quintals of green fodder per hectare.

Pusa Phalguni: The plants are dwarf with bushy habit. The crop becomes ready for harvest in 65 days. This variety is suitable for sowing in February-March. Under normal conditions this variety gives about 50-60 quintals of green pods per hectare. It is a white seeded variety. Grain yield is 10-12 quintal per hectare. It is suitable to be grown in Uttar Pradesh, Punjab, Haryana, Delhi and Madhya Pradesh.

Pusa Barsati: It is a selection from seed material imported from the Philippines. This is an early dwarf variety which takes about 45 days for first flush (fruiting). The pods are light straw coloured and about 20-25 cm long. This is one of the best variety for June-July sowing. The average—yield of this variety is 60-75 quintals of green pods per hectare. This variety is suitable for growing in Delhi, Punjab, Uttar Pradesh, Madhya Pradesh and even some parts of South India.

Pusa Dofasli: This variety is suitable to be grown in summer as well as Kharif seasons. It is an improvement over Pusa Phalguni for pod quality. Plants are dwarf and bushy. It is a photo-insensitive variety and hence can be grown both during rainy and spring seasons. Pods are yellowish green, erect and seeds are creamy with red coloured hilum. It gives an average green pod yield of 60-70 quintal per hectare. It is suitable to be grown in Punjab, Haryana, Delhi, Uttar Pradesh, Madhya Pradesh and Rajasthan.

Pusa Rituraj: This variety can be grown in summer as well as Kharif due to its highly photo thermo-insensitive nature. It gives comparatively better performance even under severe summer conditions. It gives an average green pod yield of 80-85 quintal per hectare. Pods are 22-24 cm long, thin and less fibrous. Pods become ready for first picking in 45-50 days after sowing. The plant is bushy and bears pods so profusely as to cover the foliage, appearing like fan. It is suitable to be grown in most parts of North India.

F.S-68: This variety is well suited for spring season. It is about a week late than Pusa Dophasli. Its grains are attractive white. Pods are small and green with small white seeds. It is suitable for both grains and vegetable. It yields about 10-12 quintals of grain per hectare. This variety is suitable for cultivation in North India.

Gwalior K 3B: This variety can be grown in both the seasons and pods are ready to harvest 65-75 days after sowing. The seed colour is creamy with brown hilum. Average seed yield is about 12 quintal per hecatre.

Gwalior K 11: It can also be grown in both the seasons with the same duration as of above variety. The seeds are smaller than the above one.

Gwalior K 14: It can also be grown in both the seasons with the same duration as of above varieties. The seeds are medium in size, attractive, creamy white in colour with black hilum. The average seed yield is about 10 quintal per hectare.

Pusa Komal: It is a very promising unreleased culture. However, it will be released shortly. It is suitable for summer as well as rainy season cultivation. The plants are dwarf and produce about 25-30 cm long pods. The grains have pink pigment in some portions. This culture is resistant to wilts and yields about 80-85 quintal of green pods or 15-16 quintal grains per hectare. The pods can be harvested 60 days after sowing.

SEED AND SOWING

Sowing time

Suitable time for sowing summer cowpea crop is mid-February to mid-March. It varies according to field availability. The sowing for Kharif crop starts from middle of June and extends up to the end of July. In hills, this crop is sown in April-May. For green manuring, the crop should be sown from middle of June to first week of July.

Seed rate and method of sowing

For grain or vegetables purposes, 20-25 kg seed is required for sowing one hectare pure crop. When sown with crops, the seed rate is reduced proportionately. Variation in seed rate depends on several factors such as method of sowing, availability of soil moisture and the seed size of a variety. For green manuring about 35-40 kg seed shall be needed for one hectare.

The row spacing 30-45 cm and plant to plant distance of 8-10 cm may be maintained for Kharif planting. The row spacing in spring and summer planting should be kept 25-30 cm as the plants do not make much growth. Seeds should be treated with Thiram at the rate of 3 g per kg of seed before sowing. Crop can be sown either with seed drill or behind desi plough.

MANURES AND FERTILISERS

Being a leguminous crop, it needs small quantity of nitrogen for early growth period on those soils which are poor in organic matter. Such soils should get about 15-20 kg nitrogen per hectare as a starter dose. Application of phosphorus is very important as it promotes proper development of roots and activity of Rhizobium bacteria. Apply 50-60 kg phosphorus per hectare in the soil before sowing in case soil test values are not available. It is advisable to apply phosphatic fertilisers according to soil test recommendations. The fertiliser should be applied by drilling at the time of sowing in such a way that it is placed about 5-7 cm below the seed.

IRRIGATION AND DRAINAGE

The rainy season crop requires no irrigation but good drainage is essential. The early sown rainy season crop may need one or two irrigations in the pre-monsoon period. For raising summer crop, 5 to 6 irrigations may be given. The number and frequency of irrigation depend upon the soil type and weather prevailing during the growth period. Generally, the crop should get irrigation at an interval of 10-15 days during summer.

WEED CONTROL

Effective control of weeds in the first 20-25 days of the crop season is essential. At least two weedings and hoeings are required to check the weeds. During rainy season weeds can be controlled by the use of chemicals too. Use Baslin 1 kg a.i. perhectare in 800-1000 litres of water as pre-planting spray. It should be well incorporated in the soil before sowing.

DISEASES AND THEIR CONTROL

Bacterial blight of cowpea

It is caused by *Xanthomonas vignicola*. Symptoms of this disease first appear on the cotyledons and primary, and the new trifoliate leaves. The affected cotyledons are red and shrivelled. Necrotic spots are found on the margins of the primary leaves. Thereafter, the causal bacterium affects the stem and finally covers other parts of the plant. Growing points of the affected leaves are destroyed resulting into quicker death of plants. Cankers are also found on stem from where the plant may break because of the wind.

Control Measures

❖   Grow resistant varieties.

❖   Use healthy seed from disease–free field.

❖   In case of severe infection crop may be sprayed with 0.2% solution of Fytolan.

Cowpea mosaic

It is a disease caused by a virus transmitted by aphids. The affected leaves become pale yellow and exhibit mosaic and vein banding symptoms. The affected leaves become reduced in size and show puckering. Pods are also reduced and become twisted.

Control Measures

❖ Use healthy seed from healthy crop.

❖ For controlling aphids, spray 0.1 per cent solution of Metasystox or any other systemic insecticide.

Powdery mildew

This disease is caused by a fungus *Erysiphe polygoni*. Powdery mildew symptoms are visible on all the aerial parts of the affected plants. Symptoms first start from leaves and then spread to stem, branches and pods. Symptoms start with white powdery growth on leaves which may coalesce and cover the whole leaf with the white powdery growth. This white growth consists of the fungus and its spores. Affected leaves become twisted and smaller in size.

Control Measures

❖ After harvest, collect the plants left in the field and burn them.

❖ The disease can be controlled by spray of wettable sulphur like Sulfex, Elosal or Hexasual at the rate of 2-3 kg per hectare in 800-1000 litres of water.

Rust

This disease is caused by a fungus *Urontyces appendiculatus*. The disease affects the leaves, pods and sometimes new shoots. Symptoms on the leaves are very clearly visible and start from the lower surface of the leaf where very small white pustules are found. These pustules contain uredia of the fungus. Brown coloured urediospores come out of these uredia. At the end of the season these urediospores may be replaced with black coloured telia.

Control Measure

❖ Spray crop with Dithane M-45 at the rate of 2 kg per hectare in 1000 litres of water.

INSECT PESTS AND THEIR CONTROL

Hairy caterpillar

It is one of the most important pest of cowpea crop. It causes severe damage to the crop by eating away green portions of leaves. The adult moth of this caterpillar lays eggs in large clusters and the young larvae are also congregated. They may damage the crop at seedling stage. Damage can be so severe that sometimes re-sowing may be necessary.

Control Measures

❖ Collect and destroy the eggs and young larvae.

❖ The young caterpillars can be killed by dusting 10 per cent BHC dust at the rate of 25-30 kg per hectare. For full grown caterpillars, spray 1.5 litre Endosulfan (35 EC) in 1000 litres of water per hectare. Trenches all around the field may be dug and 10 per cent BHC put in trenches to check migration of caterpillars to field.

Leaf hoppers, jassids and aphids

The adults and Mymphs of these pests suck the juice from the leaves and the damage is more severe when the plants are young. As a result of sucking up of the sap, the leaves turn brown and crumpled, and plants look sick.

Control Measures

❖ Spray the crop with 0.1% solution of Metasystox or 0.04 per cent solution of Monocrotophos (40 EC))

❖ Give basal application of Thimet 10% granules at the rate of 10 kg per hectare.

HARVESTING AND THRESHING

Green pods for use as vegetable can be harvested 45 to 90 days after sowing depending on the variety. Pods should be harvested while tender otherwise yield may be poor and pods may develop fibres due to longer retention on the plant. For grains, the crop can be harvested in about 90-125 days after sowing when pods are fully matured. The crop should be then dried and threshed. The threshed grains should be dried in sun before storage.

For fodder, the cutting of the crop depends upon the need and the stage of growth of the component crop sown with it. In general, the crop should be cut when it attains the age of 40-45 days.

YIELD

A good crop of cowpea yields about 12-15 quintals of grain and 50-60 quintals of green pods per hectare. If crop is raised for fodder purpose, 250-350 quintals of green fodder is obtained from one hectare pure crop.

PREPARATION FOR MARKET

After pod harvest, they should be kept in shade and all diseased and damaged ones should be removed. Washing can also be done if they are covered with dust. In the morning, these can be sent to market after filling in baskets.

STORAGE

The pods can be, stored at room temperature for two to three days provided they are frequently sprayed with of cold water. In cold storage, pods can be stored for 15-20 days at 0°C with 85 to 90 per cent relative humidity.

SEED PRODUCTION

It is a self–pollinated crop and requires 50 and 250 metres solutionis distance for foundation and certified seed respectively. The crop should be inspected thrice during the crop period. First, before flowering, and on the basis of external characters, all off types and diseased plants should be removed. Secondly, at the time of flowering, and on the basis of flower characters, off types and diseased plants should be removed. Finally at the time of pod ripening, and on the basis of pod characters the off types and diseased plants should be removed. Dried pods are plucked from time to time, these are dried and seeds taken out by beating with a stick or on largescale by tractor.

POLE BEAN

Botanical name	-	Dolichos lablab
Family	-	Leguminosae
Synonymous	-	Sem, Baloor, Indian Bean, Wal

IMPORTANCE AND UTILITY

It is one of the excellent pod vegetable crops grown in India. Its green pods are used as vegetable alongwith potato or alone. Mature seeds are also used as vegetable. It is very popular in villages as well as cities where less area is available for cultivation. Its single plant supplies half kg pods every third day or so and can be grown even in pot. Its fresh green pods contain 86.1 per cent moisture, 3.8 per cent protein, 6.7 per cent carbohydrate, 0.7 per cent fat, 0.9 per cent mineral matter, Vitamin A 312 I.U. It is good source of Vitamin B and C also. Its pods are available regularly for 3 to 5 months and cultivation cost is very less.

ORIGIN AND HISTORY

It is supposed to have originated in this part of the world. Wild forms of beans are found in India and this country is probably the centre of its origin. At present it is a common vegetable grown in all Asiatic and African countries. In India, it is grown all over the country but compact large acreage for commercial production is uncommon.

CLIMATIC REQUIREMENTS

It is relatively a warm-season crop and it can be kept alive in summer to provide pods in the next season but bearing is poor and hence a new planting should done every year. Some of the strains are highly drought resistant and are often grown alongwith castor or sorghum. The best temperature for its seed germination is 18^0C to 27^0C and better growth and development takes place at 21^0C to 27^0C. For better fruit set the temperature should be 12^0C to 18^0C. Its seeds can be kept viable for two to three years at room temperature.

SOIL AND ITS PREPARATION

It can be grown on all types of soils from light sandy loams to heavy clay.

Fairly rich and well drained soil is better for pole beans. Very rich soil leads to more vegetative growth and less pod formation. Very heavy soils are not good for cultivation of pole beans. Prepare the soil well for sowing the seeds by repeated harrowings and plankings.

VARIETIES

Pusa Early Prolific: It was developed at I.A.R.I., New Delhi and is an early variety. It bears long, thin pods in bunches and is suitable for sowing in early spring and autumn.

Blue lake: It is an early variety, a preading in nature, having white flowers. The colour of seed is brown. The average weight of pod is about 15 to 20 g and average length of pod is 6 to 8 cm. It becomes ready to harvest 70 to 80 days after sowing.

F 54: Pods are ready to harvest 90 to 100 days after sowing. Pods are green, smooth and average length is 8 to 10 cm. Each pod contains 4 to 6 seeds and colour of seed is light brown.

SEED AND SOWING

The best time for its sowing is June-July and February to March also. It can be planted at a distance of 1 to 1.5 metre apart between the rows and one metre apart between the hills. Hills are prepared at proper distance, 10 to 15 cm raised from the surrounding area. Ten to 15 kg farmyard manure is mixed in each hill. Five to six seeds are sown in each hill, thus about 6 to 8 kg seed is sufficient to sow one hectare. Generally, seeds germinate 3 to 5 days after sowing.

MANURES AND FERTILISERS

For better growth and development of crop, heavy dose of nutrients during early stage is essential. About 200 to 300 quintals of well rotten farmyard manure should be added in the field during field preparation. At the time of sowing, 50 kg nitrogen, 60 kg phosphorus and 50 kg potash per hectare may be given as basal dressing. About 10-15 kg nitrogen may be given in the form of top dressing about 40 to 50 days after sowing. Spraying of micronutrients to the crop sixty days after sowing is also beneficial as it increases the size and weight of the pod.

IRRIGATION AND DRAINAGE

After germination, crop should be irrigated if moisture is insufficient. During summer season frequent irrigations are needed. During winter season two to three irrigations are sufficient at an interval of one month. Drainage facilities during rainy season are essential otherwise excess water may damage the crop.

WEED CONTROL

Normally, two or three hand hoeings and weedings should be done, depending upon soil type and extent of weed infestation. Effective control of weeds in the first 20-25 days of the crop season is essential.

DISEASES AND THEIR CONTROL

Powdery mildew

It is caused by *Erysiphe polygoni*. It appears late in the season during flowering and podding stage. White powdery particles are formed on both the sides of the leaves as well as on flower stalks and pods. It can be controlled by spraying the crop with 0.06 per cent solution of Karathane at 15 days' interval during flowering stage.

Downy mildew

It is caused by *Pernospora* spp. White cottony, patches are formed on the lower surface of leaflets, while upper surface turns yellow, brown and dries up. It can be controlled by spraying the crop with 0.2 per cent solution of Dithane M-45 at 15 days' interval during growth period.

Foot rot and blight

It is caused by *Ascochyta pinodella*, *Ascochyta pisi* and *Ascochyta pinodes*. Light brown lesions appear on the stems and pods. This disease can be controlled by spraying the crop with 0.2% solution of Dithane M-45 during the incidence of disease.

INSECT PESTS AND THEIR CONTROL

Stem fly

It is a small blue–black fly which lay eggs on the stem of young plants and its pale yellow maggots bore into stems, causing an early death of the young plants. This insect can be controlled by soil application of 20 kg Furadan per hectare at the time of sowing.

Aphid

They are very small insects which suck the cell sap from leaves, stem and pods. These can be controlled by spraying the crop with 0.1 per cent solution of Metasystox at 15 days' interval.

HARVESTING

The first picking is obtained after 75 to 90 days of sowing depending upon the variety and climatic conditions. Only the well matured pods should be harvested. Harvesting is down entirely by hand and that is why largescale cultivation is not followed. Interval between two pickings is about 15 to 20 days. The crop lasts up to the end of February or latest by second week of March if frost does not kill the vines. Maximum pickings are eight to ten, giving pods mostly during September-January.

YIELD

It produces an average of 60 to 80 quintals of green pods per hectare depending upon the variety and soil type.

PREPARATION FOR MARKET

Hard and damaged pods are removed from the harvested lot and if required, washed in running fresh water. Pods are put in baskets and sent for market. Minimum time should be taken during harvesting and marketing.

STORAGE

Pods can be kept longer than shelled grains. The best storing temperature is 4.5^0C to 7^0C with a relative humidity of 65 to 70 per cent. Fresh pods can be kept for about 15 to 20 days in cold storage.

Dried seeds can be kept for two to three years at room temperature under dry conditions.

SEED PRODUCTION

Seeds can be produced freely in the plains of the country as well as on the hills. It is a self–pollinated crop and requires only 25 metre isolation distance between the two varieties. Same cultural practices are to be followed for the seed crop. Three roguings have to be done, before flowering, at the time of flowering and last at the time of maturity. Spraying of fungicide against powdery mildew and downy mildew have to be done at proper time. Generally, seed crop matures in about 100 to 125 days after sowing depending upon the climatic conditions and variety of the crop. Completely dried pods are harvested and seeds are extracted by threshing. Seeds are dried completely and put in cloth bags or in tin containers at cool and dry conditions.

CLUSTER BEAN

Botanical Name	-	*Cyamopsis Tetragonoloba* L.
Family	-	Leguminoceae
Synonymous	-	Guar, Thupi, Guara, Urahi, Koth Avarai, Gavar, Gor Chikudu, Gorikaya, Kothavara, Guvar.

IMPORTANCE AND UTILITY

It is one of the important vegetable crops of northern India. It is grown for its tender green pods which are used as vegetables like French bean. Among leguminous crops it is comparatively more drought resistant and is cultivated on a large scale as a forage crop in dry regions. Among dry land crops, it occupies an important place in the national economy because of its industrial importance mainly due to the presence of gum in its endosperm. Guar gum is highly mucilaginous, which is being used in various industries such as textiles, cosmetics, explosives, paper, food processing etc. Today it is one of the significant foreign exchange earner of the country. According to Dr. Aykroyd (1941), fresh pods contain 82.5 per cent water, 9.9 per cent carbohydrates, 3.7 per cent protein, 0.2 per cent fat, 2.3 per cent fibre and 1.4 per cent mineral matters. Dried pods can also be used as vegetable in off season.

ORIGIN AND HISTORY

Cluster bean (Guar) is being grown India since ancient times for vegetable and fodder purposes. Therefore, some people believe that cluster bean is probably indigenous to India. It is occasionally found growing in its wild state in some parts of India. Gillette (1958) pointed out that tropical Africa is its probable centre of origin because of more occurrence of wild species in that country.

BOTANY

Cluster bean belongs to family Leguminosae. Plant is robust, erect, annual which usually grows to a height of 90 to 180 cm. Certain varieties may grow even taller than this. Plant has a well developed tap root system. Leaves are trifoliate and toothed. The flowers are borne in short axillary racemes and are generally purplish in colour. The pods are somewhat flattened and are borne in a cluster, hence the plant is known as 'cluster bean'. Pods are fleshy beaked, 2.5 to 13 cm long containing 5-12 seeds inside. When the pods are tender they are used as vegetable. The seeds are square in size and compressed.

CLIMATIC REQUIREMENTS

Cluster bean (Guar) is a drought resistant crop and can be grown successfully in areas where average annual rainfall is 30-40 cm. It is cultivated mostly as rainfed crop in semi-arid zones of northern India. Proper germination of seeds and root development takes place between 25^0C to 30^0C temperatures. It cannot stand waterlogging conditions at all. It is a photo-sensitive crop, and comes into flowering and fruiting when sown in Kharif season only.

SOIL AND ITS PREPARATION

Cluster bean can be grown on all types of soils except heavy and poorly drained ones. It thrives best on well drained medium to light soils with pH range of 7.0 to 8.5.

Clusterbean does not require much field preparation. Two or three ploughings with desi plough or two cross harrowings and a planking are sufficient. There should be enough moisture in the field at the time of sowing.

VARIETIES

Description of some of the recent promising varieties is given below.

Pusa Sadabahar: It is a day neutral variety and can be grown in spring as well as rainy season. It gives about 50-55 quintals of green pods per hectare. This variety can be grown on saline soils too.

Pusa Mausmi: It is suitable to grow in Kharif season only. Pods are shining, smooth and long. It gives about 50-55 quintals of green pods per hectare.

Pusa Naubahar: This variety has been evolved by selection from the progenies of a natural cross between 'Pusa Sadabahar' and Pusa Mausmi'. It has shining, smooth, long and tender pods. It yields about 60-65 quintals of green pods per hectare.

SEED AND SOWING

Sowings are usually done in March for the summer crop in northern India and in June-July for the rainfed kharif crop. It has been observed in experiments conducted at various places in northern India that for sowing of cluster beans first week of July to July 25 is the best time for obtaining higher yields. Early planting results in more vegetative growth, leading to lodging and ultimately low yields. The crop for fodder may be sown from April to mid July. The early sown crop makes luxurient growth under irrigated conditions and gives a high yield of fodder.

Fifteen to 20 kg seed per hectare is sufficient for vegetable and grain crop while 40-45 kg seeds per hectare should be used in case of fodder crop. A combination of 45 cm row to row and 15 to 20 cm plant to plant distance is best for normal sown crop. In late sown crop a row spacing of 30 cm in stead of 45 cm should be recommended. Closer spacing is good for fodder crop.

MANURES AND FERTILISERS

Being a leguminous crop, cluster bean does not require additional nitrogen. Only on extremely poor soil (sandy with very low organic matter content) 20 kg nitrogen should be used as starter dose at the time of planting. It is desirable to apply 40-60 kg phosphorus per hectare to ensure good yields. All the fertiliser should be applied at the time of sowing in furrows 4 to 5 cm below the seed.

When cluster bean is sown on poor soils after an exhausting crop, it is desirable to apply about 100-125 quintals of farmyard manure or compost about one month before sowing.

IRRIGATION AND DRAINAGE

The crop sown in July does not require any irrigation if the rains are normal and timely; otherwise one or two irrigation may be needed. For a summer crop, irrigations should be given at 10-12 days' intervals. During kharif season, drainage is more important than irrigation as cluster bean does not tolerate water stagnation in the field. Excess—water should be removed from the field during rainy season.

WEED CONTROL

One or two weedings are essential in kharif season crop to control the weeds in initial stage of plants growth. Basalin can also be used at the rate of

I kg a.i. per hectare. It should be used as pre-planting and incorported well in upper 10 cm of soil prior to sowing. It controls annual grasses as well as broad leaved weeds.

DISEASES AND THEIR CONTROL

Bacterial blight

It is the most serious disease of cluster bean caused by *Xanthomonas cyamopsidis*. It occurs mostly in kharif season. The spots are intraveinal, round and well defined on the dorsal surface of the leaf. They may enlarge or coalesce and result in blight phase. The pathogen invades vascular tissues and causes flaccidity of the affected portion. The flaccid spots become necrotic and turn brown. From the leaf, infection advances to petiole and stem and causes longitudinal streaks which result in blackening and cracking of stem.

Control Measures

❖ Seed treatment with hot water at 56^0C for 10 minutes controls the disease.

❖ Grow resistant varieties.

Alternaria leaf spot

It is caused by a fungus *Alternaria cyamopsidis*. Dark brown, round to irregular spots varying from 2 to 10 mm in diameter appear mainly on leaf blade of leaves. These water soaked spots later on turn greyish to dark brown with concentric zonations with light brown lines inside the spots. In severe cases spots merge together and the leaflets become chlorotic and usually drop off. If the plants are infected in the early stages of growth, there may not be any flowering.

Control Measure

❖ Spray 0.2 per cent solution of Dithane Z–78 at an interval of 15 days twice or thrice.

Anthracnose

It is caused by a fungus *Colletotrichum capsici f. Cyamopsicola*. Black spots on leaves, petioles and stems are seen during rainy season. This disease can be controlled by spraying 0.2 per cent solution of Dithane Z–78.

There are some other diseases of minor importance such as Myrothecium leaf spot, Curvularia leaf spot, Cercospora leaf spot and powdery mildew etc.

INSECT PESTS AND THEIR CONTROL

There is not much problem of insect pests in cluster bean crop. Sometimes Bihar hairy Caterpillar and jassids may attack the crop. Bihar hairy caterpillar can be controlled by spraying 1.25 litres of Endosulfan (35 EC) in 1000 litres of water. Attack of jassids can be checked by 2 or 3 sprayings of 600-1000 ml of Malathion (50 EC) in 600 to 1000 litres of water per hectare, depending upon the height of the crop with a manually operated sprayer at 15 days' intervals. The fodder crop, should not be fed to cattle up to about one week of spraying. There should be no spray on vegetable crop.

HARVESTING

Tender green pods are picked from the plant by twisting or by cutting. Harvesting or picking of green pods is continued over a period of long time because they continue arising as the plant grows. When crop is grown for seed, the crop is left until the plants are mature. Crop is harvested with the help of sickles and then dried and threshed.

YIELD

A good crop of cluster bean yields about 10-15 quintals of grain or about 50 to 60 quintals of green pods per hectare.

PREPARATION FOR MARKET

The pods should be kept in shade after harvest and over–mature, diseased and damaged ones should be removed. Early in the morning the pods can be sent to market in baskets or in gunny bags.

STORAGE

At room temperature, the pods can be stored for two days with frequent spraying of water on them and can be kept in cold storage at 0^0C with 85 to 90 per cent relative humidity for 15 to 20 days.

SEED PRODUCTION

It is a self–pollinated crop and only 25 to 50 metres isolation distance is required for foundation and certified seeds. The crop should be inspected thrice during its growing period. Once before flowering when on the basis of foliage characters, off types and diseased plants should be removed. Second roguing should be done at the time of flowering when on the basis of flower characters, all off types and diseased plants should be taken out. Finally, at the time of maturity the crop should be inspected and on the basis of pod characters, all off types and diseased plants should be removed. When 60 to 70 per cent pods change their colour from green to light brown the crop should be harvested and kept on the floor for 8 to 10 days for drying. Later on threshing can be done by sticks or by tractor.

OKRA

Botanical name	-	*Abelmoschus esculantus* Moench.
Family	-	Malvaceae
Synonymous	-	Bhindi, Bhendi, Dheras, Tori, Dhenrosh, Venda, Vendi, Safed tori, Benda Bendakaya, Vendaikkay, Bhinda, Bhida, Okra, Bendekayi Ramturai, Tindisha, Gandhmula, Babniyah, Bandaka, Ladies finger, Gumbo, Youn-padi-si, Kachang-lindir.

Importance and Utlity

Okra is an important vegetable crop of rainy as well as summer seasons. It is grown in all tropical and subtropical parts of the country. Its pods are used for vegetable in curries, stewed with meat, cooked into soups and also canned and dried. Fruits with its fibrous stalks are used in paper and Gur making industries. The seeds roasted and ground to powder are used as a substitute of coffee. Fruits have 2 per cent protein and are also a good source of minerals like calcium and magnesium. They also contain potash and iodine. Dried fruits contain 2 to 2.4 per cent nitrogen. Tender pods are used in cases of spermatorrhoea. The mucilage from the fruit and seeds or the fresh meshed capsules acts as an efficient emollient poultice. This mucilage has aphrodisiae effect. The pods are very useful in fever and problems of genito-urinary organs such as gynorrhoea, leucohoea and pains in passing urine. According to Dr. Akyroyd (1941) the fruits of okra contain the following nutrients in 100 g edible portion. Water 88 per cent, carbohydrates 7.7 per cent, protein 2.2 per cent, fat 0.2 per cent, fibre 1.2 per cent, mineral matters 0.7 per cent, calcium 0.09 per cent, phosphorus 0.04 per cent, iron 0.0015 per cent, Vitamin A 58 I.U., Vitamin B 63 I.U., Vitamin C 16 mg. It also contains iodine and potash.

ORIGIN AND HISTORY

It is essentially a native of Africa but a few wild types are found in India also. It spread to America probably with the slave trade. It is one of the popular vegetable crops in Africa, America, Turkey, India and other neighbouring countries.

BOTANY

The plant bears flowers in the axil of leaves which are large and hermaphrodite. Anthesis takes place in the morning and most of the flowers open between 9 to 10 AM. Dehiscence commences at the initiation of flowers and is completed with the full bloom of flower. Dehiscence takes place between 6 to 11 AM and is at its peak between 8 to 9 AM.

CLIMATIC REQUIREMENTS

The crop is basically adapted to tropical climate and requires warm humid weather for best growth and production. The minimum temperature tolerated by this crop is around 18^0C but unless the temperature is above 20^0C the seeds do not germinate. The optimum temperature range for growth is 20^0-30^0C. Maximum temperature tolerated without any setback to growth and fruiting is 34. 5^0C. Continuous rains are harmful to the crop.

SOIL AND ITS PREPARATION

It can be grown in all kinds of soils ranging from sandy loam to clay. However, high yields can be obtained in loose friable, well manured loam soils having better facilities for irrigation and drainage. The soil should be ploughed 3-4 times and levelled properly. After the land is prepared, beds of suitable size, according to source of irrigation should be made for effective irrigation. The optimum soil pH for okra ranges between 6 to 6.8.

VARIETIES

Pusa Sawani: It was developoed at I.A.R.I., New Delhi by a cross between "IC 1542" and "Pusa Makhmali". The pods are edged, smooth and dark green in colour. The length is about 10 to 15 cm at the marketable stage. It is high yielding variety and is good for rainy as well as summer season cultivation. The average yield is about 80-100 quintal per hectare.

Pusa Makhmali: It was bred at I.A.R.I., New Delhi from the varieties collected from West Bengal. It has proved superior to all the indigenous and foreign materials under Delhi conditions. It can be grown in both the seasons. In summer, the first harvest is taken in 50 days whereasein monsoon, the crop takes about 10 days more. The pods are 15 to 20 cm long, straight, smooth with attractive green colour. The average yield is about 80-90 quintal per hectare.

Bhindi No. 13 : It is evolved at P.A.U., Ludhiana and is popularly grown in Punjab. Pods are soft, smooth and dark green in colour. The average yield is about 75 to 80 quintal per hectare. The first harvest is taken 50 days after sowing.

Punjab Padmini: It is developed at P.A.U., Ludhiana and is very popular in North India. The pods are straight, smooth and dark green in colour. The average yield is about 90 to 100 quintal per hectare. The first harvest is taken 50 to 55 days after sowing.

Red Bhindi: The fruits are red, large and slender with less seeds than "Pusa Sawani". It is very common in south India.

Selection 1: It is developed at I.A.R.I., New Delhi and is resistant to some extent to yellow vein mosaic. The pod length is about 18 to 20 cm, and the colour of pods is light green. The average yield is about 100 to 120 quintal per hectare.

IHR 20-31: It remains free from the attack of yellow vein mosaic virus. The pods are five-ribbed and ready to harvest 45 to 55 days after sowing. The average number of pods per plant varies from 20 to 25, giving an average yield of 350 to 375 g per plant.

Parbhani Kranti : It is resistant to yellow vein mosaic. First picking can be done 40-45 days after sowing. Pods are medium in size, soft and dark green in colour.

Arka Anamika: It is recommended from I.I.H.R., Bangalor and is found to be resistant to yellow vein mosaic. Pods are soft and medium in size.

Arka Abhay: It is a sister line of orka Anamika and resistant to fruit borer.

Varsha Uphar: It is recommended in H.A.U., Hisar. First picking can be done 45 days after sowing. Pods are medium in size and dark green in colour.

Perkins Long Green : Plants are very tall with dark green foliage. The pods are long, smooth, tapered, bright green and spineles especially suitable for northern hilly areas.

SEED AND SOWING

Sowing time

In plains and frost free areas the first sowing is done in the month of February and March for summer crop. The best time is from 15th February to 15th March. The second sowing is done in the month of May-June. The best time is from 25th May to 25th June. The crop sown earlier in season will be less affected by yellow vein mosaic virus than the July-sown one. On hills the crop is sown from April to July.

Seed rate

The seed rate depends upon the season and germination percentage. Seeds having 80 to 90 per cent germination will be needed to the extent of 15 to 20 kg per hectare for spring sowing and 10 to 12 kg per hectare for rainy season sowing.

Seed treatment

The seed coat is hard and needs more moisture and time for germination. To avoid delay in germination the seeds should be soaked in water for 15 to 20 hours before sowing. The floating seeds should be removed since they are not suitable for sowing.

Sowing

Seeds are sown 15 to 30 cm apart on the ridges which are 30 to 45 cm apart. But this method of sowing is costly and time consuming. The sowing can also be done in flat field in lines 30 to 45 cm apart depending upon the season and variety. During rainy season, the distance between the lines should be 45 cm while in summer 30 cm. Plant to plant distance may vary from 15 to 45 cm. Besides dibbling, the sowing may be done with seed drill of behind a plough at required inter-row spacing. Later on the spacing can be adjusted by thinning. The seed should be sown at a depth of 2.5 cm.

MANURES AND FERTILISERS

The quantity of manures and fertilisers depends upon the type of soil but in normal condition 200 to 250 quintals farmyard manure should be added at the time of last harrowing. In addition to this, 50 kg nitrogen, 40 kg phosphorus and 40 kg potash per hectare will be required in medium type of soils. Half of the nitrogen and full amount of phosphorus and potash should be applied as basal dose while remaining half dose of nitrogen should be given as top dressing 35 to 40 days after sowing the seeds.

IRRIGATION AND DRAINAGE

Pre-sowing irrigation is essential for proper germination. The interval of irrigation and amount of water depend upon the season of crop and type of soil. In summer season the crop should be irrigated at every 5th day while during rainy season the crop should only be irrigated if rains are irregular. Excess water is harmful to the crop during rainy season hence it is essential that proper drainage is arranged.

WEED CONTROL

In both the season the crop suffers badly due to weeds. For better yield and quality the crop should be free from weeds during early stage, hence, three to four weedings should be done at 10 to 15 days' interval depending upon the intensity of weeds. Weeds can also be controlled by use of Basalin weedicide. Chemical at the rate of 1.0 kg ai, dissolved in 1000 litres of water, is sprayed in one hectare and mixed in the soil before sowing the seed.

DISEASES AND THEIR CONTROL

Yellow Vein Mosaic

It is a viral disease in which the leaves show prominently yellowish veins. In case of severe infection, the stem as well as fruits are affected and their colour is also changed to yellowish green and yellow. This disease is very common in rainy season.

Control Measures

❖ Grow resistant varieties.

❖ Spray the crop with Metasystox at the rate of 0.1% concentration. It will check the white flies which spread this disease.

❖ The crop sown in the middle of June is less affected by yellow vein mosaic as compared to July sowing.

Powdery mildew

White greyish powdery mass is seen on the under surface of the leaves. Severely attacked leaves may turn yellow and drop off.

Control Measure

❖ Spray the crop with Karathane at the rate of 0.06% concentration, repeat the spray 12 days after first spray or dust the crop with sulphur powder at the rate of 25 kg per hectare.

Cercospora leaf spot

It is caused by *Cercospora abelmoseki* fungus. The lower side of affected leaves become black and finally drop off Very less flowering and fruiting takes place on the affected plants.

Control Measure

❖ Crop should be sprayed with Blitox at the rate of 0.3% concentration at 15 days' interval.

Root knot

It is caused by *Melaidogyne* species of nematodes. Small swelling like structures are found on the roots of affected plants. Affected plant does not grow properly and very less yields are obtained.

Control Measures

❖ Mix neem cake or saw dust in the field at the rate of 25 quintal per hectare.

❖ Use Nemagon at the rate of 12 litres per hectare in the soil.

INSECT PESTS AND THEIR CONTROL

Short and fruit borer

It is one of the main insect pest causing heavy losses to the fruit. It is very common in early stage of growth and fruiting. Its dirty brown spotted caterpillars damage the crop by boring into growing points of the plants and later on into the fruits.

Control Measures

❖ Spray the crop with Thiodan 35 EC at the rate of 0.2 per cent concentration at weekly interval.

❖ Spray the crop with Sevin at the rate of 0.2%

Jassids (*Empoasea* sp.)

The adults and nymphs such the sap of the plant and leaves start curling or become cup shaped.

Control Measures

❖ Spray the crop with Sevin at the rate of 0.2% and repeat it 2 to 3 times but picking of pods should be done before each spray. Even after spray the picking should be stopped for a week.

Red cotton bug (*Dyodercus* sp.)

The clusters of nymph and adults suck the sap from mature fruit and damage the seed crop by reducing the seed germination.

Control Measure

❖ Spray the crop with Sevin 0.2% concentration.

Aphid

Adults and nymphs both suck the cell sap from the leaves of young growing branches. They leave sticky material on the leaves which develop black fungus on the surface and ultimately there is reduction in photosynthetic activities and plants become very weak.

Control Measure

❖ Spray the crop with Endosulfan 35 EC at the rate of 0.2% concentration or with Sevin at the rate of 0.2% concentration.

HARVESTING

The pods should be harvested when they immature and green and havge attained edible size (10 cm in Pusa Sawani). The growth of pods in rainy season crop is very fast and they are ready to harvest at 24 to 48 hours' interval.

Delay in harvesting causes fibrous and matured fruits of poor edible quality. Such fruits get very poor price in the market and ultimately poor income to the growers. Ten to fifteen pickings are done during the crop period. The best length at which the pods should be harvested is 8 to 10 cm.

YIELD

The yield depends upon the season, variety and cultural practices followed for the crop cultivation. On an average 50 to 75 quintals of green pods per hectare are obtained from summer crop while 100 to 125 quintal from rainy season crop.

PREPARATION FOR MARKET

After harvesting, the pods should be kept in the shed and damaged, diseased and over mature pods should be removed. The selected pods can be packed in baskets or gunny bags depending upon the quantity to be sent to market.

Storage

The pods can be stored at room temperature for 2 to 3 days if water is sprinkled on the pods during day and once in night to keep them cool and fresh. At 0^0C to 2^0C temperature with 60 to 75 per cent relative humidity the pods can be stored for 8 to 10 days.

SEED PRODUCTION

It is an often cross pollinated crop and to get pure seed isolation distance of 400 and 200 metres should be maintained for foundation and certified seeds, respectively. Same cultural practices should be followed as recommended for normal crop. However, rainy season crop is good for seed. All recommended control measures for insect pests and diseases should be followed strictly. Crop should be inspected thrice during the crop period. First before flowering and on the basis of foliage characters, off types and diseased plants should be removed. Secondly at the time of flowering and on the basis of flower characters, off types and diseased plants should be removed. Finally at the time of pod ripening and on the basis of pod characters, off types and diseased plants should be removed. When pods are brown, they should be consisdered for harvesting. Harvest them at 4 to 6 days' interval depending upon the maturity. Keep them in sun for drying and thresh them. Clean the seed and dry it up to 10 per cent available moisture. Keep it in cool and dry place. The average seed yield is about 10 to 15 quintal per hectare.

CUCUMBER

Botanical Name	-	*Cucumis sativus* Linn.
Family	-	Cucurbitaceae
Synonymous	-	Cucumber, Khira, Dosakaya, , Sukasa, Kakri, Vellarikkai, Kakrikai

IMPORTANCE AND UTILITY

It is one of the oldest vegetable crops grown widely throughout the country, tropical and sub-tropical parts of the world. Fruits are eaten raw with salt and pepper at the immature and mature stages. Mostly, the small fruits are used for pickling and big fruits are used for salads and for cooking curries. A portion of stem-end of the fruit is cut crosswise and rubbed together to remove the white bitter substance that comes out. Later on, the fruit is peeled and sliced without removing the seeds for the table. Its fruits have a cooling effect and prevent constipation and are useful in jaundice and allied diseases. The mature fruits are not so beneficial. Its edible portion contains 96.3 per cent water, 2.7 per cent carbohydrates, 0.4 per cent protein, 0.1 per cent fat and 0.4 per cent mineral matters. It is a good source of vitamin B and C.

ORIGIN AND HISTORY

It is probably indigenous to North India, and from here it was introduced in Asia and Africa, and then to Europe. Cucumber was cultivated by Greeks and Romans in about 300 B.C. It was grown in France in the ninth century and was grown in England in 1327.

BOTANY

It is a trailing or climbing annual, bearing elongated, thick cylindrical fruits of varying sizes and forms. The leaves are simple, palmately five-lobbed, sharply angled when young but subcordate at maturity. Tendrils are simple. The colour of the fruits varies from pale whitish green to dark green turning brownish yellow or rusty brown when mature. The plants are monoecious bearing male and female flowers. The flowers do not open at temperature below 12^0C, dehiscence and nectar secretion begins at 16^0C to 17^0C. The minimum temperature for pollen germination is 22^0C and optimum 24^0C and

25^0C.The dehiscence occures when temperature ranges from 20.5 to 21.5^{0}C between 2.30 to 3.45 A.M. and dehiscence completes before 5 A.M.The stigma becomes receptive 12 hours before and remains so 24hours after opening of flowers at moderate temperature. Cucumbers are mostly pollinated by honey bees.

Gynoecious lines have also been evolved in foreign countries. The plants produce only female flowers and seeds of monoecious lines are mixed at the time of sowing for providing male flowers for pollination purposes.

CLIMATIC REQUIREMENTS

It is a warm season crop and cannot tolerate even slightly lower temperature. The best termperature for its growth is 27^0C to 35^0C. High humidity and high temperatures are not suitable for better fruit set, and such climate increases the infection of powdery mildew.

SOIL AND ITS PREPARATION

Though it can be grown on a variety of soils from heavy clay to sandy loam but for early production a sandy or sandy loam soil is better. The soil should be free from hard layer with a high amount of humus. The best soil pH is between 5.5 to 6.5. The field should be harrowed four to six times and planked properly to prepare a good seed bed. At the time of last harrowing, 200 to 250 quintals of farmyard manure should be added in the soil.

VARIETIES

Following are the important varieties grown in the country.

China: Its fruits are about 50 cm long, slender in shape with deep green skin. Flesh is white, firm and crisp. It is a medium late straight variety and very hard and prolific in bearing.

Balam Khira: It is an old variety grown in all parts of the country. Its fruits are small, tender, oval in shape with light green skin at immature stage and light brown at ripening.

Sheetal : It is recommended from Kokan Vidhya Peeth' Dapoli. Its fruits are light green in colour, cylindrical and medium in size. Average weight of the fruit is 300-350 g.

Poinselle: It is an introduction from outside. Fruits are dark green in colour, cylindrical and are 25-30 cm large.

Khira-75 : It is recommended from Solan University It is found suitable for mid hills of Himachal Pradesh.

Khira-90 ; It is also recommended from Solan University fruits are lurg and thick as compared with other varieties.

Pusa Sanyog : It is recommended from I.A.R.I., New Delhi (Katrayain). It is an early and high yielding veriety.

Poona Khira : It is commonly grown in central part of the country. Its fruits are small to medium in size, oval in shape with light green skin at immature stage and light brow at ripening.

Japanese Long Green: It is an early variety and its fruits are ready to harvest after 45 to 50 days of sowing. Fruits are about 30 to 40 cm long, with green skin. The flesh is light green and crisp.

Straight Eight: It is also an early variety and its fruits are ready to harvest after 50 to 55 days of sowing. Fruits are medium long, thick, straight and cylindrical with round ends. The skin colour is green.

Sikkim cucumber : This variety is generally grown in hills. Its fruits are large in size, redish brown in colour and inferior in fruit quality. Its fruits can be stored for longer period at normal temperature.

Spineless Long Green: Its fruits are longated, smooth with dark green skin colour.

Long Spined Green type: It is an ordinary field cucumber having long spines with white or black colour. At the time of fruit maturity the spines fall down.

SEED AND SOWING

Time of sowing

Cucumbers are grown twice in a year in the plains and the sowing for spring crop is done in February-March while for rainy season crop in May and June. On the hills, only one crop is taken and sowing is done from March to May.

Seed rate

Seed rate depends upon the germination percentage, season and distance of sowing. On an average 3 to 4 kg seeds are sufficient for sowing one hectare field.

Method of sowing

Sowing of seed is done in hills and about 4 to 6 seeds are sown and later on 3 to 4 plants are maintained in each hill. Furrows are made at 1.5 metre and on both sides of these furrow mounds are prepared at one metre distance. The seeds are sown at a depth of 2 to 3 cm.

MANURES AND FERTILISERS

As already indicated, 200 to 250 quintals of farmyard manure should be applied 20 to 25 days before sowing. Sixty kg nitrogen, 50 kg phosphorus and 50 kg potash per hectare should be applied in the form of chemical fertilisers. Half of the nitrogen and full dose of phosphorus and potash should be given at the time of sowing while rest half dose of nitrogen should equally be applied as top dressing 40 and 60 days after sowing.

IRRIGATION AND DRAINAGE

The amount of water and interval of irrigation depend upon the season of the crop and type of soil. During dry season the crop should be irrigate every fourth or fifth day. During rainy season the crop does not require irrigation if rains are regular and adequate. The irrigation water should be allowed in furrows only but should not be allowed to touch the plants. With more water, foliage becomes yellow and the growth is retarded. During rainy season proper drainage facilities should be provided to remove excess water from the field.

WEED CONTROL

Better yield and quality of fruits can only be obtained if the crop is maintained weed-free. Two to three weedings are required for spring crop and four to five for rainy season crop. Large weeds can be removed by hand when the plants have covered the beds.

DISEASES AND THEIR CONTROL

Damping off

Young plants start wilting and die due to rotting of the stem near the ground. The disease is more prevalent in moist soils.

Control Measures

❖ Seed should be treated with Thiram (2 g/kg seed) before sowing.

❖ Spraying the plants with 0.2% solution of Dithane M-45.

Powdery Mildew

The leaves are covered with white mouldy growth and the plants are stunted and weakened. The fruits dot not reach the proper size.

Control Measures

❖ Dusting the crop with Sulphur dust @ 10 to 15 kg per hectare.

❖ Spraying the crop with 0.06% solution of Karathane.

Mosaic

It is caused by cucumber mosaic virus. The young levaes of the plants are stunuted, deformed and mottled with yellow and light green colour. The fruits get mid-shaped and mottled in colour.

Control Measure

❖ Spray the crop with 0.15% solution of Metasystox to check its spread.

INSECT PESTS AND THEIR CONTROL

Cucumber beetle

The larvae feed on the roots and the adults feed on leaves and stems. Sometimes cent percent plants are damaged during early stage.

Control Measure

❖ Spraying the crop with 0.2% solution of Sevin or Melathion (50 E.C.)

Aphid

It is one of the most destrictive insect of cucumber. Aphids suck the plant sap causing curling and distortion of the leaves as well as spreading of mosaic disease.

Control Measure

❖ Spraying the crop with 0.15 per cent solution of Rogor or Metasystox.

HARVESTING

Green fruits of proper size should be picked up from the vines. As the size of the fruit vary with variety, therefore, it should be known for the particular variety. The fruits can be cut, clipped or broken from the vines, avoiding injury to the plants. Picking should be done at 2 to 3 days' interval. If the fruits are allowed to ripen the growth of the plants and setting of new fruits are checked.

PREPARATION FOR MARKET

Harvested fruits should be kept in shade or cool place and soil particles removed by a piece of cloth from the surface of fruits. Diseased, damaged ripe and undersized fruits should be sorted out from the bulk. The selected fruits are then packed in mulberry or bamboo baskets. Use of gunny bags is not desirable because it may affect the appearance of fruits.

YIELD

Fruit yield may vary according to variety, season and cultural practices adopted for its cultivation. The average yield of fruits varies from 75 to 150 quintal per hectare.

STORAGE

At normal room temperature the fruits can be kept for two to three days by frequently sprayings them with fresh water. In cold storage, fruits can be kept for 10 to 14 days at 7.5^0C to 10^0C temperature with 85 per cent relative humidity. If the fruits are kept below $7.5\ ^0$C temperature they become dark coloured with watery areas which soon become mouldy.

SEED PRODUCTION

It is a cross-pollinated crop and requires 400 and 800 metres isolation distance for certified and foundation seed production, respectively. During crop period sufficient sprayings of insecticides and fungicids should be done to control the insect pests and diseases. Plants affected by virus should be removed regularly. Three roguings should be done, first before flowering, second at the time of flowering and thrid at the time of fruit maturity to remove the off types. Completely ripended fruits should be harvested. Seeds are removed after cutting the fruits. The seeds should be washed immediately by clean water and dried properly.

MUSK MELON

Botanical Name - *Cucumis melo*

Family   - Cucurbitaceae

Synonymous   - Musk melon, Bachang, Melonegurke, Chiral, Sweet melon, Kalinga, Chira, Kharbooj, Khurmuj, Kharbuja, Kasturi tarabuja, Velapandu, Velapalam, Thai kumbalom Kharbuj, Sakkartoti, Kekkarike, Kharbuza.

IMPORTANCE AND UTILITY

It is an important cucurbitaceous vegetable crop grown throughout India, particularly in hot and dry areas of Uttar Pradesh, Punjab, Rajasthan, Madhya Pradesh and Bihar. From these growing areas it is exported to the large consuming centres in the north. Its fruits are used as dessert and also eaten alone. Sometimes a small quantity of sugar is sprinkled on the flesh to make it sweet before eating. Fruits in green stage are sometimes used as cooked vegetable in rural areas. The ripened fruits are consumed by poor as well as rich people. Its seeds contain 40 to 44 per cent oil and are used as a substitute of almond and pistchio. The fruit pulp or juice is used in cooling drink and is also beneficial as a lotion in chronic and acute eczema as well as tan freckles and internally in case of dyspepsia. Its seed oil is useful in relieving painful discharge and suppression of urine. Its edible portion contains 94.0 per cent water, 5.0 per cent carbohydrates, 1.0 per cent protein, 3420 I.U. of Vitamin A, 33 mg of Vitamin C.

ORIGIN AND HISTORY

It is a native of northwest India, while its primary centre of origin seems to be the hot valleys of Iran (Persia) and adjacent areas. From India it has spread to China, Europe, Japan and Turkey. Columbus first took it to New World where at present it has a considerable importance.

BOTANY

It is an annual climbing or creeping herb having large hairy leaves. Its fruits are generally sphercial, oval or elliptical, of varying size and colour. Flowers are mostly andro-monoecious and sex form is similar in most of the Indian varieties. Male flowers are borne first in cluster on main as well as secondary branches while hermaphorodite ones on secondary branches as solitry ones. Petals start opening from the top between 9 P.M. to 10. P.M. and clear flowers open from 5.30 to 6.30 A.M. The dehiscence takes place before anthesis. Anthers dehisce at 21.8^0C to 23^0C, high fertility can be observed up to 10 A.M., after which it goes down. At 6 P.M. the fertility is negligible. The stigma remains receptive for two hours before and two to three hours after anthesis.

CLIMATIC REQUIREMENTS

It can grow well in hot and dry climate where temperature varies from 22^0C to 26^0C. Bright sunny days with high temperature and low relative humidity are best to produce sweet fruits with less foliar diseases. High humidity during its growing period may delay ripening and increase the incidence of foliage diseases. It is very susceptible to frost.

SOIL AND ITS PREPARATION

It can be grown on a variety of soils but loam and silt loam soils are found to be best for better growth and yield. The soil should be deep, well drained, rich in organic matter, free from hard layer and exposed to sun. Also, it does well on the beds of big rivers where soils are sandy with high organic matter. The best soil pH is 6.0 to 6.7. The soil should be prepared well by repeated harrowing and planking. During its preparation, residue of previous crop and stone pieces should be removed. Farmyard manure at the rate of 200 to 250 quintal per hectare should be incorporated in the soil during its preparation.

VARIETIES

Following are the improved varieties of musk melon grown in different parts of the country.

Hara Madhu: It is a very good variety recommended by Punjab Agricultural University, Ludhiana. The fruits are round in shape having white rind with green furrows. The flesh is light green having about 11 per cent T.S.S. It is a late variety and fruits do not slip from vine at maturity stage. It has a wider adaptability. The average fruit weight is about 800 to 900 g.

Pusa Sharbati: It is a variety developed from I.A.R.I., New Delhi by crossing a line of "Kutana" with American variety "Cantaloupe Resistant". It has round to oval fruits with netted rind and green furrows. The flesh is orange in colour and the seed cavity is small. The average fruit weight is about 800 to 850 g and fruits can be stored at room temperature for three to four days.

Durgapur Mathu: It is a mid season variety recommended by the Agriculture Department of Rajasthan Government, Jaipur. The fruits are oblong in shape having light green rind with green furrows. The flesh colour is light green and is very sweet (12 per cent TSS). The average fruit weight is about 500 to 700 g.

Arka Rajhans: It is an early medium variety recommended by I.I.H.R., Bangalore. The fruits are oval in shape having dirty white rind with fi9ne nets. The flesh is thick, white and very sweet (12 to 14 per cent TSS). Fruits have good keeping and transport qualities. It is resistant to powdery mildew disease. The average fruit weight is 1.0 to 1.5 kg.

Arka Jeet: It is also recommended by I.I.H.R., Bangalore. It is a short duration variety having small, round fruits with orange yellow rind colour. Flesh is very sweet (15 to.17 per cent TSS) with high Vitamin C.

Hisar Madhur: It is recommended from H.AU., Hisar. It is a cross between Pusa Sharvati x 75-35. Fruits are round, dark red in colour with green lining. Pulp is orange in colour with smell.

Punjab Rasila: It is a cross between Hara Madhua and W.M.R-29 and recommended from P.A.U., Ludhiana. Fruits are round and light yellow in colour. The average weight is 600 g.

Amritsari: The fruits of this variety are very large having orange rind with green furrows. The flesh colour is light green.

Lucknow sweet: The fruits are small, round in shape having yellow rind colour. The flesh is white and very sweet.

SEED AND SOWING

Time of sowing

On hills, the seed is sown from April to may while in the plains the seed sowing is done from mid January to 15th March but the best time is around 15th February. In river beds the seed can be sown even in December. Seed can also be sown in polyethylene bags in November and December and can be kept in hot place in order to protect from frost. Later on, these plants can be transplanted along with this ball of soil.

Seed rate

Three to four kg seed having 80 to 90 per cent viability will be sufficient for sowing one hectare area.

Method of sowing

Flat or raised beds 1.5 metres wide having 45 to 60 cm wide furrows in between two beds, are prepared. At both the sides of furrows the seeds can be sown mounds at one metre distance. Later on the same furrow is used for irrigation while vines are spread on the flat/raised surface. The depth of seed should not be more than 3.5 cm and 5-8 seeds should be sown in each mounds. The seeds can also be sown by broadcasting in the moist well prepared soil.

MANURES AND FERTILISERS

In case the previous crop is potato or any legume crop, the fertiliser requirement will be very less. If such crop is not taken then 200 to 250 quintals of farmyard manure should be incorporated 20 to 25 days before sowing the seeds. Eighty kg nitrogen, 50 kg phosphorus and 50 kg potash per hectare should be added in the form of fertilisers. Half dose of nitrogen and full dose of phosphorus and potash should be added at the time of last harrowing. Remaining half dose of nitrogenmay be given as to dressing four to six weeks after sowing the seeds.

IRRIGATION AND DRAINAGE

During its growing period the crop requires heavy amount of moisture. Therefore, till fruit set, the crop should be irrigated at the interval of 7-8 days. it is better to irrigate the crop only in furrows. It helps to avoid foliage diseases and reduces the quantity of water. In river beds only two-three irrigations are required. Excess water is always harmful to the crop, hence excess water should be drained out immediately to avoid spread of foliage disease. Irrigation should be stopped when fruits start ripening.

WEED CONTROL

Better yields and high quality of fruits can be obtained only if the crop is free from weeds. Weeding should be done twice or thrice as required by the crop till the vines are fully spread.

DISEASES AND THEIR CONTROL

Powdery mildew

It is caused by a fungus *Erysiphe cichoracearum* and is one of the most common disease of musk melon. A white powdery coating of fungal growth appears on the leaf surface, mostly seen on the upper surface, but also found on lower surface and stem. In case of severe attack the yield is very much reduced and fruits remain smaller in size.

Control Measures

❖ Sulphur dust can be used @ 15 to 20 kg per hectare.

❖ Karathane (0.06%) can be sprayed on the crop at 15 days' interval.

Downy Mildew

It is caused by *Pseudoperonospora cubensis* and infection is found only on leaves. Yellowish spots are observed on older leaves and lateron spots become large and turn dark brown in colour. This disease causes severe damage in several years.

Control Measure

❖ Spray the crop with Dithane Z-78 (Zineb) 0.2% solution.

Anthracnose

It is caused by a fungus, *Colletotrichum lagenarium*. Spoting and decay of fruits make them unmarketable. The disease is more prominent during warm and humd climate.

Control Measures

❖ Use resistant varieties.

❖ Follow crop rotations.

❖ Spray the crop with Zineb or Maneb 0.2% solution.

INSECT PESTS AND THEIR CONTROL

Epilachna beetle

Both grubs and adults feed on leaves, causing characteristic skeletonized patches on the leaves. The affected leaves become dry and drop down.

Control Measures

- ❖ Spray the crop with Malathion 0.2 per cent or Sevin 0.2 per cent solution.
- ❖ Dusting with Malathion (5 per cent dust) is also effective in controlling the beetle.

Red Pumpkin beetle

Beetles damage the leaves, flower buds and flowers. They make holes in them causing severe damage, especially to young plants. Later on, defoliation takes place.

Control Measures

- ❖ Spray the crop with 0.2 per cent solution of Sevin (50 W.P.)
- ❖ Dust the crop with Carbaryle 5% dust.

Fruit flies

The maggots of the flies bore into the ripening fruits causing rotting. The damage not only reduces the yield but also affects the quality.

Control Measures

- ❖ Grow resistant varieties
- ❖ Spray the crop with Sevin 0.2% from flowering to fruit set stage.

HARVESTING

The fruits fully ripened on the vine should be harvested to obtain best quality. Over ripened fruits do not get good price in the market. Varieties may differ in certain characters to indicate the maturity. Experienced workers have various ways of determining maturity. Following are the main indication indicating the maturity of fruits.

Aroma : Ripened fruits usually emit a nutty pleasant flavour.

Softening of the rind : The softening of rind can be observed by pressing the fruits with the fingers. There is change is rind colour, generally from green to light green or yellowish, depending upon the variety. Shining surface of the rind is also indication of ripening.

Change in TSS : The TSS of ripened fruits is much more than that of unripened fruits. The TSS of ripened fruits varies from 10 to 18 per cent depending upon the variety.

Development of the abscission layer : The abscission layer forms at the junction of fruit and vine attachment. When the fruits start ripening sugar percentage in the fruits reachers its maximum level. At this time the fruits can easily be separated out from the vine. This indicates the fruit maturity and the stage is known as "Full slip stage".

YIELD

Though varieties and improved package and practices followed are the main factors affecting the yield of musk melon, however, 125 to 200 quintals of fruits may be obtained from a normal crop of musk melon.

PREPARATION FOR MARKET

Fruits should be kept in cool place after harvesting and dust should be removed by cloth or washing in running water. Damaged, diseased and undersized fruits should be sorted out and sound ones taken to the market in baskets by a suitable transport.

STORAGE

In a cool place, fruits can be stored for two to three days while at $0^{0}C$ to $1^{0}C$ with 90 per cent relative humidity the fruits can be stored for one to two weeks.

SEED PRODUCTION

It is a cross, pollinated crop and requires 400 and 800 metres' isolation distance for certified and foundation seed production respectively. Sufficient care should be taken for cotrolling insect pests and diseases. At least three roguings should be done in the seed crop, first before flowering, second at the time of flowering and third at the time of fruit maturity. Seed can be extracted from completely ripened fruits.

WATER MELON

Botanical Name	-	*Citrullus vulgaris*
Family	-	Cucurbitaceae
Synonymous	-	Tarbooj, Kalinda, Jamaika, Matira, Paniphal, Karigu, Turmuj, Kalingad, Tarubhuj, Purcha, Palam Panna, Thannir Mathan, Kallangadi, Chayapula Kuttoowombi, Tandur, Belikh, Zichi, Watermelon, Pilchagnadi, Komardu, Pha-rai, Melond can pasteque, Wasser malone.

IMPORTANCE AND UTILITY

It is one of the most important fruit vegetables, being grown in all parts of the country up to the elevation of 1500 metres above sea level. It is a drought resistant crop and can be grown even in hot and dry regions of Rajasthan. It can be grown in extremely sandy soils where other crops can not be grown successfully. It is grown for its juicy flesh which is very sweet. Its fresh juice with salt and pepper is used as cool and refreshing drink during summer season. The juice is useful in quenching the thirst and is also used as an antiseptic in typhus fever. Small unripe watermelons are also cooked as a vegetable. Its seed kernels are used in medicine and in the preparation of sharbats. Edible watermelon contains 95.8 per cent water, 3.3 per cent carbohydrate, 0.2 per cent protein, 0.2 per cent fat and has a trace of mineral maters.

ORIGIN AND HISTORY

It is supposed to be a native of tropical Africa but it has a Sanskrit name indicating its ancient cultivation in India. It was quite unknown in Europe till the sixteenth century. In U.S.A. it has been cultivated since 1629.

BOTANY

It is a trailing or climbing hispid annual with deeply or moderately divided leaves and has small to large sized fruits. The fruit colour varies from light green to dark green or mottled green. It is monoecious and female flowers appear on the main branches. Karptrdia *et al* (1952) studied that corolla becomes compact one day before and on the day of anthesis. Anthesis continues from 6 A.M. to 7.30 A.M. The anthesis is completed in a short time. The dehiscence starts one hour before anthesis and continues up to 6.30 A.M. At high temperature, stigmatic fluid starts drying and stigma become non-receptive by 3 P.M. Maximum fruit set was recorded in first hour after anthesis and minimum 2 hours before anthesis. Padda *et al.* (1968) also made almost similar studies on floral biology of watermelon.

CLIMATIC REQUIREMENTS

It is a hot season crop and can be grown successfully at temperatures ranging from 25^0C to 30^0C. Humid regions are not suitable for its cultivation. Hot weather and dry winds during fruit ripening favour the development of flavour and high sugar content.

SOIL AND ITS PREPARATION

Sandy loams, deep, well-drained, rich in organic matter, free from hard layer and exposed to sun, are the best soils for its cultivation. Generally it does well on the bank of big rivers where soils are sandy. The best soil pH is 5.5 to 6.0 but it can be grown at 5.0 pH also. The crop raised in well-drained, sandy, alluvial and dry soils of river belt gives early and big sized fruits of good quality. The soil should be prepared well by repeated harrowings and plankings. Four to six harrowings and two to three plankings will be sufficient. Farmyard manure at the rate of 200 to 250 quintal per hectare should be mixed in the field at the time of field preparation.

VARIETIES

Following are the improoved varieties of watermelon grown in different parts of the country.

Sugar baby: It is introduced from U.S.A. It is a mid season variety having medium-large sized fruits weighing 2-3 kg with dark green rind colour. The flesh is red very sweet and seeds are small and dark brown in colour. Fruits are ready to harvest after 30 to 35 days of pollination and 95 to 100 days after sowing.

Ashai Yamato: It is introduced from Japan. It is also a mid season variety having medium-large sized fruits weighing 7 to 8 kg with light green rind colour. The flesh is deep pink with small seeds. Fruits are ready to harvest after 95 to 100 days of sowing.

Durgapura Meetha: It is recommended from Durgapur Research Station. It is a late variety and fruits are ready 125 days after sowing. Fruits are round with an average weight of 6.8 kg.

Arka Manik: It is recommended from I.I.H.R., Bangalore. Fruits are round and oval with green colour, having dark green strips.

New Hampshire Midget: It was introduced from U.S.A. It is an early variety and fruits are ready to harvest after 80 to 85 days of sowing. The fruits are small, weighing 1.5 to 2.0 kg. The shape is oval with bright green rind colour having dark green lacerations. The flesh colour is red. This variety is most suitable for kitchen garden. The fruits are ready to harvest after 28 to 30 days from the date of pollination.

Pusa Bedana : It is a hybrid between Tetra-2 of the U.S.A. and Pusa Rassal a local purified material developed at I.A.R.I., New Delhi. Due to triploidy nature, it is a seedless variety having pink and sweet flesh.

Arka Jyoti: It is hybrid developed from Indian Institute of Horticultural Research, Bangalore. It is a mid season hybrid, having round fruits weighing 6 to 8 kg. The rind colour is light green with dark green stripes and flesh colour is deep pink. The fruits are very sweet (13 per cent TSS). It has better keeping and transporting qualities.

IHR 6 x Charleston Gray : It is developed from Indian Institute of Horticultural Research, Bangalore. It is a mid season hybrid with oblong fruits weighing 8 to 10 kg. The rind colour is green with dark green lacerations. The flesh colour is red.

SEED AND SOWING

Time of sowing

In plains of the country, sowing is done in December-January. Seeds can be sown in polyethyiene bages and can be kept in hot place in order to protect from low temperatures. Later on seedlings are planted in field.

Seed rate

Five to six kg seeds having 80 to 90 per cent germination are sufficient to sow on hectare field.

Sowing

It can be sown in hills on raised beds or on levelled ground. The beds are prepared two metres wide having 30 cm wide furrows between two beds. At both the sides of furrow the seeds are sown at one metre distance. Later on the same furrow is used for irrigation while vines are spread on the raised surface. The depth of seed should not be more than 3.5 cm. In the river belts deep pits are prepared and a basket of farmyard manure is added in the pit and seeds are sown in it. If the sowing is done by this way the crop does not require irrigation.

MANURES AND FERTILISERS

The crop does well on soils well supplied with organic matter. About 200 to 250 quintal of farmyard manure should be mixed in the soil at the time of field preparations. Later on 60 to 80 kg nitrogen, 50 kg each of phosphorus and potash per hectare will be needed for better growth and production. Half dose of nitrogen and full dose of phosphorus and potash should be mixed on last harrowing while half dose of nitrogen may be given as top dressing four to six weks after sowing the seeds.

IRRIGATIN AND DRAINAGE

The crop needs heavy amount of moisture during early stage of growth. Therefore, till fruit set the crop should be irrigated at weekly interval. During early stage individual hill can be irrigated by pitcher or by water can. Irrigation should be stopped when fruits start ripening. It is better to irrigate the crop only in furrows where roots are there. Excess water should be drained out immediately to abvoid disease spread.

WEED CONTROL

High yields and high quality of fruits can be obtained only if weeds are effectively controlled. Hoeing and weeding should be done twice or thrice as required for complete control of weeds till the vines cover the surface of the bed. Pre-emergence application of NPA (N-I- naphthylphthalamic acid) at the rate of 2 kg per hectare on loam soils and 3 kg on clay and muck soils are effective in controlling weeds that germinate and emerge with the crop. The chemical should be applied just after sowing the seeds. The quantity of chemical is dissolved in 600 litres of water and sprayed on the soil.

DISEASES AND THEIR CONTROL

Anthracnose

It is caused by a fungus *Colletotrichum lagenarium*. It also attacks cucumber, musk melon and squash. Spotting and decay of fruits make them unmarketable. The disease is more prominent during warm humid climate.

Control Measures

❖   Use resistant varieties.

❖   Follow crop rotations.

❖   Spray the crop with Zineb or Maneb 0.2 per cent solution.

Fusarium wilt

It is caused by *Fusarium oxysporium* and the disease is most severe on light sandy soils and it develops most rapidly at 25^0C to 30^0C temperature. The entire vine may suddenly wilt and die or at first there may be wilting only during the day and some recovery at night but finally the plants wilts and die.

Control Measures

❖   Grow wilt resistant varieties.

❖   Follow crop rotations.

Downy mildew

It is caused by *Pseudoperonospora cubensis* and attacks only on the leaves. The symptom is yellowish spots on the older leaves and later on the spots large and turn dark brown in colour.

Control Measure

❖   Spray the crop with Zineb 0.2% solution.

Mosaic

It is caused by virus and is transmitted by certain species of aphids. It causes mild mottling of some leaves and a shortening of the internodes of the runner. If the plants are infected in early stages then they do not produce fruits.

Control Measure

❖ Spray the crop with Metasystox 0.15% solution to avoid its spread.

INSECT PESTS AND THEIR CONTROL

Aphids

There are very small insect and damages the leaves by sucking the juice. They are found in groups and feed from lower side of the leaf.

Control Measure

❖ Spray the crop with Metasystox 0.15% solution or 0.2% Malathion solution.

Cucumber beetle

They attack the plants as soon as they come up and may kill them. As the plants grow, the beetles feed upon the leaves, flowers, tender shoots and fruits.

Control Measure

❖ Spray the crop with Malathion or Thiodan or Parathion 0.2% solution.

Cutworms

They are very destructive to small melon plants. They cut them from soil surface during early stage.

Control Measure

❖ Mix Heptachlore 5% dust 20 to 25 kg per hectare before sowing the seeds.

HARVESTING

The fruits should be harvested at the right stage of maturity. They should be ripe enough to be sweet but not so mature as to be over-ripe. Varieties may differ in certain character to indicate the maturity. Experienced workers have various ways to determine the maturity. The most common field test of maturity probably is the change in the colour of the rind, especially the part of it in contact with the ground. This part of the rind changes from white to pale yellow colour with maturity. However, the best test of ripeness is by cutting and tasting of a few melons taken at random from various parts of the field. It these are ripe, it is likely that others of similar appearance will also be ready for harvest.

YIELD

Yield depends upon the variety, type of soil and management practices followed for its cultivation. Normally, 250 to 350. quintal per hectare fruits can be obtained.

PREPARATION FOR MARKET

Fruits should be kept in a cool place after harvesting. Damaged, disased and undersized fruits should be sorted out. The fruits can be loaded in trucks or cart as such or after filling in gunny bags. If they are loaded as such, a 15 cm thick layer of straw should be put on the bottom of truck or cart, sent to market.

STORAGE

In a cool place, fruits can be kept for two to three days, while at 2.2^0C to 4.4^0C temdperature and 85% relative humidity fruits can be kept for one to three weeks.

SEED PRODUCTION

It is a cross-pollinated crop and requires 400 and 800 metres of isolations distance for certified and foundatin seeds. In a seed crop, sufficient care should be taken for controlling insect pests and diseases. Minimum three roguings should be done. First before flowering, second at the time of flowering and third at the time of fruits ripening. Completely ripened fruits should be harvested and seeds can be extracted by fermentation method easily. The flesh may be kept for 36 hours to complete the fermentation process. Later on ,by running water the seeds can be washed.

BOTTLE GOURD

Botanical Name - *Lagenaria siceraria*

Family - Cucurbitaceae

Synonymus - Lauki, Chia, Doodhi, Jatilao, Jatilas, Tikatalana, Lau, Anapa, Sorakaya, Surakai, Dudhya, Bhopla, Sorekayi, Sorakaya, Surakai, Alabu, Dhudhya, Halagumbla, Ghai Kadu, Kashisore, Gurde, Flaschenkurbis, Bitter bottle gourd, White pumpkin, Lauka, Daani, Aal.

IMPORTANCE AND UTILITY

Among cucurbitaceous vegetable crops, it is one of the important one grown throughout the country and its fruits are almost available in the market throughout the year. Fruits are used for cooking, rayata, kapoorkand, pickles (especially on hills), kofta, petha, halwa and paratha etc. It has a cooling effect and prevents constipation. It is digestible easily, therefore, it is recommended during convalescence. Leaf extract with sugar is used against jaundice. Its seed oil is iused in headache. Fruit pulp is used as purgative and is very useful in coughs. It is an antidote to certain poisons. Pulp is also used as poultice during hot season, the cut surface of small sized fruit is rubbed on the underside of the feet and hands to reduce the effect of heat. The fruit ash with honey is useful to eyes for night blindness. Its edible portion contains 96.3 per cent water, 2.9 per cent carbohydrates, 0.2 per cent protein, 0.5 per cent fat, 0.5 per cent mineral matter, Vitamin A in traces and Vitamin B 10 I.U.

ORIGIN AND HISTORY

Bottle gourd is found in wild condition on the coast of Malabar and in the humid forests of Dehradun (India). From India and Africa, it spread to other warm countries. As literature shows, it was cultivated in India even before 2000 B.C. At present it is cultivated almost in all warm countries.

BOTANY

It is monoecious in nature and anthesis takes place from 5 P.M. to 7.30 P.M. When the maximum and minimum temperature range from 37^0C to 45^0C and 13^0C to 25^0C respectively. In winter season crop it occurs between 6 to 8 P.M. when temperature varies from 32^0C to 35^0C (maximum) and 18^0C to

20^0C (minimum). The staminate and pistillate flowers open at the same time. However, the opening of the petals starts earlier in pistillate flowers than in staminate ones. The dehiscence takes place between 12 noon and 1.30 P.M. when the maximum temperature ranges between 16^0C to 20^0C. The stigma remains receptive 36 hours beofe and 48 hours after anthesis. It fruits are long round, or oval to oblong in shape.

CLIMATIC REQUIREMENTS

It is warm season crop and grows well in a warm humid climate and is very susceptible to frost. The seeds germinate well at 30^0C to 35^0C and better growth takes place at 32^0C to 38^0C. High rainfall and cloudy weather promote the infection of insect pests and diseases.

SOIL AND ITS PREPARATION

Bottle gourd can eb cultivated in a variety of soils but thrives best in fertile sandy loam soils which are rich in organic matter, free from hard layer and have better irrigation and drainage facilities. The crop does well at 5.5 to 7.0 soil pH. The land should be prepared well by repeated harrowings and plankings. It should be levelled well before sowing. Well rotten farmyard manure at the rate of 250 to 300 quintal per hectare should be added in the field 25 to 30 days before sowing the seed.

VARIETIES

The following varieties of bottle gourd are recommended for cultivation.

Pusa Manjari: It is a hybrid produced by the cross between Pusa summer Prolifi Round and S1. 11. Its fruits are round in shape and light green in colour. The yield per hectare is about 253 quintal per hectare. The fruits can be dharvested 70 to 80 days after sowing the seed.

Pusa Meghdut: It is also a hybrid produced at I.A.R.I., New Delhi by the cross between Pusa Summer Prolific Long and SI.2. Its fruits are long in shape and light green in colour. The average yield is about 258 quintal per hectare. The iruits can be harvested 65 to 75 days after sowing the seed.

Arka Bahar: It is recommended from I.I.H.R., Bangalore. Fruits are long, cylindrial with an average weight of 1 kg.

Pusa Naveen: It is recommended from I.A.R.I., New Delhi . It can be grown in both the seasons. Fruits are smooth, green in colour, long with an average weight of 250 gm.

Punjab Komal: It is recommended from P.A.U., Ludhiana. It is a cross between LCII and AC -5. Fruits are long, medium in size and light green in colour.

Pusa Summer Prolific Long: It is an old variety recommended by I.A.R.I., New Delhi. Its fruits are long in shape and light green to yellowish green in colour. The length of the fruit varies from 60 to 75 cm with medium girth (20-25 cm). It can be grown in summer as well as in rainy season.

Pusa Summer Prolific Round: It is also an old variety developed at I.A.R.I., New Delhi. Its fruits are round in shape with green colour. It is a high yielding variety and can be grown in summer as well as in rainy season. The average girth varies from 15 to 18 cm.

SEED AND SOWING

Sowing time

In the plains, the sowing is done in February-March for summer crop and in June-July for rainy season crop. Sometimes, for early production in the summer the sowing is done in the month of October and November, but the crop has to be protected against frost. On the hills, the crop is sown from March to May.

Seed rate

The seed rate varies from season to season. For summer season crop 4.5 to 5.5 kg and for rainy season crop 3 to 4 kg seed having above 90 per cent germination percentage is sufficient for sowing one hectare.

Method of sowing

In rainy season, the seeds are sown in pits at the distance of 2 x 2 metres. The pits are prepared at proper distance (generally 15 cm raised pits are preferred) and 4 to 5 seeds are sown in each pit. Later on 2 to 3 plants are allowed to grow. In summer season, furrows are made at 2 metre distance and the pits are prepared by the side of furrows at 1.5 metre distance. During summer season, the furrows are used for irrigation and the area between two furrows is used for speading the vines. This system reduces the water requirement and checks the spread of foliage diseases. During winter season sowing can be done in polyethylene bags and these are kept in hot place for proper germination. Later on transplanting alongwith the ball of soil can be done in the permanent field.

MANURES AND FERTILISERS

About 250 to 300 quintals of farmyard manure should be added at the time of field preparation and in addition to it 60 kg nitrogen, 80 kg phosphorus and 60 kg potash per hectare should be added by chemical fertilisers. Half dose of nitrogen and full dose of phosphorus and potash should be given at the time of sowing. Rest half dose of nitrogen should be given by top dressing in two doses, first 25 days after sowing and second at flowering stage.

IRRIGATION AND DRAINAGE

Frequency of irrigation and quantity of water depends upon the season and soil type. During summer season, the crop should be irrigated every fourth or fifth day while during rainy season the crop does not require irrigation if rains are adequate and frequent. Excess water helps in the spreading of foliage diseases during rainy season. Therefore, the excess water should always be drained out from the field.

WEED CONTROL

For better yield and quality of fruits, the crop should remain free from all types of weed. During summer season two to three weedings and in rainy season four to five weedings are sufficient. During early stage (before spreading the vines) grasses can be controlled by spraying Gramaxone (0.15%) between the furrows.

STAKING

The crop should be staked for better yield and quality of fruits, especially during rainy season. The crop can be staked with bamboos or with poles. These are fixed at proper distance and ropes are tied on the poles at 60 cm distance.

DISEASES AND THEIR CONTROL

Downy mildew

It is caused by *Pseudoperonospora cubensis.* Yellow, more or less angular leaf spots are formed with a downy growth on the lower surface of the leaves. Affected vines do not set fruits properly.

Control Measures

❖ Crop should be sprayed with 0.2% solution of Dithane M-45 or Dithane Z-78.

❖ Crop rotation and sanitation reduce the severity of the disease.

Powdery Mildew

It is caused by *Erysiphe cichoracearum.* A white powdery coating of fungal growth appears on the leaf surface, generally on upper surface but sometimes also on lower surface and the stem. The affected leaves become yellow and later on fall down. The vines do not set fruits properly.

Control Measures

❖ Spray the crop with 0.06% solution of Karathane.

❖ Use sulphur dust at the rate of 15 to 20 kg per hectare.

❖ Spray the crop with 0.3% solution of wettable sulphur such as Sulfex etc.

Mosaic

It is a viral disease, caused by number of viruses. The most common symptoms are irregular light-green or dark-green mottling, occasionally with pale-yellow chlorotic areas on the leaves. Affected vines do not set fruits. These viruses are transmitted by insects.

Control Measure

❖ Spray the crop with 0.2% solution of Metasystox or Rogor or Dimecron.

INSECT PESTS AND THEIR CONTROL

Red Pumpkin beetle

It is a red beetle, about 7 mm long and 2.5 mm wide and its entire body is covered by hard wings. Beetles feed on the leaves, flower buds and flowers and make holes in them. In case of severe damage complete defoliation takes place.

Control Measures

❖ Spray the crop with 0.2 per cent solution of Sevin or 0.05 per cent solution of Endosulfan 35 EC.

❖ Plough the field just after harvest. By this method the pupae and larvae are killed.

Epilachna beetles

Both grubs and adults feed on the leaves and eat entire chlorophyll portion. The attacked leaves gradually dry up and drop down.

Control Measures

❖ Spray the crop with 0.2% solution of Sevion or 0.1 per cent Nuvan or 0.05 per cent Endosulfan or Melathion.

❖ Follow crop rotations.

❖ Dusting with 5% Malathion dust should be done @ 10 to 15 kg per hectare.

Fruit fly

The damage done by the maggots of the flies which bore the fruit and cause fruit rotting. The attack not only reduces the yield but also affects the quality adversely.

Control Measures

❖ Collect the affected fruits and bury them deep in the soil.

❖ Spray the crop with 0.2% Sevin or 0.1% Malathion solution.

❖ Grow resistant varieties.

Aphids

Sometimes there is very high population of these insects and they suck the juice from the leaves and stem. Affected plants become yellow. This insect also transmits viral diseases.

Control Measure

❖ Spray the crop with 0.15% Metasystox or 0.1 per cent Rogor or 0.1% Malathion solution.

HARVESTING

The tender fruits should be harvested. After this stage the seeds becomes hard and the flesh coarse and dry. Tender fruits get good price in the market, while hard fruits cannot be used for cooking. The fruits should be removed carefully from the vine with the help of a knife so that the plant is not uprooted or injured.

YIELD

Yield varies from variety to variety and from season to season. Normally, yield of 100 to 125 quintal per hectare in summer season and 125 to 150 quintal in rainy season can be obtained.

PREPARATION FOR MARKET

After harvesting, hard and damaged fruits should be removed to get better price in the market. Selected fruits can be put in baskets or in the gunny bags and sent to market.

STORAGE

The fruits can be stored for 2 to 3 days without any damage under shade provided they are sprinkled with fresh water. The fruits can also be stored at 5°C to 8°C in cold storage for 20 to 25 days.

SEED PRODUCTION

It is a cross-pollinated crop and requires 400 and 800 metres' isolation distance for certified and foundation seed production, respectively. Off type plants should be removed, first before flowering, second at the time of flowering and last at the time of fruit maturity. Better control measures against insect pests and diseases should be adopted. Completely ripened fruits should be harvested and seeds be extracted. The average seed yield is about 5 quintal per hectare.

PUMPKIN

Botanical Name	-	*Cucurbita moschata*
Family	-	Cucurbitaceae
Synonymous	-	Sitaphal, Kaddu, Kadua, Kashiphal, Mitha kaddu, Saphurii Kumra, Pilum Kohalum, Lal Phopla, Gummadi Kayi, Poashani, Gumbala, Kannada, Duddini, Prala Kalu, Red Gourd, Lal Bhopla, Lal Kumhara, Meetha Kaddu.

IMPORTANCE AND UTILITY

Pumpkin is important and most extensively grown cucurbitaceous vegetable in the country. It is grown during summer and rainy seasons. During summer it is used commonly in North India in marriage parties. Its fruits are used for cooking, for rayata making in both the stages—green as well as ripe. Edible portion of pumpkin contains 92.5 per cent water, 1.4 per cent protein, 4.6 per cent carbohydrates, 0.1 per cent fat, 0.6 per cent mineral matters. Sometimes the leaves and fruits are also used as vegetables. Cooked vegetable prepared from the fruits reduces the effect of hot weather. Its seeds along with sugar are taken to kill tape worms and are useful in urinary diseases. The fruit pulp is used for poultice for boils, carbuncles and ulcers etc.

ORIGIN AND HISTORY

Pumpkin is reported to have originated in America. Its probable native place is Guetemala and Central Mexico or Colombia. It is still found there growing in wild condition. It was used as vegetable in 2000 B.C. in America. It has been cultivated in India and China since long back.

CLIMATIC REQUIREMENTS

Pumpkin requires much longer season than other cucurbits and takes about 80 to 120 days from seed sowing to first fruit harvest. The abundance of light gives rise to male flowers though within limits. High temperature and long days help to increase the number of male flowers and reduce the number of female flowers. Rainy season crop is more successful than the summer one. The favourable temperature range for their growth and development is minimum 18.5°C. Optimum 25-27°C and maximum 34-35°C. Better seed germination takes place at 26°C to 30°C.

BOTANY

The leaves are five lobed, simple, non-hirsute and soft textured. The flowers are mostly monoecious and pollination is mostly done by insects. Anthesis starts in the early morning at 3.30 A.M. and the maximum number of flowers open between 3 A.M. and 4 A.M. The flowers remain open for about 8 to 10 hours after which they start losing their yellow colour and wither. Higher temperature seems to hasten the time of anthesis. The dehiscence takes place from 9 P.M. to 3 A.M. with its maximum at 11 P.M. to 1 A.M.

SOIL AND ITS PREPARATION

The crop does well in a variety of soils ranging from sandy to moderately heavy soils provided the drainage system is quite efficient. Better yield can be obtained in sandy loam soils which are free from hard layer, rich in organic matter and have better irrigation and drainage facilities. The best soil pH is 6.0 to 6.8. The soil should be prepared well by repeated harrowings followed by planking. During its land preparation the residues of previous crops and pieces of stone etc. should be removed. About 250 to 300 quintals per hectare of farmyard manure should be added in the soil 20 to 25 days before sowing the seeds.

VARIETIES

Following are the improved varieties of pumpkin grown in the country. Besides these, many local varieties are also cultivated.

Arka Suryamukhi : This variety was developed at I.I.H.R., Bangalore. Fruits of this variety are small (1 to 1.5 kg in weight), round with flat ends in shape. Rind colour varies from deep orange to yellow, with discontinuous thin creamy lining alongwith shallow furrows. Linings originate from the blossom end whereas the furrows originate from the stem end. It has excellent flavour, firm texture and bright orange flesh colour. It is highly resistant to fruit fly. Yield varies from 200 to 250 quintal per hectare and the crop is harvested in about 100 days.

Pusa Vish Wash: It is recommended from I.A.R.I., New Delhi. Fruits are round with yellow pulp. The average weight of fruit is 5 kg.

Pusa Vikas: It is also recommended from I.A.R.I., New Delhi. Fruits are small, flat with an average weight of 2 kg. Pulp is yellow in colour. It can be cultivated in both the seasons.

Arka Chandan: It was also developed at I.I.H.R., Bangalore. Fruits are medium sized (2 to 3 kg in weight), round with slightly pressed poles and rind colour is light brown with creamy patches at maturity. It has excellent flavour, firm texture, bright orange flesh and yield varies from 300 to 325 quintal per hectare. Crop is harvested in 125 days.

IHR 83-1-1-1: It was also developed at I.I.H.R., Bangalore. Its fruits are medium in size varying from 2 to 3 kg in weight. Fruits are round with flat poles. Stem colour is light brown to yellow.

Co 1: It was developed from the Agricultural Research Institute, Coimbatore. It is a late variety and takes about 175 days from sowing to complete harvest of the fruits. Fruits are large in size varying from 7 to 8 kg in weight. They are attractive and globular in shape. Each vine produces 7 to 9 fruits. The yield varies from 250 to 300 quintal per hectare.

Co 2: It was developed at Agricultural Research Institute, Coimbatore. The fruits are small in size weighing not more than 2.0 kg and slightly ridged with orange coloured flesh. Normally, a vine produces 10-12 fruits, weighing 20 to 24 kg. The average yield varies from 225 to 250 quintal per hectare. The total duration of crop is 130 days. The keeping quality remains quite good for over 4 to 5 months under ordinary storage conditions.

SEED AND SOWING

Seed rate

Seed rate varies from season to season and depends on germination percentage of the seed. Normally, 6.5 to 9 kg seed is sufficient for one hectare area.

Sowing time

In the plains, summer crop is sown from January to March while the rainy one from June to July. In frost-free areas, sowing can be done in October which gives edible fruits in February-March. On hills the sowing is done from March to July. In North India, due to low temperature, early production is not possible.

Method of sowing

Furrows are made at a distance of 2 metres and on the side of these furrows mounds are prepared at 1.5 metre distance. Generally, mounds are prepared 15 centimetre raised from the surrounding areas. Four to five seeds are sown in each mounds and later on 2 to 3 plants per mounds are allowed to grow. During summer the furrows are used for irrigation while during rainy season the furrows are used for drainage purpose.

MANURES AND FERTILISERS

The doses of manures and fertilisers depend upon the soil type, climate, soil test value and variety. About 250 to 300 quintals of farmyard manure should be added during soil preparation. Besides this 60 kg nitrogen, 80 kg phosphorus and 60 kg potash per hectare should be applied in the form of chemical fertilisers. Full dose of phosphorus and potash and half dose of nitrogen should be given as basal whereas rest half dose of nitrogen should be given as top dressing in two splits, first 25 to 30 days after sowing and second at flowering stage.

IRRIGATION AND DRAINAGE

Interval and amount of water in each irrigation depends upon the season and type of soil. During summer season the crop should be irrigated at four to five days' interval while the crop sown during rainy season should be irrigated when there are no rains. During rainy season the excess water should be drained out immediately after rains.

WEED CONTROL

For better yield and quality fruits, weeding should be done regularly and crop should remain free from weeds. Normally 2 to 3 weedings in summer season and 3 to 4 weedings in rainy season are required. Weeding can be done by *khurpi* or by hand hoe. During early stage the weeds may be controlled by the use of chemicals like Gramaxone (0.2% solution).

DISEASES AND THEIR CONTROL

Powdery mildew

It is one of the most common disease of pumpkin. A white powdery coating of fungal growth appears on the leaf surface. The growth is mostly on upper surface but is also found on the lower surface and the stem.

Control Measure

❖ Spray the crop with 0.03% solution of Karathane at weekly interval, or any wettable sulphur compound like Sulfex or Elosal.

Anthracnose

Sometimes small fruits are affected by this disease and black spots are formed and finally the fruits do not achieve proper size.

Control Measure

❖ Spray the crop with 0.2 to 0.3% solution of Dithane M-45 or Dithane Z-78 at an interval of 15 to 20 days.

INSECT PESTS AND THEIR CONTROL

Red Pumpkin beetle

The damage is caused by beetles which feed on leaves, flower buds and flowers and make holes in them. During heavy infestation, defoliation takes place.

Control Measures

❖ Dusting the crop with Sevin 5 per cent dust @ 10-15 kg per hectare.

❖ Spraying the crop with 0.2% solution of Sevin (50 W.P.) during early stage.

Epilachna beetle

Both grubs and adults feed on leaves causing skeletonized patches on them. The affected leaves gradually dry up and drop down.

Control Measures

❖ Dusting the crop with Malathion or Sevin dust.

❖ Spraying the crop with 0.3% solution of Malathion (50 W.P.).

❖ Spraying the crop with 0.2% Sevin (50 W.P.).

HARVESTING

The pumpkin fruits are harvested at full maturity or at complete ripening stage. At ripening, there is change in colour from green to brown or yellow. If there is a demand of green fruits in the market, the fruits can be harvested even before reaching full maturity stage. The fruits should be handled carefully during transport.

YIELD

Soil fertility, cultural practices and crop season are the factors affecting the yield of pumpkin. Normally the fruit yield varies from 200-300 quintal per hectare.

PREPARATION FOR MARKET

The fruits affected by insects and diseases should be sorted out, because they start rotting during transit. Selected fruits can be packed in gunny bags before sending to market.

STORAGE

Pumpkin fruits can be kept for 2 to 4 months without any damage at room temperature but the fruits should not be kept in heaps. It is better to keep them in shelves where they can be spread out in one single layer with a space between the fruits. In cold storage, the fruits can be kept at 8°C to 12°C with 70 to 75 per cent relative humidity for 6 months.

SEED PRODUCTION

It is a cross-pollinated crop, therefore, 400 and 800 metres' isolation distance should be maintained for certified and foundation seed production. It is better to produce the seed of one variety in one village. Crop should be inspected frequently and off types removed. Proper control measures against insect pests and diseases should be adopted. Completely ripened fruits should be harvested and seeds extracted from them. The pulp can be sold in the market after extracting the fruits.

BITTER GOURD

Botanical Name   -   *Momordica charantia* Linn.

Family   -   Cucurbitaceae

Synonymous   -   Karela, Karavella, Cherbal samapfel, Kerula Uchche, Quisaulbarri, Kakara, Pavakka, Balsamper, Karathi, Momordique charandia, Kareli, Tita, Kakarakaya, Pakarkai, Pavakka, Balsampear.

IMPORTANCE AND UTILITY

It is grown throughout India for its ridged, bitter and immature fruits. Fruits are highly nutritive and are relatively high in proteins, minerals and vitamins. They are used for cooking as vegetables, pickles and consumed after drying. It has some medicinal properties and is recommended for curing bllod diseases, rheumatism, diabetes and asthma. Its pulp, leaf juice and seeds are anthelmintic, leaves act as galactagogue and its root is astrigent. The whole plant powder is used for dusting over leprous and ulcers. Its fruits contain, 83.2 per cent water, 2.9 per cent protein, 1.0 per cent fat, 1.4 per cent mineral matter, 1.7 per cent fibre, 9.8 per cent carbohydrates, 0.05 per cent calcium, 0.14 per cent phosphorus, 9.4 per cent iron and traces of Mg (Aykroyd *et al.,* 1962).

ORIGIN AND HISTORY

It is considered to be an old world species with its native in the Tropical Africa and Asia. At present it is grown almost in all countries. It is cultivated in each state of India and also found growng wild in many areas of the country.

BOTANY

Its leaves are deeply lobed and tendrils simple. Flowers are monoecious which start opening at 5 A.M. and completely open between 9.30 to 10.00 A.M. Lowering of atmospheric temperature delays flower opening and shedding by one hour. Anthers dehisce about two hours before blooming i.e. between 7 to 8.0 A.M. Male flower drop in the evening. The viability of pollen grains and receptivity of stigma are optimum about two hours before the flower fully opens i.e. 7 to 8 A.M. The pollens become non-viable as the day advances and after 12 noon not a single pollen grain is found to germinate and the stigma retains its receptivity for a much longer period. There is normal fruit setting after crossing between varieties.

CLIMATIC REQUIREMENTS

It has a wide range of adaptability yet it thrives best in warm humid regions. Its seed has a hard seed coat and germinates slowly due to slow absorption of water. Germination takes much more time at low temperature. It cannot tolerate temperature below 10°C during growth period.

SOIL AND ITS PREPARATION

It can be grown in all types of soils but well-drained loam soil rich in organic matter is found to be most suitable for its better yield and quality. The soil should be prepared well by harrowings followed by plankings and residues of previous crops should be removed during the field preparation. The best soil pH is 6 to 7 for better growth and yield. Well rotten farmyard manure at the rate of 200 to 250 quintal per hectare should be mixed at the time of field preparation.

VARIETIES

Kalyanpur Baramasi: It is recommended from Vegetable Research Station, Kalyanpur, Kanpur. Fruits are 20-25 cm long, thin, dark green in colour and the fruits are available almost around the year.

Priya: It is recommended from Kerala. Fruits are 40 cm lony, thin with an average weight of 200 gm. In South India it is cultivated all around the year.

Pusa Vishesh: It is recommended from I.A.R.I., New Delhi. Fruits are soft, green and medium in size. The average fruit weight is 150 gm.

Pusa Do Mausmi: It was developed from the I.A.R.I., New Delhi. Its fruits are long, green and medium in size. The variety is suitable for both summer and rainy seasons. The first picking can be done after 55 to 60 days of sowing. The average yield of this variety is about 100 quintal per hectare.

Coimbatore long: It was developed from the Agricultural Research Institute, Coimbatore. This variety is good for rainy season. Its fruits are long, tender and slightly whitish in colour. The average yield is about 80 to 100 quintal per hectare.

Arka Harit: It was developed from I.I.H.R., Bangalore and can be grown in summer and rainy seasons. Its fruits are medium in size, green in colour and have less seeds. The average yield is about 90 to 120 quintal per hectare.

SEED AND SOWING

Time of sowing

In hills, only one crop is taken and sowing of seed is done from April to May. In the plains, two crops are grown i.e. summer as well as rainy season. The seed sowing is done in February-March for summer crop and in June-July for rainy season crop.

Seed rate

Four to five kilograms of seed having 80 to 90 per cent germination is sufficient to sow one hectare area.

Sowing

At 1.5 metre distance, furrows are made and seeds are sown at one metre distance at both the sides of furrows. This system is very useful for summer season. At the same distance seeds can be sown in flat beds for rainy season crop.

MANURES AND FERTILISERS

As already mentioned above, 200 to 250 quintals of farmyard manure should be mixed in the soil during field preparation. In addition to this, 60 kg nitrogen, 60 to 80 kg phosphorus and 50 to 60 kg potash per hectare should be added. Full dose of phosphorus and potash and half dose of nitrogen should be given at the time of last harrowing, while rest half dose of nitrogen should be given by top dressing 3 to 4 weeks after sowing the seeds.

IRRIGATION AND DRAINAGE

Quantity of water and interval of irrigation depend upon the season and type of soil. Crop sown in June and July will not require irrigation but better drainage facilities should be provided to drain out excess water from the soil. The crop sown in February-March will require frequent irrigations at an interval of 7-8 days.

WEED CONTROL

Weeding should be done when required to keep weeds under control. During rainy season atleast 3 to 4 weedings and in summer season 2 to 3 weedings will be required.

STAKING

For better yield and quality, staking must be provided specially in rainy season crop. Dried branches, arhar sticks and bamboos can be used for this purpose.

DISEASES AND THEIR CONTROL

Powdery mildew

It is one of the most common disease of bitter gourd. A white powdery coating of fungal growth appears on the leaf surface, mostly confined to the upper surface but also found on the lower surface and stem. The affected leaves turn yellow and drop. In severe infections the yield is very much reduced and the fruits remain small in size.

Control Measure

❖   Karathane (0.06% solution) should be sprayed at 15 days' interval during growth period.

Downy mildew

This is more common during rainy season crop. Yellow spots appear on the upper surface of leaves and purplish spots on lower surface. In case of severe infection the yield and quality goes down.

Control Measure

❖   Dithane M-45 (0.2% solution) should be sprayed at 15 days' interval.

INSECT PESTS AND THEIR CONTROL

Red Pumpkin Beetle

Both larvae and adult damage during seedling stage by eating young leaves. Sometimes the fruits are also damaged.

Control Measure

❖ Sevin (0.2% solution) should be sprayed or Sevin 10% dust may be used during early stage.

Cut worm

The larvae cut the young seedlings from the soil surface during night.

Control Measures

❖ Heptachlore 5% dust @ 20 to 25 kg per hectare should be mixed in the soil before sowing or when the damage is observed.

Epilachna beetle

The beetle damages the young seedlings just after germination.

Control Measure

❖ As followed for Red Pumpkin beetle.

Aphid

They suck the juice from the leaves and reduce the photosynthetic activities.

Control Measure

❖ Metasystox (0.15% solution) should be sprayed on the crop during active period of insect pest.

Fruit fly

It is one of the serious insect pest of bitter gourd and during rainy season the infection reaches upto 100 per cent. The maggots of the fly bore into fruits and flowers are also damaged by them.

Control Measure

❖ Sevin (0.2% solution) should be sprayed on the crop from flowering stage to fruit set.

HARVESTING

Dark green, tender, medium sized fruits should be harvested at an interval of 3 to 4 days. Light green or light yellow fruits do not get good price in the market. For crop grown for seed purpose, completely ripe yellow red fruits should be harvested.

YIELD

Yield depends upon the variety, season, soil and management practices followed for the cultivation of the crop. Normally 80 to 100 quintals of fruits per hectare from summer crop and 100 to 125 quintals of fruits per hectare from rainy season crop can be obtained.

PREPARTION FOR MARKET

The plucked fruits should be kept under shade in a cool place. Damaged undersizeed and semi ripened or ripened fruits should be sorted out. Selected fruits are packed in baskets and sent to the market.

STORAGE

The fruits can be kept for three to four days at normal room temperature under ordinary conditions of storage, provided with normal spraying of water at regular interval. Fruits can be stored for 15 to 20 days in cold storage at 5°C to 8°C.

SEED PRODUCTION

It is a cross pollinated crop and requires 400 and 800 metres isolation distance for certified and foundation seed production, respectively. Minimum three roguings should be done, first before flowering, second at the time of flowering and third at the time of fruit ripening. Completely ripened fruits should be harvested and seeds extracted. Seed crop should be protected from insect pests and disease.

SPONGE GOURD AND RIDGE GOURD

Botanical name - *Luffa cylindrica* (Sponge gourd)

Luffa acutangula (Ridge gourd)

Family - Cucurbitaceae

Synonymous - **(a) Sponge gourd:** Kali Torai, Ghia torai, Ramtori, Tarada bhol, Torai, Turaia, Nemia, Chiora, Rajakosa taki, Gilki, Dhundul, Thuppa, Heere, Kayi, Gosali, Gilka, Punibeera, Patola, Liasada, Palo.

(b) Ridge gourd: Torai, Mongi torai, Araturai, Jhingotori, Dorkavidarbha, Turi, Ghoshalata, Janhi, Beera, Peerkankai, Pechanga, Peecha kam, Cherupee rum, Dharnagava, Jhingaka, Junhi, Ribbed leefa, Scur feekige gurke.

IMPORTANCE AND UTILITY

Both the gourds are commonly grown throughout the country and used for culinary purpose. They are cultivated easily. Therefore, each house or hut owner grows them at the corner of his house or hut. The vines can be spread over the roof or thatch or on any other structure. Both these gourds can be identified from each other because ridge gourd has ribs on the fruits while sponge gourd does not possess them. Fresh edible luffa contains, 95.4 per cent water, 0.5 per cent protein, 0.1 per cent fat, 0.3 per cent mineral matters, 3.7 per cent carbohydrates, 0.04 per cent calcium, 0.04 per cent phosphorus. It has some iron and vitamins A and C also.

The sponge of the dried fruits is used for various purposes such as bath sponge, cleaning utensils, brush making, scrubber, pad and pot holder, rug, door mat, stuffing material for pillows, saddles, and mattresses etc. In U.S.A., it is used as sound absorbing material in different ways. Its seed oil is used in cutaneous complaints, the roots are used as laxative in dropsy and fruit juice is used in adrenal type diabetes. The leaves are used in splenitis, haemorrhoids and leprosy and the leaf juice is used in eyes of children in granular conjcutivities.

ORIGIN AND HISTORY

The sponge gourd is probably a native of South Asia and Africa, while ridge gourd seems to have originated from India, Sunda Islands and Java because it is still found in wild condition in these places. Both these gourds are almost cultivated in all the tropical countries of the world.

BOTANY

Monoecious, dioecious, hermaphrodite and gynoecious sex forms are found in *Luffa acutangula* and only monoecious sex form in *Luffa cylindrica*. Flowers of *L acutangula* open in the evening (4 to 6 P.M.) while those of *L cylindrica* in the morning (2 to 6 A.M.). Temperature and humidity are found to play a prominent role in the anthesis and anther dehiscence. Pollen grains remain viable for 2 to 3 days during winters and 1 to 1½ days in rainy season. The stigma become receptive 6 hours before and 84 hours after flower opening in *L. acutangula* and 10 hours before and 120 hours after anthesis in *L cylindrica*.

CLIMATIC REQUIREMENTS

These are warm season crops but have a wide range of adaptability. They thrive best in humid and warm regions. They are very susceptible to frost. Germination of seeds takes place at 28°C to 34°C and better growth takes place at 31°C to 37°C. High rainfall and cloudy weather promote the infection of insect pests and diseases. Host winds during fruit set reduce the setting percentage of fruits.

SOIL AND ITS PREPARATION

Both these species can do well in all types of soils but good yields are obtained in fertile sandy loam soils which are rich in organic matter and free from hard layer. They grow well at soil pH between 6 to 7. The soil should be ploughed three to four times and planked twice or thrice to pulverize the soil for making a smooth and fine seed bed. Well rotten farmyard manure at the rate of 250 to 300 quintal per hectare should be added in the field 25 to 30 days before sowing the seed.

VARIETIES

The fruits of sponge gourd are smooth, cylindrical and light green in colour. The seeds are black or white but smooth. The fruits of ridge gourd are club-shaped, sharply ribbed and the ridges running lengthwise. They are green in colour. The seeds are black having rough dotted surface. Ridge gourd takes less time in fruiting as compared with smooth gourd. Following varieties are commonly grown.

Kalyanpur Dharidar: It is recommended from Vegetable Research Station, Kalyanpur, Kanpur. It is an early variety with light green fruits.

Punjab Sadabahar. It is recommended from P.A.U., Ludhiana. Fruits are dark green in colour, 3-5 cm long, smooth and soft.

Arka Sumeet: It is released from I.F.R.I., Bangalore. It is the cross of early I.I.H.R. 54 and I.I.H.R. 24 (long fruits variety). Fruits are ready for first plucking after 52 days of sowing. Weight of fruit on an average is 380 g and every vine bears about 13-15 fruits. Fruits are of light green colour, cylindrical and have less seeds. It is recommended for Karnataka.

Pusa Chikni (smooth): It is an early variety and starts fruiting in 50 to 55 days after sowing. Fruits are smooth and green and about 15 to 20 fruits per plant can be obtained.

Pusa Nasdar (Ridge gourd): It is a mid-early variety and starts fruiting after 60 days of sowing. Its fruits are ridged and light green in colour.

Satputia: It is a commonly grown variety in eastern U.P. and Bihar. Five to seven fruits per cluster are obtained. Its fruits are riged and have light green colour.

SEED AND SOWING

Sowing time

In the plains, sowing is done in February-March for summer and June-July for rainy season crop. In Mysore, the crop is sown from February to October. Sometimes, for early production in summer, the sowing is done in the month of October and November between the furrows of potato crop, but the crop should be protected against frost. On the hills the crop is sown from March to June.

Seed rate

The seed rate varies from season to season and also depends on percentage of seed germination. It is normally 4 to 5 kg per hectare for summer crop and 3 to 4 kg per hectare for rainy season crop.

Method of sowing

In rainy season, 15 cm raised pits are prepared at 2.0 x 1.0 metre distance and 4 to 5 seeds are sown in each pit. Later on 2 to 3 plants are allowed to grow. In summer season (February-March sowing) the furrows are made at 2 metre distance and pits are prepared by the side of furrows at one metre distance. Five to six seeds are sown in each pit and 3 to 4 plants are allowed to grow. During summer the furrows are used for irrigation and area between two furrows is used for spreading the vines. This way, the water requirement during summer can be reduced. During winter season, the seed sowing can also be done in polyethylene bags and these can be kept in hot place for proper germination. Later on in February-March, transplanting can be done in permanent field along with the ball of soil.

MANURES AND FERTILISERS

As already indicated, 250 to 300 quintals of farmyard manure should be added during field preparation. In addition to this, 60 kg nitrogen, 80 kg phosphorus and 60 kg potash per hectare should be applied in the form of chemical fertilisers. Half dose of nitrogen and full dose of phosphorus and potash should be applied at the time of last harrowing and remaining half dose of nitrogen should be given in two split doses, first 20 days after sowing and second at the time of flowering.

IRRIGATION AND DRAINAGE

Amount of water and its frequency depend upon the season of crop and soil type. During summer season the crop should be irrigated every third or fourth day in loam soil while in heavy soil the irrigation should be given at weekly intervals. During rainy season, normally the crop does not require irrigation because of sufficient rains. Excess water during rainy season promotes spreading of foliage diseases, hence, excess water should be drained out effectively from the field.

WEED CONTROL

The crop should be free from the weeds all the time during the growth period. When the vines are spreading the crop does not require weeding and hoeing. During summer season the crop requires less weeding as compared to rainy season crop. During early stage (before spreading the vines) the weeds can be controlled by spraying 0.15 per cent solution of Gramaxone between the furrows. Hand weeding is best for weed control.

STAKING

For better yield and quality of fruits, the crop should be staked during rainy season Bamboos or wooden poles are fixed at proper distance along the row and ropes are tied on them. The vines are spread on the ropes. Some other kind of staking can also be used.

DISEASES AND THEIR CONTROL

Diseases and their control is same as for bottle gourd mentioned earlier.

INSECT PESTS AND THEIR CONTROL

Similar to bottle gourd.

HARVESTING

The fruits should be harvested when they are still tender and half to one-third grown. The mature fruits are useless for cooking and also get less price in the market. The fruits should be removed carefully from the vine without uprooting or injuring them.

YIELD

The yield varies from variety to variety and from season to season. The spongl gourd gives more yield as compared to ridge gourd. In rainy season crop, more yield is obtained as compared to summer season. Normally, fruit yield of 50 to 75 quintal in summer season and 75 to 100 quintal in rainy season crop is obtained from one hectare.

PREPARATION FOR MARKET

Hard, diseased and damaged fruits should be removed to get better price in the market. Selected fruits should be packed in baskets and sent to market.

STORAGE

The fruits can be kept under shade for one to two days while these can be stored at 5°C to 8°C in cold storage for 15 to 20 days.

SEED PRODUCTION

It is a cross pollinated crop and requires 400 and 800 metres isolation distance for certified and foundation seed production, respectively. Off type plants should be removed, first before flowering, second at the time of flowering and finally at the time of fruiting. Heavy roguing should be done before and at the time of flowering. Control measures against insect pests and diseases should be adopted. When the colour of fruits turn brown, they should be harvested and kept in sunlight for about a week for complete drying. Seeds can be extracted very easily only by removing the tip of the fruits. About 3 to 5 quintals of seed is obtained from one hectare.

POINTED GOURD

Botanical name - *Trichosanthus dioica* Roxb.

Family - Cucurbitaceae

Synonymous - Patol, Adavi patola, Peyupadal, Parmal, Parwal, Kabi padavala, Kadapaddoola, Patola, Wild snake gourd, Trichosanthes contourne, Schlangen fruchtigahaar blume.

IMPORTANCE AND UTILITY

It is cultivated mainly in the eastern part of India particularly in Bengal, Assam, Bihar and Uttar Pradesh. Its unripe fruits are used for culinary vegetable in our country. It is most useful for the convalescent. Leaves and tender stems of its vine are also used for soup preparation. Prepared vegetable is very digestible, diuretic, laxative and very good source of carbohydrates, Vitamin A and C. It is also used for sweet dish. It is good for heart and brain disorders. The plant is a semi-perennial creeper, dioecious. Leaf lamina is cordata ovale, oblong with basal lobes narrow round at base. Its fruits are "pepo", small, round or thick long. Fruits contain 92.3 per cent water, 2.0 per cent protein, 0.3 per cent fat, 0.5 per cent mineral matter, 3.0 per cent fibre, 1.9 per cent carbohydrate, 0.03 per cent calcium, 0.04 per cent phosphorus (Aykroyd, 1941).

ORIGIN AND HISTORY

Pointed gourd is a native of India and Assam is considered to be the primary centre of its origin.

CLIMATIC REQUIREMENTS

It prefers warm and moist climate with abundant rainfall for better growth and yield. Leaves fall down when temperature goes below 7°C. Better growth takes place at 21°C to 27°C and better fruit set takes place at 21°C to 24°C.

SOIL AND ITS PREPARATION

It can be grown on a variety of soils except the very heavy ones. The best growth and yield are obtained in sandy loam soils where better irrigation and drainage facilities are available. It is very susceptible water logging and land selected for its cultivation should be higher than the surrounding land. The land should be well prepared before planting. At least three to four ploughings are given during the hot weather followed by two to three ploughing at the time of planting.

VARIETIES

No improved variety has been recommended for pointed gourd but few local varieties are cultivated in our country such as:-

Patar: It is commonly grown in eastern U.P. its fruits are small, roundish and dark green striped.

Local un-named variety: Its fruits are about 10 cm long with pointed ends and swollen in the middle and are pale green when young, changing to deep orange colour when ripe.

F.P.1: Fruits are round and dark green in colour.

F.P.3: Fruits are pointed and light green in colour.

V.R.P.101: Fruits are medium in size and light green in colour. Average yield is about 250-300 quintal per hectare.

V.R.P.102: Fruits are long, having minimum seeds and light green in colour.

V.R.P. 103: Fruits are round, dark green in colour with well developed stripes.

V.R.P. 104: Fruits are long (10-25 cm) with well developed stripes.

SOWING AND PLANTING

Method of planting

The cuttings are planted by the following two methods.

(i) Straight vine method

About 30 cm deep furrows are prepared and farmyard manure is mixed in these furrows. During rainy/cloudy days the cuttings are planted 15 cm deep in furrows at a distance of 2 metre by end to end method.

(ii) Ring method

As the name indicates, the cuttings are made into the ring form and planted in mounds at 2 metre by 2 metre distance. Irrigation just after planting in both the methods is very essential.

One year old fruiting vines are used for making cuttings and 60 cm long cuttings are prepared. It is a dioecious plant (male and female flowers are found separately) therefore, for better fruit set male and female plants should be planted. On an average 5 per cent male plants are sufficient. Female flowers possess ovary at base and thus are longer in size, whereas male ones are smaller. Flowers open during the night and are pollinated by insects. Female flowers open in 8 to 12 days and male flowers open 13 to 16 days after appearance. The stigma remains receptive from 7 hours before opening till 51 hours after opening of flowers.

MANURES AND FERTILISERS

About 200 quintals of farmyard manure per hectare may be mixed in the soil one month before planting the cuttings. Later on 50 g urea, 150 g superphosphate and 2 kg farmyard manure should be given to each plant in the beginning of March.

IRRIGATION AND DRAINAGE

During rainy season the crop does not require irrigation. But till monsoon starts, five to six times, or as the need may be, the crop should be irrigated. During rainy season drainage is very essential to avoid foliage disease infection and root rot.

WEED CONTROL

Regular hoeing and weeding are necessary for proper aeration of the roots. At least at one month interval, hoeing around the plants should be done.

DISEASES AND THEIR CONTROL

Powdery mildew

It is caused by *Erysiphe cichoracearum* and this is a common disease of pointed gourd. A white powdery coating of fungal growth appears mostly on upper side of leaf surface but is also found on the lower surface and on the stem. Severely attacked leaves become brown and shrivelled.

Control Measures

❖ Spray the crop with 0.06% solution of Karathane.

❖ Dust the crop with Sulphur dust @ 40 kg per hectare.

❖ Spray the crop with 0.5% solution of Solbar (wettable sulphur).

Downy mildew

It is caused by *Peronoplasmopora cubensis* Berk and Curt. The fungus attacks only on lower surface of leaves. Symptoms appear as yellow to brown angular spots. During severe stage it attacks the stems, petioles and tendrils.

Control Measure

❖ The crop should be sprayed with 0.25% solution of Dithane M-45.

Anthracnose

It is caused by *Colletotichum* sp. The fungus attacks the stem and fruits. Brown spots are formed on the fruits which become black later ones.

Control Measures

❖ The seed should be treated with Agrosan G.N.

❖ Spray the crop with 0.2% solution of Dithane Z-78.

INSECT PESTS AND THEIR CONTROL

Fruit fly (*Docus* sp.)

Maggots of this fly cause severe damage to the fruits. The affected fruits carry sunken spots and under severe cases the fruits shrivel or rot.

Control Measure

❖ Spray the crop with 0.2% solution of Sevin (50 W.P.).

Aphid (*Aphis* sp.)

These are small green insects which suck the sap from leaves. They multipley very fast. Affected leaves turn yellow and the plant losees its vigour.

Control Measure

❖   Spray the crop with 0.1% solution of Malathion of Rogor or Metasystox.

HARVESTING

Fruits reaching full size but slightly green are picked up from the vines. Containers having water are used for keeping the fruits. Fruits are available from April to September.

YIELD

The fruit yield varies from 100 to 150 quintal per hectare with an average yield of about 125 quintals.

PREPARATION FOR MARKET

Harvested fruits are washed in running tap water and kept in shade for drying. For nearby markets, they are packed in baskets and bags and for distant markets in crates.

STORAGE

At normal temperature, the fruits can be kept for 96 hours provided with light sprinkling of water. At 7°C with 80% humidity, the fruits can be kept for 10-12 days.

SEED PRODUCTION

The best method of its multiplication is by stem cutting, hence seed production is not a problem. Healthy and diseasefree desirable plant material is selected and cuttings are prepared.

ASH GOURD (WAX GOURD)

Botanical name	-	*Benincasa hispida* Thumb. Cogn.
Family	-	Cucurbitaceae
Synonymous	-	Petha, Kumhra, Panikumhra, Kalyana, Pusineekai, Elavan.

IMPORTANCE AND UTILITY

It is generally grown on a small scale all over North India for its fleshy fruits. Its immature fruits are used as vegetables and for making "rayata" while the ripe fruits are preparinig used for sweetmeat known as "petha". Sometimes petha mash cakes (Beri of warian) are prepared in villages and used during off season. It is a good source of Vitamin A, B and C. Its seeds are used for oil extraction and eaten after frying. According to Aykroyd (1941) its fruit has 96 per cent water, 0.1 per cent protein, 3.2 per cent carbohydrate, 0.3 per cent mineral matter and Vitamin B_1 21 A.U.

ORIGIN AND HISTORY

Its original home is believed to be Java and Japan, where still it is found in wild form. It is cultivated almost in all tropical and sub-tropical countries and in many parts of India. It is used in confectionary and as vegetable.

CLIMATIC REQUIREMENTS

It prefers a warm climate and does well in plains and hills of low elevation. Better growth and fruit set takes place at 21°C to 27°C. Too much humidity spoils the fruit quality and fruits become watery. Seeds germinate within seven days after sowing at 15.5°C to 18°C.

SOIL AND ITS PREPARATION

Like other cucurbits, it thrives well in a wide variety of soils ranging from sandy to moderately heavy soils provided irrigation and drainage facilities are available. Sandy loam soil gives a heavy and early yield. It is very susceptible to waterlogging thus land selected for its cultivation should be higher than the surrounding land. The land should be prepared well before sowing. At least four to six harrowings are given and stone pieces and residues of the previous crop are removed. Prior to planting, pits are prepared and 15 kg farmyard manure per pit is mixed in the soil.

VARIETIES

Generally, round and oblong varieties described on the basis of shape are grown commercially. The normal weight varies from 4 to 10 kg per fruit and generally all the types are usually smaller than that of pumpkin. Following improved varieties have been recommended by Prem Nath (1976).

Co 1: Medium early variety, produces attractive and globular fruits ranging from 5 to 6 kg with lesser seeds and more flesh. It yields 204 quintal per hectare and crop duration is 140 days.

Co-2: It is recommended from Coimbatore. It is an early variety and ready to harvest 120 days after sowing. The fruits are round with an average weight of 2-3 kg.

S-1: It is recommended for Punjab. Fruits are medium in size.

Mudliar: Fruits are big in size, and light green in colour. It is recommended for Tamil Nadu.

SEED AND SOWING

An early crop can be produced by sowing the seeds from February to March, provided better irrigation facilities are available. The main crop is sown from the beginning of June to the end of July.

Seed rate

About 6 to 10 kg seed is sufficient for sowing one hectare land. Seven hundred seeds are present in 100 g weight.

Method of sowing

It is sown in heavily manured small but raised pits which are about 30 cm in diameter. For February and March sowing, the pits are prepared at 1.5 metre x 1 metre distance while in June-July sowing pits are prepared at 1.5 metre x 1.5 metre distance. Fifteen to twenty days before sowing 15 kg farmyard manure per pit is mixed. Four to five seeds are sown in one pit at 2.5 to 3 cm depth.

MANURES AND FERTILISERS

Ash gourd responds to manures and fertilisers. The amount required depends upon the soil type, climate and variety. About 150 to 175 quintals of farmyard manure per hectare is applied 15 to 20 days before sowing and 40 kg phosphorus and 25 kg potash per hectare is given as basal dose. Forty days after sowing 25 kg nitrogen per hectare may be given as top dressing for better growth and yield.

IRRIGATION AND DRAINAGE

Ash gourd does not require much irrigation, except in summer crop which may be irrigated immediately after germination and later on the crop should be irrigated at 8 to 10 days' interval. During rainy season excess water should be drained out by providing suitable drainage facilities. Due to excess water the crop starts wilting.

WEED CONTROL

It is useful to keep the field free from weeds especially in early stages. Frequent hoeing and weeding promote better growth and heavy fruiting. When vines are fully grown up only large weeds may be pulled out.

DISEASES AND THEIR CONTROL

Powdery mildew

It is caused by *Erysiphe cichoracearum* and it is common during rainy season crop. A white powdery coating of fungal growth appears on the leaf surface which is mostly confined to the upper surface but sometimes it is also found on the lower surface and stem. During heavy infection the leaves become brown and shrivelled.

Control measures

❖ Spray the crop with 0.06% solution of Karathane.

❖ Dusting the crop with Sulphur dust at the rate of 40 kg per hectare is beneficial.

❖ Spray the crop with wettable sulphur such as Sulfex or Elosal at the rate of 3 kg per hectare in 1000 litres of water.

Downy mildew

It is caused by *Peronoplasmopora cubensis* Berk and Curt. Generally fungus attacks only on lower surface of leaves and yellow to brown angular spots appear. During heavy infection it attacks the stems, petioles and tendrils.

Control measure

❖ The crop should be sprayed with 0.25% solution of Dithane M-45 at 15 days' interval.

INSECT PESTS AND THEIR CONTROL

Fruit fly (*Docus* sp.)

Sometimes during early stage the maggots of this fly cause severe damage to the fruits. The affected fruits carry sunken spots and under severe cases the fruits shrivel and rot.

Control measure

❖ Spray the crop with 0.2 per cent solution of Sevin (50 W.P.) at 15 days' interval.

Aphids (*Aphis* sp.)

These are small green insects which suck the sap from leaves. They multiply very fast. Affected leaves turn yellow, curl and plants lose vigour.

Control Measure

❖ Spray the crop with 0.1 per cent solution of Malathion, Rogor or Metasystox.

HARVESTING

Immature green fruits are preferred for cooking and fully grown ones are picked from the vines. However, fruits should be green at the time of picking. For confectionary, mature ripe light green fruits are preferred.

YIELD

The yield of the fruit varies from 200 to 400 quintal per hectare with an average of about 250 quintals.

PREPARATION FOR MARKET

The fruits of summer crop become ready in the month of June and due to starting of rains quick disposal is very essential. Hence, fruits are washed, dried, packed in gunny bags and sent to the market. The fruits of rainy season crop are ready for harvesting in the month of September-October and can be kept at room temperature during winter. These can be kept well for a long period if the stem ends are covered with wax or some such material.

STORAGE

Fully ripe fruits can be stored at room temperature for 4 to 6 months if humidity is not more than 30 to 35 per cent. The fruits affected by insects may start rotting during storage.

SEED PRODUCTION

It is a cross pollinated crop. Nandpuri and Singh (1967) reported that anthesis takes place between 5.45 A.M., and 7.15 A.M., dehiscence starts from 3.15 A.M. and stigma remains receptive 12 hours before and 36 hours after anthesis. The staminate and pistillate flowers open at the same time. About 800 and 400 metres isolation distance is required for foundation and certified seed production respectively. Roguing should be continued till harvesting and at least three roguings should be done, first before flowering, second at the time of flowering and third at the time of harvesting. Ripened fruits are harvested and seeds are taken out by cutting the fruits. Seeds are washed, dried and stored at cool and dry place.

ROUND GOURD

Botanical Name	-	*Citrullus vulgaris* var. *Fistulosus*
Family	-	Cucurbitaceae
Synonymous	-	Tinda, Dilpasand, Round gourd, Round melon, Tindu, Tendsi, Tindas, Tendu, Dhemsa, Indian squash, Squash melon.

IMPORTANCE AND UTILITY

It is one of the most popular and commonly grown summer vegetable crop of Punjab, Uttar Pradesh, Maharashtra and Rajasthan. It is one of the main crops grown in Aligarh and Bulandshahr districts of Uttar Pradesh. Immature fruits are used for cooking. When the seeds are mature, they are usually taken out before the fruit is cooked, but it does not make a delicious dish. Fruits are also cooked together with pulses like lentil, moong and gram. Its fruits are also used for pickles. Its edible portion contains 92.3 per cent water, 1.7 per cent protein, 0.1 per cent fat, 0.6 per cent mineral matters, 5.3 per cent carbohydrates and sufficient quantities of Vitamin A.

ORIGIN AND HISTORY

It is believed to have originated in North India (Purewal, 1957) and spread to all warm countries of the world.

BOTANY

It is an annual creeping herb having green or light green hairy leaves. The fruits are round having hairs or sometimes smooth with blackish seeds. Anthesis takes place from 6 A.M. to 8.30 A.M. The dehiscence starts one hour before anthesis and continues up to 7.30 A.M. At high temperature, stigmatic fluid starts drying and stigma becomes non-receptive by 2.0 P.M. Maximum fruit set is recorded during first hour after anthesis.

CLIMATIC REQUIREMENTS

Like water-melon it is a warm season crop and cannot be grown in areas where temperature is too low. Seeds germinate successfully at 25°C. Better growth and fruit set takes place at 30°C to 35°C.

SOIL AND ITS PREPARATION

It can be grown on a variety of soils but better growth and yield can be obtained in loam or silt loam soils. The soil should be deep, well drained, rich in organic matter, free from hard layer and exposed to sun. The best soil pH for this crop is 6 to 6.5. The soil should be prepared well by repeated harrowings etc. At the time of soil preparation 200 to 250 quintal per hectare of farmyard manure may be added in the field.

VARIETIES

Very less attention has been given towards this crop by the vegetable breeders. Though there are large number of local varieties grown in our country but improved varieties are only few. Following are the improved varieties of round gourd grown in India.

Whitish Green: The fruits are medium in size, pale or light green in colour and are ready for harvest after 50 to 55 days of sowing. The leaves are light green in colour.

Dark Green: The fruits are medium in size, dark green or slightly blackish in colour, and are ready for first harvest after 55 to 60 days of sowing. The leaves are dark green in colour.

Arka Tinda: This variety has been developed at I.I.H.R., Bangalore. It is an early summer season variety with large tender fruits having light green colour. It attains a marketable size in five days from the date of pollination.

Tinda-S-48: It produces medium sized fruits, weighing on an average 50 g each. The fruit colour is light green and they are ready for first harvest after 65 to 70 days of sowing.

SEED AND SOWING

Time of sowing

The seeds are sown in February-March for summer crop and in June-July for rainy season crop in the plains of the country while sowing is done from March to July on hills. Sometimes the crop is grown as mixed crop in maize and cotton.

Seed rate

Four to five kg seeds having 80 to 90 per cent germination are sufficient for sowing one hectare field.

Method of sowing

The seeds can be sown in channels, beds or in mounds. During summer season channels are prepared at one metre distance with 30 cm or 45 cm width and the seeds are sown on both the sides at one metre distance. At one place 6 to 8 seeds should be sown and finally 3 to 4 plants should be maintained at one place. During rainy season, sowing should be done in beds. Beds are also prepared with drainage facilities and mounds are prepared at 1 x 1 metre distance. In each mounds 6 to 8 seeds are sown. Later on 3 to 4 plants per mounds are maintained.

MANURES AND FERTILISERS

As already indicated, 200 to 250 quintal per hectare farmyard manure should be mixed in the field during its final preparation. In addition to that, 45 kg nitrogen, 40 kg phosphorus and 25 kg potash per hectare should be applied at the time of last harrowing.

IRRIGATION AND DRAINAGE

Interval of irrigation and quantity of water to be applied depend upon the season and soil type. Crop grown in summer will require irrigation each week while crop grown in rainy season will depend upon rains. During the period of heavy rains the excess water should be drained out.

WEED CONTROL

Crop should be free from weeds in the early stage of its growth and fruiting period. During rainy season at least 3 to 4 weedings will be required while 2 to 3 weedings will be enough in summer.

DISEASES AND THEIR CONTROL

Powdery mildew

It is one of the most serious disease of round gourd, observed in humid and hot period. A white powdery coating of fungal growth appears on the leaf surface, mostly on upper surface, but also on the lower surface and stem. The affected plants do not produce normal fruits and leaves turn yellow and drop down.

Control Measures

❖   Sulphur dust can be used for dusting the crop @ 15 to 20 kg per hectare.

❖   Spray 0.06% solution of Karathane at 15 days' interval during growth period.

Downy mildew

It is common in rainy season crop and yelloowish brown spots appear on the lower surface. In severe infections, yield as well as quality both go down.

Control Measure

❖   Crop should be sprayed with 0.2% solution of Dithane M-45 at 15 days' interval.

INSECT PESTS AND THEIR CONTROL

Red Pumpkin beetle

It is one of the serious beetle damaging the crop during early stage. Damage is done by adults and larvae both. Sometimes fruits and flowers are also damaged by them.

Control Measure

❖   Spray 0.2% solution of Sevin or use Sevin 10 per cent dust for dusting the crop during early stage of growth.

Epilachna beetle

Young germinated seedlings are eaten by the beetle just after their germination. If control measures are not adopted at right time the entire crop may be damaged.

Control Measure

Same as for Red Pumpkin beetle.

Aphids

During March and July the population of aphids is at peak. They suck the juice from leaves and stem and reduce the photosynthetic activities.

Control Measure

❖ Spray 0.15% solution of Metasystox on the crop during attack period of the insect.

Fruit fly

It is not very common insect of round gourd but sometimes damage from it is observed. The maggots of the fly bore into fruits and sometimes flowers are also damaged by them.

Control Measure

❖ Spray 0.2% solution of Sevin on the crop during flowering stage.

HARVESTING

The first fruit is borne on the vine very early as the vine starts spreading. This fruit should be picked immediately otherwise it may delay bearing. Later on actual fruiting will start. Tender fruits having soft seeds should be harvested at right time. Delay in harvest even for one day may reduce its quality. The fruits can be removed from the vine by a slight pressure of the thumb on the peduncle.

YIELD

Yield depends upon the variety, season, type of soil and management practices followed for the cultivation of crop. Normally 80 to 100 quintals of fruits from summer crop and 100 to 120 quintals of fruits from rainy season crop can be obtained from one hectare.

PREPARATION FOR MARKET

As soon as the fruits are harvested, they should be kept under shade in a cool place. Damaged, diseased and under/over sized fruits should be removed.

Desired fruits are packed in baskets and taken to the market in fresh stage.

STORAGE

The fruits can be kept under shade for two to three days by providing with frequent spraying of water on the basket. These can be kept for 10-15 days in cold storage at 4°C to 6°C.

SEED PRODUCTION

It is a cross pollinated crop and requires 400 and 800 metres isolation distance for certified and foundation seed production, respectively. Minimum of three roguings should be done, first before flowering, second at the time of flowering and third at the time of fruit maturity. Completely ripe fruits, after the seed colour becomes black, can be harvested and seeds can be extracted by breaking the outer hard rind. The seed crop should be free from insect pests and diseases.

SPINACH BEET

Botanical Name	-	*Beta vulgaris*
Family	-	Chenopodiaceae
Synonymous	-	Palang sag, Palang, Meetha palang, Teegabatchali, Dumpabucchale, Vusavyeley, Pasalai, Spinak soppu, Palak, Spinach, Keerai.

IMPORTANCE AND UTILITY

It is commonly grown in all parts of the country for its tender leaves. It can be grown in both the seasons, hot as well as cold. It is allied to beet root and has long leaves with entire margins. Leaves and tender stem are used for cooking and pakora making. It is mildly laxative, diuretic and stringent in fevers, inflamations of lungs and bowls and as lithontriptic in urinary calculi. It is a rich source of Vitamin 'A', calcium and iron, therefore, it is recommended for pregnant ladies. It's 100 g edible leaves contain 92.7 g water, 2.3 protein, 0.7 g fat, 10.9 mg iron, 80 mg Vitamin 'C', 73 mg calcium and 25000 I.U. Vitamin 'A'.

ORIGIN AND HISTORY

It is probably the native of Indo-Chinese region and it was known in China as early as 647 A.D.

BOTANY

The floral development occurs in six stages and takes 35 days from bud initiation to opening. Anthesis takes place between 8 A.M. to 5 P.M. with the peak at 11 A.M. to 1 P.M. In most of cases flowers open during mid day. In individual flower, the anthesis is completed within two hours and hastened by temperature and low humidity. Anther dehiscence occurs between 8.30 A.M. to 6.30 P.M. with the peak dehiscence during 12.30 P.M. to 2.30 P.M. depending upon the temperature and low humidity. Stigma receptiveness begings 8 hours before anthesis and reaches a maximum just after anthesis and continues for further 10 hours.

CLIMATIC REQUIREMENTS

Palak (Spinach beet) is normally grown during moderate winter season and up to some extent it can tolerate frost. It is very susceptible to waterlogging and poor drainage. Under warmer conditions and long days it starts bolting. The best temperature for its growth and development varies from 15°C to 22°C.

SOIL AND ITS PREPARATION

Though palak can be grown in any type of soil which is free from poor drainage, but sandy and alluvial soils have been found to be better for its better growth and quality. Acidic soils are not at all suitable for its cultivation. The soil should be rich in organic matter with adequate irrigation and drainage facilities. The best soil pH for its optimum growth is between 6 to 7.5. The soil should be prepared well by repeated ploughings and harrowings. The crop residue and stone pieces should also be removed during field preparation. About 100 to 150 quintals per hectare of farmyard manure should be mixed in the soil at the time of last harvesting.

VARIETIES

All Green: This variety was released from I.A.R.I., New Delhi in 1960. It produces uniform green, tender leaves and yields about 125-135 quintals green leaves per hectare. In winter, it gives 6 to 7 cuttings at 15 to 18 days interval. First cutting can be done 50 to 55 days after sowing.

Jobner Green: It has been recommended from Udaipur in 1967. It does well in Jobner area. The leaves are thick, large-sized, tender, soft and dark green in colour. It is a high yielding variety and first cutting can be done after 50 to 55 days of sowing. In winter, 6 to 8 cuttings are done. The average yield varies from 100 to 125 quintal per hectare.

Pusa Jyoti: It is a new selection made at I.A.R.I., New Delhi. The leaves are succulent, thick, long, soft with dark green colour. This variety contains more potash, calcium, sodium, iron and ascorbic acid than All Green. The first cutting can be done after 45 to 50 days of sowing. In winter it gives 6 to 8 cuttings at 12 to 15 days' interval. The average yield varies from 100 to 110 quintal per hectare.

Pusa Harit: It is also recommended from I.A.R.I., New Delhi and is a cross between local variety and Chukandar. It is a late bolting variety and gives normally 8 to 10 cuttings in the season. The leaves are upright, uniformly thick, big in size and dark green in colour. The first cutting can be done 45 to 50 days after sowing. In comparison to other varieties it does well in alkaline soils. The average yield varies from 150 to 200 quintal per hectare.

Banerjee Giant: It is very popular in West Bengal. It is cross between Local and beet root. Leaves are bigm, thick and soft.

Palak 51-16: It is developed from Maharashtra. Leaves are green in colour and medium in size.

S 23: It is a selection from H.A.U., Hisar. The leaves are broad, dark green, soft and big in size. Normally 7 to 8 cuttings can be obtained. The first cutting can be done 45 to 50 days after sowing. The average yield varies from 120 to 130 quintal per hectare.

SEED AND SOWING

Seed rate

Seed rate depends upon the germination percentage and method of sowing. In case germination percentage is poor, higher seed rate should be used. Similarly, if the sowing is done by seed drill the seed rate shall be more than in hand sowing. Normally 30 to 45 kg seed is sufficient for sowing one hectare area.

Time of sowing

In the plains, sowing can be done from August to November and sometimes in February and March also (only in kitchen gardens) while on hills sowing can be done from March to May but in valleys from September to October.

Method of sowing

The method of sowing depends upon the area to be sown. If the area is more then it should be sown by seed drill in rows made at 20 to 30 cm distance. If the area is small the sowing can be done by hand hoes in lines made at 15 to 20 cm distance. The furrows are opened at the required distance and sowing is done in the furrows. Finally, the furrows are covered. There should be sufficient moisture in the soil at the time of sowing.

MANURES AND FERTILISERS

From better yield and quality view point, sufficient farmyard manure and fertilisers should be used in this crop. In addition to farmyard manure, 100-150 kg nitrogen, 80 kg phosphorus and 100 kg potash per hectare should be applied in the form of chemical fertilisers. Half dose of nitrogen and full dose of phosphorus and potash should be applied at the time of sowing and remaining half dose of nitrogen should be divided into six equal doses and each dose should be given by top dressing just after the each cutting. After top dressing light irrigation should be given.

IRRIGATION AND DRAINAGE

Normally, this crop requires more number of irrigations than other vegetable crops grown in winter season. The interval and amount of water depend upon the type of soil. In case of sandy and sandy loam soils, the interval should be less while in heavy soils the interval should be more. Normally, the crop should be irrigated at 12 to 15 days' interval. Excess water is very harmful to the leaves since it helps in increasing the incidence of fungal diseases and in reducing the leaf quality. Therefore, proper drainage facilities should be provided.

WEED CONTROL

For proper growth and development of the leaves the crop should remain free from weeds during early stage of growth. If the weeding is not done at right stage the grasses will be cut down alongwith spinach leaves which will reduce the quality. Normally, first weeding should be done 25 to 30 days, second at 40 to 45 days and third 60 to 65 days after sowing. Later on it does not require any weeding.

DISEASES AND THEIR CONTROL

Damping off

It is caused by *Pythium ultimum* and sometimes the crop suffers badly due to attack of this disease. At the time of girmination the small growing plants start falling down from the base of the soil.

Control Measures

❖ Seed should be treated with Thiram at the rate of 0.25%.

❖ The crop should not be irrigated just after sowing.

❖ Thick sowing should be avoided.

Downy mildew

It is caused by *Peronospora* sp. and sometimes causes heavy damage to the crop. The symptoms occur on the outer leaves as pale yellow spots of irregular shape which increase in size in the wet weather. Petioles may also be affected and become yellowish. The affected leaves do not get better price in the market.

Control Measures

❖ The affected plants should be removed and burnt.

❖ The crop should be sprayed with 0.2% solution of Dithane M-45 or Dithane Z-78 or Blitox at 10 to 15 days' interval. Usually two sprayings are sufficient.

Leaf spot

It is caused by *Cercospora beticola*. Round brown spots appear on the leaves and in later stage they become purple in colour. The affected leaves cannot be sold in the market.

Control Measures

❖ The seed should be treated with Thiram at the rate of 0.25%.

❖ The affected leaves should be collected and burnt.

❖ The crop should be sprayed with 0.2% solution of Dithane M-45 or Dithane Z-78 or Blitox.

INSECT PESTS AND THEIR CONTROL

Grasshopper

Sometimes during September and October the small grasshoppers eat the green leaves and damage the crop but in late sown crop they do not damage the crop.

Control Measures

❖   The crop should be sprayed with 0.2% solution of Nuvan in early stage.

Bihar hairy caterpillar

It is a serious pest. A single female may lay 1000-1500 eggs on the lower surface of the leaves. These eggs hatch in three to five days. Newly-emerged caterpillars are gregarious feeders on the leaf epidermis, skeletonising entire leaves. Sometimes the attack is so heavy that the entire crop is eaten up by them in a single night.

Control Measure

❖   The crop should be sprayed with 0.2% solution of Nuvan in early stage.

HARVESTING

Normally, the first cutting is done 40 to 60 days after sowing and later on cuttings are made at 15 to 20 days interval depending upon the variety. The average number of cuttings vary from 5 to 10.

YIELD

The yield depends upon the variety and the cultural practices followed for its cultivation. Normally, the yield varies from 100 to 150 quintal per hectare.

PREPARTION FOR MARKET

Palak leaves should be sent to market immediately after cutting. At the time of cuttings, weeds and diseased leaves should be removed. Small bundles weighing about 250 to 300 g should be made at the time of cutting and packed in baskets or gunny bags before sending them to market. To maintain freshness, water should be sprinkled on the baskets or gunny bags.

STORAGE

Normally it cannot be stored at room temperature for long time but it can be kept in shade for one day provided frequent sprinkling of water is done. It can also be kept for three to four days at 6°C to 10°C with 80 to 85 per cent relative humidity.

SEED PRODUCTION

It is a highly cross pollinated crop and requires 1000 and 1600 metres isolation distance for certified and foundation seeds, respectively. Palak crop takes about 180 to 200 days for its seed production. Almost same cultural practices are followed for seed crop as are followed for normal crop. After second cutting, the crop is left for seed production. Weeding, hoeing, top dressing and irrigations etc. should be given as per crop requirement. Sufficient crop protection measures have to be followed against insect pest and diseases. The seed crop should be inspected thrice during its entire life cycle. First, before flowering, and on the basis of external characters, off type plants have to be taken out. Secondly, at the time of flowering and on the basis of flower characters, off types have to be removed. The final inspection is done at the time of seed set and on the basis of seed colour, the off types have to be removed. The crop starts maturing about 180 days after sowing when stem becomes yellowish. It can then be harvested and left for complete drying. Later on the crop can be threshed for seed extraction.

FENU GREEK

Botanical name	-	*Trigonella foenum-graecum*
Family	-	Leguminosae
Synonymous	-	Methi, Menti, Mentulu, Vendayam, Venthayam, Menthya, Hulabaha, Shamlita, Fenu Greek, Sag, Menthai, Uluva, Vendia, Keerai.

IMPORTANCE AND UTILITY

There are two types of methi, one is Fenu Greek (*Trigonella foenum-graecum*) and the other Champa or Kasuri methi (*Trigonella corniculata*). First one is cultivated almost in all parts of the country while Kasuri gives better performance in cooler parts. Its green leaves are used as vegetable while its seeds are used as spice and as pulse. According to Aykroyd (1943) methi contains 81.8 per cent moisture, 4.9 per cent protein, 0.9 per cent fat, 1.6 per cent mineral matter, 1.0 per cent fibre, 9.8 per cent carbohydrate, 0.47 per cent calcium, 0.05 per cent phosphorus, Vitamin A 3900 I.U. and Vitamin C 14 mg per 100 g fresh leaves. Its testa cells contain tannin and its seeds contain a foetid, 6 per cent bitter fatty oil, 28 per cent resin and mucilage, 22 per cent albumin, 7 per cent ash and 25 per cent phosphoric acid. Its chemical composition is almost similar to Cod liver oil and like that the Fenu Greek alkaloids stimulate appetite by their action on the nervours system or produce a diuretic or ureopoietic effect. Its leaves are cooling and mild aperient. The powder of its seeds if applied on head promotes growth of hair and prevents their falling off.

ORIGIN AND HISTORY

It originated from China and has be cultivated in India from seventeenth century. Besides India, it is cultivated in Burma, Pakistan, Turkey, Palestine, Russia, Balkan States and in North Africa, principally in Morocco.

CLIMATIC REQUIREMENTS

The seeds of Fenu Greek do not germinate properly when temperature is above 27°C and below 12.5°C. The plants grow better at 15°C to 18°C. Heavy rains and humid climate reduce its quality and increase fungal infection on the leaves and stem. At very high temperature, the plants are affected by fusarium wilt. During early stage of growth the plants dry up due to attack of stem fly.

SOIL AND ITS PREPARATION

It can be grown on a variety of soils ranging from heavy to sandy but loamy soils are best suited for its cultivation. A satisfactory growth and yield can also be obtained in alluvial and heavy clayey soils if they are prepared well and are provided with proper drainage facilities. For better and early growth, the field should be prepared well in order to have fine seed bed. The field should be well levelled and beds should be made according to source of irrigation. At the time of field preparation, 200 to 300 quintals of farmyard manure should be incorporated and mixed well in the soil. Residues of previous crop and stone pieces etc. should also be removed from the field at the same time.

VARIETIES

Pusa Early Bunching: It is a quick growing variety producing upright shoots in bunches and having white flowers, yellow and bold seeds. Its pods are 6 to 8 cm long, green in colour having 10 to 12 seeds per pod. First cutting can be made after 55 to 60 days of sowing. It is a heavy yielder.

Pua Kasuri: It is a slow growing variety and remains in a rosette condition during most of its vegetative growth period. Its seeds are small and dark brown in colour, and its flowers are yellow. Its pods are smaller in size than the former variety. It is a heavy yielder. Leaves of this variety have special fragrance. It becomes ready for first harvest after 60 to 65 days of sowing.

Prabha: It is resistant to insects. Leaves are soft, sweet with dark green colour.

Co. 1: It is recommended from Tamil Nadu Agricultural, University, Coimbatore. It is lights yielding variety having leaves that are soft, sweet and dark green in colour.

Lam Selection n-1: Plents are bushy in nature with medium height, It is a high yielding variety with better leaf quality.

SEED AND SOWING

Pusa Early Bunching can be sown for leaves from middle of September to January end, while for seed it is sown from middle of September to middle of November. Pusa Kasuri can be sown for leaves and seed from middle of September to middle of November. Both the varieties are sown in hills in autumn or early spring in the first week of March. The seed rate per hectare for Pusa Early Bunching is 30 to 35 kg while for Pusa Kasuri 20 to 25 kg per hectare.

On small scale the crop can be sown by hand hoes in linen 20 to 30 cm apart. On largescale, the crop can be sown by seed drill in lines 30 cm apart. The crop can also be sown by broadcasting in beds and then the surface is raked to cover the seeds with soil. This method is not good because later on it creates problem during weeding and hoeing etc.

MANURES AND FERTILISERS

The soil should be fertile enough for better growth and yield. About 200 to 300 quintals of farmyard manure should be added to the field during field preparation. According to Singh and Joshi (1960), an ample supply of nitrogen helps in the production of more succulent leafy matter in all the leafy vegetables. Fifty kg nitrogen, 80 kg phosphorus and 80 kg potash per hectare should be added at the time of last harrowing, while 15 kg nitrogen per hectare should be given after each cutting in the form of top dressing.

IRRIGATION AND DRAINAGE

Its germination is completed within a week in the early sowings, while in late sowing, due to low temperature, it takes a few days more. Frequent and light irrigations are necessary for obtaining a quick growth and better yield. Crop should be irrigated at 7 to 10 days' interval. Heavy irrigation should be avoided. Excess water from the field should be drained out otherwise it will reduce the plant growth and quality of leaves.

WEED CONTROL

Fenu Greek plants give ample time for weed growth up to the time of first cutting. If crop is sown in lines, weeding and hoeing become easier. First weeding should be done 15-20 days after sowing. Later on Fenu Greek plants suppress occasional weeds which come out. Weeds like *Chenopodium alba* (bathua), *Fumaria parviflora* (gajri), *Circium arvense* (kateli), *Melilotus alba* (senji) and *Lathyrus* spp.(chatri matri) etc. should be pulled out when the first cutting is done. Weedicide like Basalin @ 0.75 kg ai in 800-1000 litres of water as pre-planting spray may be used as an effective herbicide. It should be well incorporated in the soil before sowing.

DISEASES AND THEIR CONTROL

Leaf spot

It is caused by *Cercospora traversinia*. Due to attack of this disease, in the beginning, spots on leaf are light brown in colour and later on these turn black. This disease can be controlled easily by spraying the crop with 0.2% solution of Dithane M-45 at 15 days' interval.

Downy mildew

It is caused by *Perinospora trigonella* and produces on the lower side of leaves brown yellowish spots. It can be controlled by spraying the crop with 0.2% solution of Dithane M-45 at 15 days' interval.

INSECT PESTS AND THEIR CONTROL

Aphids

They are very small insect pests found generally in groups on the tender shoots and leaves of plants. They suck the cell sap and make them poor in growth. They can be controlled by spraying the crop with 0.1% solution of Metasystox or any other systemic insecticide.

Laphygma exigua

Its caterpillars attack the leaves and stems of almost all leafy vegetables and eat them very fast. They can be controlled by spraying the crop with 0.2% solution of Endosulfan (35 EC) at 15 days' interval.

HARVESTING

The first cutting can be taken generally 55 to 65 days after sowing whereas subsequent cuttings can be taken at intervals of 15 to 20 days. If this interval is increased leaves become hard and develop a somewhat bitter taste. If the crop is grown for seed then after two to three cuttings crop is left as such for seed.

YIELD

Green leaf yield varies from 100 to 125 quintal per hectare when seed is not taken. Alongwith yield of 5 to 8 quintals of seed, the green leaf yield is about 15 to 20 quintals.

PREPARATION FOR MARKETING

The picking of leaves is done by nipping at the ground level. Weeds and plants affected by disease and insect pests are removed from the lot. Small bundles of about 250 g in weight are prepared and sent for marketing. Minimum time should be taken from harveting to marketing.

STORAGE

Fully dried leaves of methi can be stored for one year without any damage. Kasuri Fenu Grek is available in this form, packed in small packets of different size and this way dried leaves can be used allround the year. Its seeds can be stored for two years.

SEED PRODUCTION

Seeds can be produced easily in the plaints of country without any problem. It is a self-pollinated crop and does not require much isolation distance between two varieties. The crop can be allowed to grow without taking any cuttings for the production of seed or two to three cuttings can be taken before leaving for seed. In case of first one, better seed yield and quality are obtained than the second one. From the seed crop, off types and diseased plants are identified and removed on the basis of external plant characters. Required cultural practices are followed according to the need of crop.

The seed crop matures in about 150 to 170 days after sowing. After threshing, seeds are dried completely and kept at low temperature. On an average, 8 to 10 quintal per hectare seed yield is obtained from the crop grown specially for seed.

CORIANDER

Botanical name	-	*Coriandrum sativum* L.
Family	-	Umbelliferae
Synonymous	-	Dhania, Dhaniya, Dhaniyalu, Kothamalli, Kottambri, Dhane, Kustumbri Dhanyaka, Coriander, Kusbara, Kishniz.

IMPORTANCE AND UTILITY

The leaves are used for flavouring soups and other foods. The fruits are an important ingredient of curry powder, usually contributing the greatest quantity of all the spices followed by turmeric. People use it as pickling spice in seasonings and sausages, and also in pastries, buns, cakes and other confectionary. It is also used in flavouring gin and other wines. It is used for medicinal purposes particularly as a carminative. Its fruit and the oil are used as a flavouring agent to cover the taste or grip qualities of other medicines. Its name is derived from the Greek word 'Koris', meaning bed bug, because of the upnpleasant, fetid, bug-like odour of the green unripened fruits. According to Aykroyd (1941) coriander contains 87.9 per cent moisture, 3.5 per cent protein, 0.6 per cent fat, 6.5 per cent carbohydrate, 1.7 per cent mineral matter, 0.14 per cent calcium, 0.06 per cent phosphorus and Vitamin A 10460 to 12600 I.U. per 100 g fresh leaves. Its 100 g dry seeds contain 11.2 per cent moisture, 14.1 per cent protein, 16.1 per cent fat, 21.6 per cent carbohydrates, 32.6 per cent fibre, 4.4 per cent mineral matter, 0.63 per cent calcium, 0.37 per cent phosphorus and 17.9 mg iron.

ORIGIN AND HISTORY

It probably originated from Mediterranean region. It is one of the earliest spices used by mankind. It was used in Egypt for medicina. and culinary purposes as early as 1550 B.C. and is mentioned in the Ebers Papyrus. It was known to the ancient Israelites and is referred to in the Bible. It is also mentioned in Sanskrit literature. It was one of the drugs employed by Hippocrates about 400 B.C. Besides India it is cultivated in Burma, Pakistan, Turkey, Palestine, Russia, Balkan States and in North Africa, principally in Morocco.

CLIMATIC REQUIREMENTS

It grows under a wide range of climatic conditions, but thrives best at 12°C to 24°C. It can tolerate frost to some extent. The seeds germinate at 12°C to 15.5°C. If temperature goes beyond 27°C the growth becomes poor and formation of stalk and early flowering takes place.

SOIL AND ITS PREPARATION

It grows well under a variety of soils, but thrives best on well-drained medium to heavy soils. In India, it also grows well in black cotton soils. It is grown in all states of India. Soil is prepared well by one ploughing followed by four to five harrowings and plankings. Soil should be well levelled. At the time of field preparation, grass and stone pieces should be removed. It can also thrive in high pH soils.

VARIETIES

Small seeded: Seeds are small with less fibre and is most suited for growing in temperate regions. Volatile oil content is higher than bold seeded ones. The seed colour is light green.

Bold seeded: Seeds are bold having more fibre and is most suited for growing in tropical and subtropical regions. Volatile oil is lesser than small seeded ones and seed colour is light brown.

NP (D) 92: It is a selection from local material grown around Delhi area. Seeds are small, light green in colour having less fibre.

Pant Haritma: This variety is developed at G.B. Pand University of Agriculture and Technology, Pantnagar. It is resistant for stem-gall and yields better as green leaf as well as seed.

SEED AND SOWING

In plains of India, it is sown from October till early December. For seed raising, the best sowing time is from second week of October to second week of November. On higher hills the crop is sown from March to September for leaf as well as for seed. In valleys, it is sown as in plains.

It is always propagated by seed. Before sowing, the seeds are rubbed into two mericarps. It is broadcasted or drilled in rows. Broadcasting creates some problems during cultural operations. At smallscale, the lines are made at a distance of 30 cm and seeds are sown 2 cm apart within the rows. Seed should not be sown more than 2 cm deep in the soil. On largescale sowing can be done by seed drill in furrows made at 30 cm distance. The seed rate varies from 25 to 30 kg per hectare for leaf and 20 to 25 kg per hectare for seed crop.

MANURES AND FERTILISERS

Though very little attention has been paid on its manurial and fertiliser requirements in India, but experience in European countries has shown that proper manuring significantly increases the yield. Significant results have been obtained when nitrogenous, phosphatic and potassic fertilisers are applied in the early stage of development. About 150 to 200 quintals of well rotten farmyard manure per hectare should be added during the field preparation. At the time of sowing 40 kg nitrogen, 50 kg phosphorus and 40 kg potash per hectare should be given as basal dose. Forty kg nitrogen should be top dresed when crop is about 50-55 days old or before flowering stage.

IRRIGATION AND DRAINAGE

First irrigation should be given when seeds have germinated fully. Later on, frequent and light irrigations are required for better growth and development of the plants. Crop should be irrigated at 12 to 15 days' interval during December-January while during February-April the interval should be one week. On hills, the crop does not require irrigation as it gets sufficient moisture through rains. Excess water, specially during Kharif season, should be drained out. Under poor drainage conditions, the crop suffers from leaf spot disease.

WEED CONTROL

Generally the crop itself suppresses the seasonal weeds which come out. But sometimes due to poorer germination in thin plant stand growth of weeds like *Chenopodium album* (bathua), *Cyperus rotundus* (motha) *Fumaria parviflora* (gajri), *Lathyrus* spp. etc. grow well and compete with the crop. The crop requires two to three weedings. Weedings can be done either by *Khurpi* or by hand operated implements. For largescale cultivation, Basalin 1 kg ai per hectare in 800-1000 litres of water can be used as pre-planting spray. It should be well incorporated in soil before sowing.

DISEASES AND THEIR CONTROL

Shoot gall

It is one of the serious disease caused by fungus *Protomyces macrosporus Unger.* Small tumour like swellings on all parts of infected plants, including the stem, petioles, veins of leaves, flower stalk and seeds are found.

Control Measure

❖ The best control measure is to grow resistant variety such as Pant D 1. The disease can also be controlled partly by seed treatment with Thiram @ 2 g per kg seed.

Wilt

It is also a serious disease and it damages the crop very quickly. It is caused by *Fusarium oxysporum.* The plants are attacked at all the stages of growth but the severity of infection increases with the age. It causes drooping of the terminal portions followed by withering and drying up of the leaves and finally resulting in the death of the plant.

Control Measure

❖ It can be controlled by seed treatment with Agrosan GN or Thiram @ 2 g per kg of seed.

Powdery mildew

This disease is caused by *Erysiphe polygoni.* It is observed during flowering of late sown crop in the month of March and April. The disease causes whitish powder on all aerial parts of the plant. Affected leaves lose their chlorophyll and dry up. Finally there is poor fruit set and whatever fruits are formed do not mature.

Control Measures

❖ Spray 0.06% solution of Karathane at 15 days' interval during flowering stage.

❖ Use sulphur dust @ 20-25 kg per hectare.

INSECT PESTS AND THEIR CONTROL

The crop is not subject to any serious pests, but occasionally stick-bug, leaf eating caterpillars and boring grubs are found on the plants. A chalcid fly has been reported as damaging the fruits. All these insect pests can be controlled by spraying the crop with 0.2% solution of Endosulfan (35 EC) as and when required.

HARVESTING

When plants attain 5 to 6 cm height, nipping can be done so that the whole plant may not be uprooted. Later on, for garnishing purpose, the leaves and stem are nipped when suitable length of the plant is reached. Seed crop matures in 100 to 125 days after sowing. To avoid shattering it is better to harvest the crop in morning hours when there is dew. It is usually recommended that the crop should be harvested when fully ripe to ensuer that the unpleasant odour of unripe fruits has disappeared. The crop should be harvested when seeds are in light green stage. After harvesting, dry it in shade for 72 hours and then put it for sun-drying. The quality of the spice is highly dependent upon the stage of fruit maturity at harvest and on the methods used for its subsequent drying and handing. Sulphur dusting against powdery mildew also maintains the green colour of seeds. After drying, threshing is done by beating the crop residue with stick or by light thresher. The seeds are sieved, winnowed and dried in sun before final packing.

YIELD

The green leaf yield varies from 30 to 40 quintal per hectare when crop is fully grown for green leaf purpose, while the seed yield varies from 15 to 20 quintal per hectare.

PREPARATION FOR MARKET

The leaves along with stems are cut and weeds and disease affected plants are removed from the lot. Small bundles of about 100 g in weight are prepared and sent for marketing.

After threshing and winnowing when seeds are fully dried, clean them properly by suitable size sieve. Make standard size packing and send them for market.

STORAGE

The whole, dried fruits/seeds are usually packed and stored in a cool, dry room. It is better that spice should be stored in sealed cans immediately after drying to ensure that quality deterioration during storage is minimum.

SEED PRODUCTION

Its seed can be produced freely in plains of the country as well as on the hills. It is a cross pollinated crop and requires 800 metres isolation distance between two varieties. Better seed yield and quality is obtained when cutting or nipping of green leaves or stem is not done. Seed crop is sown from second week of October to second week of November in the plains and 15th February to 15th March on high hills. The recommended cultural practices have to be followed during its growth period. Spraying against powdery mildew has to be done without any fail. Off types identified on the basis of external plant characters and diseased plants are removed. First roguing should be done before flowering, second at the time of flowering and third at the time of seed ripening. The seed crop matures in about 100 to 125 days after sowing depending upon the climatic conditions and variety of the crop. When crop is ready for harvest, harvesting, threshing, winnowing etc. should be done subsequently and finally dry the seed till moisture percentage comes down to ten or even below ten. On an average 15 to 20 quintals of seed yield per hectare is obtained. Seeds are stored in cool and dry room conditions.

CHAULAI (Amaranthus)

Botanical Name	-	*Amaranthus tricolor* L., *Amaranthus blitum* L.
Family	-	Amarantaceae
Synonymous	-	Khada Sag, Arakeerai, Marsa, Banopatanate, Tandalji, Elam, Chemcheera, Math, Dantinesoppu, Tandukeerai, Norpa, Tandulja, Serukeerai, Pungikeerai, Amaranthus, Chaulai.

IMPORTANCE AND UTILITY

It is one of the oldest and common vegetable crops grown in India. There are several kinds of chaulai cultivated all over the country. They all belong to the genus *Amaranthus* of the family Amarantaceae. They differ in plant height, size, shape, colour of the leaves, stem, branching habit and response to cutting. Leaves and succulent stems are used for vegetable. They are very good source of iron and Vitamin A. Hundred gram of fresh leaves contain 2500 to 11000 I.U. of Vitamin A, 130 to 173 mg of Vitamin C and 100 to 130 I.U. of Vitamin B.

The crop is cultivated twice in a year, once in the monsoon and once in summer. The crop do well in monsoon as compared to summer crop.

ORIGIN AND HISTORY

It is probably a native of India and cultivated by the ancient but was not commonly used in their common food. A few varieties are still found in wild condition. In West Bengal, it is very commonly grown and used in the daily diet.

BOTANY

The Amaranthus belongs to the family *Amarantaceae*. The plants are erect, tall, soft wooded annuals. The flowers are borne in clusters in the axils of leaves.

CLIMATIC REQUIREMENTS

The crop does well in humid tropical climate, where temperature varies from 24°C to 32°C. In cool climate, the plants do not grow properly and at 1°C to 2°C the leaves become hardy and are not fit for consumption. At very high humidity the leaves are affected by spot diseases.

SOIL AND ITS PREPARATION

This crop can be grown on a variety of soils but thrives best in well drained, deep, loose sandy loam soils, having high amount of humus and free from hard layer. The best yield is expected at soil pH 6.5 to 7.0. Organic manures are essential for better growth and development of the plants. The soil should be prepared well by repeated harrowings and plankings. About 150 to 200 quintals of farmyard manure or compost per hectare should be applied during field preparation.

VARIETIES

Chhoti chaulai: This variety is suitable for early sowing in summer. It can also be sown at the break of monsoon. The plants are erect and slightly dwarf with small leaves and respond to cuttings. The plants are all green.

Pusa chaulai: It is recommended by I.A.R.I., New Delhi. When planted in early summer it continues to supply green shoots up to the end of August and even later. Irrespective of planting time in summer it flowers only in early autumn. The leaves are medium in size, tender and green. Stem is medium thick and tender. First cutting can be done after 35 days of sowing.

Lal sag: It is a local variety grown in West Bengal. Plants are tall with light red leaves.

SEED AND SOWING

Sowing time

In North India, it is sown from mid March to end of June, while in South India it is sown almost round the year. In hills, the crop is sown in April which continues till July.

Seed rate

Amaranthus seeds are very small, therefore, only 1.5 to 2.5 kg seed is sufficient for sowing one hectare.

Method of sowing

Sufficient moisture should be there in the soil for getting better germination of seeds. The seeds should be sown shallow, not more than 1.5 cm deep. For uniform distribution, the seeds can be mixed with fine soil or in sand. It can be sown by scattering or by drilling in lines made 20 to 30 cm apart. In South India, the practice of transplanting young seedlings is also followed specially in variety Bari chaulai. The seeds are sown in nursery and young plants are later on transplanted in lines made at 30 cm distance. Plant to plant distance is also maintained at 30 cm.

MANURES AND FERTILISERS

In addition to 150 to 200 quintals of farmyard manure added in the field during field preparation, 50 kg nitrogen, 40 kg phosphorus and 45 kg potash per hectare should also be given at the time of sowing. Fifty kilogram nitrogen should be applied twice by top dressing after first and third cuttings of the crop.

IRRIGATION AND DRAINAGE

In summer, the crop should be irrigated every fourth or fifth day while in rainy season, the crop should only be irrigated as and when there is no rain. Proper drainage facilities should be arranged during rainy season.

WEED CONTROL

During summer, weeds are a great problem and they should be removed in early stage of growth for better growth and development of the crop plants. In line-sown crop, a hand hoe may be used for weeding and interculture purposes while in crop sown by broadcast method only 'khurpi' can be used.

DISEASES AND THEIR CONTROL

Damping off

It is caused by *Pythium* spp., when plant population per unit area is thick during early stage of growth, the infection of disease is more. Affected plants start rotting in the collar region of seedlings. It is generally observed when the drainage of the field is poor.

Control Measures

❖ Light irrigation should be given to the crop.
❖ The seed should be treated with Thiram or Captan at the rate of 3 g per kg of seed.

Leaf spot

During rainy season, when high humidity followed by high temperature is there, small spots are observed on the leaves which make them unfit for human consumption.

Control Measure

❖   Spray the crop with 0.2% solution of Dithane M-45.

INSECT PESTS AND THEIR CONTROL

Leaf eating caterpillars

They feed on the leaves in groups and damage the plants badly.

Control Measure

❖   Spray the crop with 0.2% solution of Sevin (50 W.P.).

HARVESTING

The plants are either cut periodically or the young plants are pulled out with the roots. For a better yield, periodical cutting of the plants is recommended. First cutting can be done after 30 to 35 days of sowing. Normally six to eight cuttings are obtained.

YIELD

The normal yield varies from 90 to 100 quintal per hectare.

PREPARATION FOR MARKET

Small bundles are prepared normally of similar size and weight. All diseased and damaged plants are removed at the time of making bundles. These bundles can be packed in baskets or in gunny bags before sending them to the market.

STORAGE

At normal room temperature, it can only be kept fresh for one to two days if sprinkling of water is done regularly at one to two hours' interval. At cold storage, it can be kept for 7 to 10 days at $5^{\circ}C$ to $8^{\circ}C$ with 85 relative humidity.

SEED PRODUCTION

It is an often cross-pollinated crop, so to maintain the purity, 100 and 400 metres isolation distance should be maintained for certified and foundation seed production, respectively. The crop should be inspected at least thrice during the crop period. First, before flowering when on the basis of foliage characters all off type plants should be removed, second, at the time of flowering when, on the basis of flower characters, all off type and diseased plants should be removed, and finally, at the time of seed maturity when, on the basis of seed character all off types and diseased plants should be removed. The seed crop is harvested when most of the leaves turn yellow. The bundles of seed bearing shoots are dried in the sun for a few days and later on beaten by sticks for seed extraction. The seed yield varies from 2 to 3 quintal per hectare.

LETTUCE

Botanical name — *Lactuca sativa* L.

Family — Compositae

Synonymous — Salad, Letus, Kahu, Letuse, Lettuce, Laitue, Bazr-ul-khas, Tukj-i-kahun, Salit, Shallathu, Shatlatuvirai.

IMPORTANCE AND UTILITY

It is grown in almost all parts of the country and is mainly used for salad purposes. It is very rich in iron but in cell sap the iron availability is very less and this is almost entirely precipitated by boiling. Mostly, it is cultivated in kitchen gardens but near big cities it is grown on large scale. It is only consumed by high class families and standard hotels only. According to Chatfield (1949), its 100 gram leaves contain 94.8 per cent water, 1.3 per cent protein, 0.2 per cent fat, 2.8 per cent carbohydrates, 0.6 per cent fibre, 540 I.U. Vitamin A, 8 mg Vitamin C, 170 mg malic acid, 140 mg potassium, 22 mg calcium, 0.5 mg iron, 25 mg phosphorus, 12 mg sulphur and 39.74 mg chlorine.

ORIGIN AND HISTORY

It is probably the native of Europe and Asia and has been in cultivation for at least 2000 years (Thompson and Kelly, 1957).

BOTANY

It is a herbaceous annual plant but biennial for seed crop. Its seeds can be produced in the plains. It is self-pollinated crop and its fruit is called "achene". There are two types of varieties, "leafy" where leaves are open and loose and may be harvested more than once, and the second type known as the "head" type which looks like cabbage head and needs to be harvested only once.

CLIMATIC REQUIREMENTS

It is a cool season crop and does well in winter season with a monthly mean temperature of 12.8°C to 15.6°C. High temperature promotes bolting (formation of seed stalk) and causes a bitter taste in the leaves and also increases the development of "tip burn". Seeds are germinated well at 15°C to 20°C soil temperature. Seeds do not germinate when soil temperature is above 30°C. Cool nights are very favourable for better growth and development of heads.

SOIL AND ITS PREPARATION

It can be grown in a variety of soils ranging from heavy clay to sandy loam but it does best in sandy loam and silt loam soils having enough organic matter. The soil should be free from hard layer with proper irrigation and drainage facilities. Where the crop matures in warm season, the crop does well in clay soils because they are cooler and hold more moisture, while for an early crop maturing in cold season, sandy loam soil is preferred. The optimum soil pH is 5.8 to 6.6.

The soil should be prepared well by repeated harrowings and plankings. At the time of field preparation, well rotten farmyard manure at the rate of 200 to 250 quintal per hectare should be mixed in the soil.

VARIETIES

Great Lakes: It is resistant to "tip burn" and marginal burning of outer leaves. It can grow better under some unfavourable conditions than other varieties. The heads are hard and slow to bolt and leaves are light green. The outer leaves are blistered.

Imperial 859: It can be grown at high temperature. The heads are medium to large in size, compact and well covered by heavily blistered outer leaves.

Slow bolt: It is a better variety for kitchen gardens since it is very slow in bolting. The leaves are broad, filled and slight yellowish green in colour.

Chinese yellow: The leaves are light green in colour, tender and crisp. It is highly productive, early in maturity and produces white seeds.

SEED AND SOWING

Sowing time

In the plains, the seed is sown in the nursery in the month of October and November and transplanted in the month of November and December. In hills, the seed is sown in February-March and transplanted in March and April.

Seed rate

The seed rate depends upon the germination percentage, variety and time of sowing. About 600 to 750 g seed possessing 80-85 per cent germination is sufficient for raising a nursery to transplant one hectare of land.

Method of sowing

The lettuce seedlings are raised in the nursery. The selected area for nursery should be prepared well by repeated spading and necessary levellings. During its preparation, stone pieces, roots and weeds should be removed. One centimetre thick layer of farmyard manure should also be mixed in the soil. Raised beds of one metre width and five metre length are to be prepared provided with 30 cm wide channel around the raised bed. Approximately twelve beds are required for raising sufficient seedlings to plant one hectare. Seeds should be treated with Thiram before sowing in the nursery @ 2.5 g per kg of seed. Half centimetre deep lines are made on the beds at a distance of 5 cm and seeds are sown in these lines at one centimetre distance and the lines covered properly. Later on the entire bed is covered by a thin layer of dry grass. Keep the beds moist till germination starts. As soon as the seeds start germinating, the layer of grass should be removed. Required cultural practices like weeding, hoeing, irrigation etc. should be done as per requirement. The seedlings become ready for transplanting four to six weeks after sowing.

Transplanting

Before transplanting, seedlings should be carefully selected, weak and diseased seedlings should not be used for planting. In the field, lines at the distance of 45 cm are made by rope and seedlings are transplanted in these lines at the distance of 30 cm. Immediately after transplanting, a light irrigation should be given. It is better to transplant the seedlings in the evening hours.

MANURES AND FERTILISERS

For better yield, a heavy dose of farmyard manure and fertilisers should be given. In addition to the farmyard manure, 100 kg nitrogen, 60 kg phosphorus and 60 kg potash per hectare is required. Half dose of nitrogen and full doses of phosphorus and potash should be given as basal at the time of transplanting and the remaining half dose of nitrogen should be given 30 to 35 and 45 to 50 days after transplanting.

IRRIGATION AND DRAINAGE

The amount of water and its interval depend upon the climate and soil types. Better growth and yield can be obtained only when the field is kept moist. Normally, the crop should be irrigated at an interval of 10 to 15 days and in total 6 to 8 irrigations are required. To avoid disease infection, proper drainage should also be provided.

WEED CONTROL

Better quality can only be obtained if the crop is kept weed free in early stage of growth. Normally, first weeding should be done 10-15 days after transplanting. Second weeding should be done 20 days after first weeding. Sometimes third weeding is also required in heavy infested fields.

DISEASES AND THEIR CONTROL

Downy mildew

It is caused by *Bremia actucae* fungus. During early stage of growth, light green or pale yellow spots appear on the upper surface of the leaves. On the reverse side a downy white growth is also seen. In later stages the entire leaf turns yellow and brown.

Control Measures

❖ Spray the crop with 0.2% solution of Dithane M-45 at an interval of 10 to 15 days.

❖ Grow resistant varieties like Imperial 17.

Mosaic

It is a very common disease of lettuce and sometimes causes considerable damage. The young leaves get distorted by inward rolling and mottling. The plants do not grow properly and turn yellow and discoloured.

Control Measures

❖ Use only disease-free seeds.

❖ Spray the crop with 0.15% solution of Metasystox to control the aphids which transmit this disease from plant to plant. The leaves should only be used 10 days after spraying.

Lettuce drop

It is caused by *Sclerotinia selerotiorum* fungus. The plants are affected at any age but more commonly in headed varieties. Older outer leaves turn pale yellow and the plant starts wilting.

Control Measure

❖   Follow crop rotations of long duration.

Tip burn

On the affected leaves, brown necrotic areas appear at the margins of younger leaves and dead areas may also develop in the interior of the head. It is very common during hot days.

Control Measures

❖   Grow resistant variety like Great Lakes.

❖   Avoid direct sunlight to the plants.

INSECT PESTS AND THEIR CONTROL

Aphids

Aphids cause heavy damage to the crop by sucking the cell sap and spread the mosaic. The affected leaves become cup shaped and are reduced in size.

Control Measure

❖   The crop should be sprayed with 0.15% solution of Sevin (50 W.P.) but the leaves should only be used 7-8 days after spraying.

Bihar hairy caterpillar

Sometimes this insect also damages the crop by eating the leaves and boring into the heads.

Control Measure

❖   The crop should be sprayed with 0.2% solution of Nuvan in early stage when caterpillars are small. In later stage, these caterpillars cannot be controlled by safe insecticides.

HARVESTING

In case of leafy varieties, tender and immature leaves are harvested while in case of headed varieties, the heads are harvested when they attain a good size and become solid.

YIELD

The yield depends upon the variety, climatic conditions and cultural practices followed. Normally 60 to 70 quintal yield per hectare can be obtained.

PREPARATION FOR MARKET

After harvesting, the leaves should be kept in shade and humid place. Damaged, diseased and outer leaves are removed to make the remaining lot look attractive. They are properly kept in baskets before sending them to the market.

STORAGE

The leaves cannot be stored at room temperature because they lose their moisture very soon. However, heads can be kept for a few days at room temperature. Leaves and heads can be kept in cold storage at 0°C with 90 to 95 per cent relative humidity for two to three weeks.

SEED PRODUCTION

It is a self-pollinated crop, even then 1 to 6 per cent cross-pollination is expected. The isolation distance for foundation and certified seeds should be 150-200 metres between two varieties. The agronomical practices are more or less the same for the crops to be raised for leaves and heads. First time, off type plants are removed on the basis of leaf and head characters. The plants affected by virus are removed. Second time, off type plants are removed on the basis of flower characters and finally, off type and diseased plants are removed at pod maturity stage. In case of headed varieties, for easy sprouting, a cross cut can also be given at the top of the head. In the months of March and April in the plains, the plants start flowering and seeds mature in the month of May. It is desirable to collect the seeds periodically by shaking the tops and collecting the seeds from the burst heads in a tray. The average seed yield is about 2 to 3 quintal per hectare.

Tuber and root crops other than potato

SWEET POTATO

Botanical name	:	*Ipomoea batata* Lam.
Family	:	Convolvulaceae
Synonymous	:	Shakarkand, Shakaria, Mitha aloo, Mishti alu, Kandamula, Chilagadadumpa, Seenikilangu, Cheenikizangu, Genasu, Ratalee, Ratalu.

IMPORTANCE AND UTILITY

It is one of the important crop of tropical and subtropical countries like Africa, China, India and U.S.A., but at present it is cultivated throughout the world. In India, U.P., Bihar, Punjab, Maharashtra and West Bengal are the main sweet potato growing states. Its roots are used after boiling or after roasting. In our country it is used for making flour, which is mixed with other types of flour and used for chapati making. Undeveloped roots and vines are used for cattle feed. Roots are rich in starch which varies from 19 to 32 per cent. Pectin of sweet potato is used for making jellies and marmalades. The crop has many industrial uses, like manufacture of starch, alcohol, syrup and in baking and confectionery.

According to Chatfield (1949 and 1954) 100 g edible roots contain 68.5 g water, 1.8 g protein, 0.7 g fat, 27.9 g carbohydrates, 1.0 g fibre, 7700 I.U. Vitamin A, 0.46 g Vitamin B, 0.6 mg nicotinic acid, 0.93 mg pantothenic acid, 22 mg Vitamin C, 40 mg Vitamin E, 530 mg K, 30 mg Ca, 12 mg Mg, 0.7 mg Fe, 49 mg P, 15 mg S and 85 mg Cl.

ORIGIN AND HISTORY

It is a native of Brazil and was probably introduced in India by Portugese. At present it is cultivated where climatic conditions are favourable.

BOTANY

The family Convolvulaceae has about 1000 species of plants which are distributed widely around the world but occur mostly in the tropics. The roots are small and fibrous and these become enlarged near the stem and form an edible root. Usually vines do not flower in high temperature but flower in short-day conditions during December and January. Leaves are alternate and heart shaped. In some varieties purple pigment is also found.

CLIMATIC REQUIREMENTS

It is a tropical plant and one of the most drought resistant vegetables. A light frost will kill the leaves and a soil temperature of 10°C or below will result in chilling damage. Better yield is secured when the rainfall is abundant in early part of the growth. The best growth takes place at 22°C to 25°C and this temperature is also good for maximum starch content.

SOIL AND ITS PREPARATION

Well drained soils are essential for better yields. The crop does well on sandy to sandy loam soils with a clay subsoil. The soil should be rich in organic matter, free from hard layer and should have better irrigation facilities. In very rich soils there is heavy vegetative growth and yields are poor and also the tubers are rough. The best pH is 5.8 to 6.7. Normally, up to 30 cm deep field preparation is sufficient, but soil should be fine. Repeated harrowings followed by plankings should be done to make the soil fine. Crop residues of previous crop and stone pieces should also be removed at the same time. Farmyard manure at the rate of 150-200 quintals per hectare should be added in the field during the land preparation.

VARIETIES

Following are the main varieties of sweet potatoes grown in India.

Pusa Safed: It is a selection from I.A.R.I., New Delhi from a white variety originally introduced from Tiawan. It is a high yielding variety with wide adaptability. Outer skin and flesh are white in colour. The variety has done well in Delhi, Punjab, Rajasthan, Uttar Pradesh, Bihar, Maharashtra and Tamil Nadu. The tubers are medium in size, somewhat elongated. The boiled flesh is creamy white, moist, sweet and very palatable.

Pusa Lal: It is a selection from I.A.R.I., New Delhi from a Japanese variety (Norin). It is a red skinned and white fleshed high yielding variety. The tubers are medium sized but thick in the middle. This variety has done well in Delhi, Punjab, Rajasthan, Uttar Pradesh, Bihar and Maharashtra.

Pusa Sunehri: It is also a selection from I.A.R.I., New Delhi from a material obtained from the U.S.A. The tubers are elongated, light brown skinned and yellow fleshed. The tubers contain 24.8 ppm carotene which is very high. The boiled flesh is attractive orange yellow, moist and sweet.

Hybrid 42 (I): This hybrid is pink-skinned and white fleshed. It is a high yielding variety producing medium sized attractive tubers. The keeping quality at room temperature is excellent. This variety is fairly resistant to sweet potato weevil. It has been bred at CTCRI, Trivandrum.

V2: The leaves of this variety are broad with dark green colour, stem is long, thick and hairy. White skinned, white fleshed and large sized tubers are produced. The average yield is approximately 150 quintal per hectare.

V6: The base of the leaves is purple. The tubers of this variety are large in size, thick, red in colour and non-fibrous. The average yield is around 100 to 125 quintals per hectare.

V_2 and V_6 varieties are recommended by Punjab Agricultural University, Ludhiana.

No. 4004: This variety is recommended by Department of Agriculture, Maharashtra State Government. It produces white skinned tubers at a shallow depth. It is a high yielding variety. The average yield is around 200 quintal per hectare.

V8: This variety was introduced in India from U.S.A. It is an early variety and takes only 120 days from transplanting to harvest. The vines are long, trailing, with a purple shade at the internodes. The stem is round, smooth and hairy. The tubers are small in size and white skinned. It is recommended for cultivation in Punjab.

V12: It is also an early variety and takes from 105 to 120 days for complete maturity. The vines are semi erect in nature. It produces big sized, elongated white skinned tubers. Tubers are very sweet in taste and non-fibrous. It is recommended for cultivation in Punjab.

Varsha: It is a red coloured variety, ready to harvest four months after planting. Average yield is 200 to 250 quintal per hectare. It is good for dry areas.

Sree Nandini: It is a white colour variety and matures early. Recommended for Kerala state. Average yield is about 200 to 250 quintal per hectare.

Rajendra Sakarkand 5: It is recommended from Rajendra Krishi Vishvavidhyala Dali. The roots are milky in colour. It is early variety ready for harvest 90-100 days after planting.

Jawahar Sakarkand 145: It is recommended from Jawaharlal Krishi Vishvavidhyalya, Dawalpur. It is early variety and ready to harvest 130 to 145 days after planting. Roots are copper red in colour.

Kiran: It is a red coloured variety. Recommended for Andhra Pradesh. It is ready for harvest 120 days after planting.

Yellow Jersey: Leaves are green but small in size. The stem is green and slender. The tubers are yellow, smooth with yellow flesh.

PROPAGATION AND PLANTING

Planting time

Planting season varies from place to place. In Central India, planting is done during October. In some parts the crop is grown in both seasons i.e. Rabi as well as Kharif. For Kharif, vine cuttings are planted in June-July and for Rabi in September-October. Normally, in North India, cuttings are planted in first fortnight of July during cloudy weather.

Planting material

Tubers with a diameter of two to three centimetre are most suitable for producing vines for further planting. Five quintals of tubers are required to produce sufficient vines for planting one hectare. Theoretically, one lakh cuttings will be required for one hectare with approximate weight of 700 to 1000 kg. These numbers can be produced in 0.15 to 0.20 hectare area nursery. The tubers are planted in the nursery in the month of April or two months before planting season. Proper irrigation and weeding is done regularly during the nursery stage.

Planting

The cuttings are prepared from the matured vines which are free from soil-borne diseases. The length of the cutting varies from 30 to 50 cm with 4 to 5 sound buds. The planting can be done in flat beds or on ridges, but better yields can only be obtained by ridge planting method. Ridges are made 60 cm apart and cuttings are planted at 20 to 25 cm distance on the ridges. Before planting, the plot is irrigated and planting is done in the mud but the best time to plant the cuttings is on rainy day.

MANURES AND FERTILISERS

For better yields, balanced fertilisation is required. The quantity of nutrients depends upon the soil type, variety and season of planting. In addition to farmyard manure, 60 kg each of N, P and K per hectare should be given. Half dose of nitrogen and full dose of phosphorus and potash should be applied as basal whereas rest half dose of nitrogen should be given by top dressing, 35 to 40 days after planting. Top dressing should be followed by light earthing.

IRRIGATION AND DRAINAGE

The interval and amount of irrigation depend upon the season and soil type. The total water requirement of the crop is 75 to 80 cm. Just after transplanting the cuttings, field should be irrigated. Later on, at an interval of 10 to 12 days, the crop should be irrigated. During rainy season, if rains are not regular, crop should be irrigated as per need. During rainy season it is essential to drain out the excess water from the field for proper growth and root development.

WEED CONTROL

Till the vines are spread over the soil, the crop should remain free from weeds. Later on the crop itself suppresses weed growth. Normally two to three weedings are sufficient.

TURNING OF THE VINES

There are different opinions regarding this operation. But during early stage this operation helps in root development. It should not be done after 60 to 65 days of transplanting, because at that stage this operation promotes the development of foliage diseases.

DISEASES AND THEIR CONTROL

Stem rot

This disease is caused by *Fusarium batata* fungus. The leaves of infected plants become dull in colour and then become yellow between the veins. Diseased stems become blackened inside. This disease is spread through soil or through seed tubers or vines.

Control Measures

❖   Grow resistant varieties.

❖ Follow suitable rotation.

❖ Treat the seed tubers with Aretan 0.2% solution.

Black rot

It is caused by *Ceratostomella fimbriata* fungus and tubers are affected. There are black spots on the affected tubers and later on the entire tuber starts rotting.

Control Measures

❖ Treat the seed tubers in 0.1% mercuric chloride solution.

❖ Sort out the infected tubers before storing.

❖ Provide better irrigation facilities.

Wilt

It is caused by *Fusarium oxysporum* fungus which mostly attacks in nursery stage. First of all the leaves become dull and later on the plants die. The stem of affected plants become black inside.

Control Measures

❖ The seed tubers should be treated with 0.1% mercuric chloride solution.

❖ Avoid high nitrogen application in the field.

❖ Follow proper crop rotation.

White rust

It is caused by *Albugo ipomoeapanduratea* fungus. Irregular yellowish white spots are observed on older leaves and later on white powder is seen on the surface of leaves.

Control Measures

❖ Use disease-free material for planting.

❖ Follow proper crop rotation.

❖ Keep the crop weed free.

Leaf spot

It is caused by *Cercospora batatae* fungus. Round and brown spots are found on the surface of the leaves. The disease is more prominent in hot and humid climate.

Control Measures

❖ Follow proper crop rotatin

❖ Spray the crop with 0.2% solution of Dithane M-45.

INSECT PESTS AND THEIR CONTROL

SweetPotato weevil

It is very common insect pest of sweet potato. It looks like a small ant and is bluish in colour. The grubs bore into the vines and kill them and the adults feed onleaves. The damages also continues in storage on the tubers.

Control Measures

❖ Spray the crop with 0.2 per cent solution of Sevin (50 W.P.).

❖ Get the tubers in storage fumigated with Methyl bromide.

Leaf eating caterpillars

Sweet potato sphinx and Bihar hairy caterpillar are the leaf eating caterpillars which damage the foliage of the vines. Sometimes they become very serious pests and become most destructive. The adults lay eggs in small cavities in the stem and after hatching in a week's time the larvae feed on the vine or in the tuber for 2 or 3 weeks.

Control Measures

❖ Spray the crop with 0.2% solution of Sevin (50 W.P.). or 0.2% Endosulfan solution.

❖ Put Aldrin 10 per cent dust in trenches around the field.

HARVESTING

Generally, the crop is ready for harvesting after 120-135 days of transplanting. There is change in the colour of leaves at maturity and also tubers become brittle when fully developed. The vines are removed before harvesting and harvesting can be done by digging out the tubers with *kudali* or spade.

YIELD

The tuber yield varies from soil to soil and variety to variety. The higher yields are obtained in irrigated areas than in rain-fed areas. Generally, in rain-fed areas, the yield varies from 60 to 90 quintal per hectare while in irrigated conditions with improved varieties, 200 to 250 quintal per hectare can be obtained.

PREPARATION FOR MARKET

After harvesting, undersized, diseased and insect damaged tubers are removed. Selected tubers are cleaned and packed in gunny bags for the market.

STORAGE

Generally, red skinned tubers store better than white skinned ones. The tubers can be stored for 2 to 3 months at 15°C with 85 to 90 per cent humidity.

SEED PRODUCTION

True to the type tubers should be selected for producing the vines. At the time of planting, selection of cuttings on the basis of leaf and stem characters should be made for the specific variety. Off types should be removed as and when observed in the field. Finally, at the time of harvesting, off types should be sorted out. Control measures should be followed for controlling insect pests and diseases.

COLOCASIA

Botanical name	-	*Colocasia esculenta* Schoot
Family	-	*Araceae*
Synonymous	-	Kachu, Kachalu, Saru, Alooka, Dasheen, Great-leaved caladium, Elephant ear, Chemadumpalu, Sambu, Sapan Kizhangu, Alu, Kannad, Kesavina gedde, Alvi, Alavu, Arvi, Ghuiya, Ghuiyan.

IMPORTANCE AND UTILITY

Among summer vegetables colocasia is one of the most paying crop to the vegetable growers. It is cultivated twice a year and planted in February-March for summer crop and June-July for rainy season crop. It is cultivated almost throughout the country but Uttar Pradesh, Bihar, Bengal and Maharashtra are the main growing states in India. In Konkan and parts of Maharashtra, almost every family grows a small plot of colocasia in its backyard for its green leaves. In early stage, they use the tender leaves for making pakoras and also for making rayata. It has some medicinal use as well as the juice of petioles is dripped in the ears of children in otorrhoea and its hot tubers are locally applied to painful parts in rheumatism whereas the ash of root stock mixed with honey is used for local application for Aphthae in the mouth. The summer crop is mostly grown around cities but due to no-adoption of scientific cultural practices a good yield is not harvested. According to Dr. Aykroyd (1941), its edible root contains 73.1 per cent water, 22.1 per cent carbohydrates, 3.0 per cent protein, 0.1 per cent fat, 1.0 per cent fibres, 1.7 per cent minerals, 40 I.U. Vitamin A, 80 I.U. Vitamin B, and Vitamin C in traces.

Its flour can be mixed with wheat flour and can be used for chapaties.

ORIGIN AND HISTORY

According to Marigowda (1952) it originated from India, and still it is found in wild condition in the forest, while according to Mehta (1959), it originated from old world tropics.

BOTANY

It is a perennial tuberous plant with large, heart-shaped leaf blade, borne on long petioles arising from underground corms. The petioles vary in size and shape, the central ones being big and conspicuous.

CLIMATIC REQUIREMENTS

It is a warm season crop and can be grown in hot and humid areas. It is well suited to tropical and subtropical regions of the country. It cannot tolerate even slight frost. The best growth takes place at 30°C to 34°C and germination at 25°C to 28°C. High rainfall and high humidity may increase the blight infection.

SOIL AND ITS PREPARATION

Although, it can be cultivated in a variety of soils, but it thrives best in deep, well manured and sandy loam to friable loam soils. The best soil pH is 6.0 to 7.0. The soil should have better facilities for irrigation and drainage and should not have hard layer. The land is prepared thoroughly by harrowings alongwith plankings and removal of grass and stone pieces. For a better yield, 150 to 200 quintals of farmyard manure should be mixed in the soil during its preparation.

VARIETIES

In our country, improved varieties are still not available and mostly local varieties are cultivated. Following varieties are, however, being grown in different parts of the country.

In North India: Selection 3, Selection 11, Goraiya, Faizabadi, Banshi, Ladhara, Deshi Banda.

In Central part of the country: Worm 1, Worm 2, Gyano Nos. 12, 22, 36 and 40.

In South India: Sarkachu, Gurri Kachu, Asu Kachu, Kalla Kachu and Char Kachu. Satmukhi, Shri Palvi and Sree Rashmi.

SEED AND SOWING

Sowing time

In the plains, the crop is planted in March-April for summer crop and June-July for rainy season crop whereas in hills, it is planted in September-October.

Seed rate

The seed rate depends upon the size of corms. Eight to ten quintals of medium sized corms are required for planting one hectare.

Method of sowing

The seed stock should be treated with 0.25 % Aretan and only sprouted corms should be used for planting. The sowing can be done by the following methods:

(1) In Flat beds

With the help of rope, lines are made at 60 cm distance and corms are planted 30 cm apart in these rows. The depth of corms should be around 8 cm.

(2) On Ridges

The ridges are made at 45 to 60 cm distance by rigger or by spade and corms are planted on these ridges at 30 cm distance. Same depth is maintained as mentioned in flat bed method. Planting on ridges gives better yield than flat planting.

MANURES AND FERTILISERS

For better yield the crop should be heavily manured and fertilised. Besides the farmyard manure, as already recommended, 100 kg nitrogen, 60 kg phosphorus and 80 kg potash per hectare will be required. Half dose of nitrogen and full dose of phosphorus and potash should be given in basal application and remaining half dose of nitrogen should be given as top dressing 45 to 50 days after planting.

IRRIGATION AND DRAINAGE

At the time of planting there should be enough moisture in the field to obtain better and uniform emergence. In case there is no emergence, after some time of planting the field should be irrigated to hasten the emergence without any danger of rotting of the corms. Summer crop should be irrigated once a week regularly but excess water should be drained out immediately. During rainy seasons, the crop does not require any irrigation. If rains are frequent, proper drainage facilities should be provided.

WEED CONTROL

One or two shallow hoeings should be done in the crop and after every hoeing or weeding the earthing of the plants should be done to cover the open roots. Periodical removal of side shoots and allowing only one or two main shoots increases the yield considerably. The weeds can be controlled by spraying Lasso at the rate of 5 litres per hectare dissolved in 1000 litres of water immediately after planting.

DISEASES AND THEIR CONTROL

Phytophthora blight

It is caused by *Phytophthora* sp. and the disease is observed in July-August. Initially leaves are affected and subsequently petiole is also affected which may cause the leaves to fall. In severe infestation even the corm is attacked by the fungus resulting in the death of the plant. The corms may either be lacking or may become small and shrunken.

Control Measure

❖ The disease can be controlled by spraying the crop with Dithane M-45 @ 2.5 kg per hectare dissolved in 1000 litres of water at 15 days' interval.

INSECT PESTS AND THEIR CONTROL

Bihar hairy caterpillar

The attack is very common in rainy season and the female lays yellow coloured eggs in bunches on the lower surface of the leaves. They start hatching after 3 to 5 days and small creamy white caterpillars come out in bunches and feed on the tender leaves.

Control Measures

❖ The crop should be sprayed with 0.2 per cent solution of Endosulfan (35 EC).

❖ During early stage the eggs should be collected and burnt.

Grass hopper

They are green insects and feed on the leaves. They always prefer tender ones.

Control Measure

❖ The crop should be sprayed with 0.2% solution of Endosulfan (35 EC).

HARVESTING

The time of harvest depends upon the variety, season, and climate. Normally, when the crop is about 60 to 70 days old, some side shoots may be removed by sickle without making any damage to main shoot. By this way the cultivator may get better price in the market by selling the shoots besides obtaining better yields.

Normally, harvesting should be done when tubers become sufficiently ripe for market and storage.

YIELD

The factors which are responsible for yield are variety, crop period, application of nutrients, irrigation and drainage facilities. The average yield may vary from 200 to 250 quintal per hectare.

PREPARATION FOR MARKET

Just after harvest the colocasia does not get good price in the market. The harvested bulk should be kept in dry and cool place and turning should be done at an interval of 3 to 4 days. Diseased and damaged corms are sorted out and the better ones kept in gunny bags before sending them to market.

STORAGE

Colocasia can be kept at cool and dry place for 4 to 5 months with proper care in storage. Normally, in villages, the growers keep them for seed in a pit which is about 50 to 60 cm deep and provided with dry grass on all sides. This method cannot be followed in heavy rainfall areas. They can be kept in cold storage at 7°C to 10°C for three to four months.

SEED PRODUCTION

Select true to the types, based on the external characters of corms. The selected corms are multiplied with recommended agronomical cultural practices. Proper spraying of fungicide should be done to control the blight. Off types and diseased plants should be removed from time to time during its growing period. During harvesting, the true to the type corms should be selected for seed purpose.

TURMERIC

Botanical name	-	*Curcuma domestica*
Family	-	*Zingiberaceae*
Synonymous	-	Holud, Manjal, Arishina, Pasupu

IMPORTANCE AND UTILITY

It is an important spice among rice eating people of India, South-East Asia and Indonesia, and is indispensable in the preparation of curry powder. Its main use in Western world is for musky flavour and yellow colour in cooking vegetable. It is also used for dyeing cotton, silk or wool without mordant, but the colour is fugitive. Rice coloured with turmeric is used on ceremonial occasion. Yellow turmeric paper can be used as a test for alkalinity when it turns brown. Among the main turmeric growing countries, India produces maximum turmeric per year which is exported to other countries also. Essential oil may also be distilled from the turmeric rhizome but this is of little importance in international market.

ORIGIN AND HISTORY

It originated from Southern or South-East Asia (Raghavan and Venkatasubban, 1943). Some of its species are the native of India and were grown here earlier. At present it is widely spread throughout the tropics but its cultivation as a spice is largely confined to India, South-East Asia and Indonesia.

BOTANY

It is an erect perennial herb, but is grown as annual. Its somatic chromosome number is 2 n = 32 (Darlington and Wylie, 1955). The plant bears 6-10 leaves with the leaf sheaths forming a pseudostem. The lamina is lanceolate, acuminate and thin. The inflorescence is cylindrical spike, 10-15 cm long and 5-7 cm wide. The bracts are adnate for less than half their length and are elliptic lanceolate and acute, 5-6 cm long and about 2.5 cm wide. The calyx is short, unequally toothed, corolla is tabular at the base. There are two lateral elliptic-oblong staminodes which are creamy white in colour. The ovary is inferior and trilocular with a slender style. Fruits are seldom, if every, produced.

CLIMATIC REQUIREMENTS

It can be cultivated well in tropical and subtropical areas having adequate rainfall or irrigation facilities. It requires hot and moist climate. On an average it requires an annual rainfall of 1000 to 2000 mm. It can be grown up to the elevation of 1220 metres. Its cultivation can be extended to wetter areas with over 2000 mm of rain per annum.

SOIL AND ITS PREPARATION

It can grow well in a variety of soils provided with better irrigation and drainage facilities. Gravelly, stony and heavy clay soils are not fit for its cultivation because they check the development of the rhizomes. It thrives best on loamy or alluvial, loose, friable, fertile soils and cannot stand waterlogging conditions. It can be grown in partial shade of orchards where other crops cannot be grown (Aiyadurai, 1966). Better yields are obtained at neutral pH of the soil.

The soil should be prepared well by harrowing followed by planking. Residues of previous crops should be removed during the field preparation. About 200 to 300 quintal farmyard manure should be mixed in the soil at the time of field preparation.

VARIETIES

Following are the main varieties of turmeric grown in India.

Deshi: It is grown in Assam and West Bengal. The fingers are of small size but possess deep yellow colour.

Patani: It is also commonly grown in Assam and West Bengal. It has better colour and flavour than the previous one.

Chinna nadom: It is grown in Bhavani and Erode taluks of Tamil Nadu. It has light yellow colour.

Patani nadom: It is also grown in Bhavani and Erode taluks of Tamil Nadu. It grows more vigorously and its rhizomes have a sweeter aroma (Sastri, 1950).

Soniya: It is recommended from Rajendra Kumar Vishvavidhyalya Dali. It is resistant to leaf spot. Tubers are medium in size with dark colour. Average yield is 45 to 50 quintal per hectare.

Co-1: It is recommend by Tamil Nadu Agriculture University, Coimbatore Tamil Nadu. It is ready to harvest 285 days after planting. Tubers are orange in colour. Average yield is 55 to 60 quintal per hectare.

Krishna: It is resistant to leaf spot and also to insects. It is ready to harvest 230 days after planting and average yield is 40 quintal per hectare.

Swarna: It is resistant to soft rot and is ready to harvest 150 days after planting. Its average yield is 46 quintal per hectare.

Roina: It is resistant to a number of diseases. It is ready for harvest 250 days after planting. Average yield is 60 quintal per hectare.

Saugandham: It is an early variety, ready to harvest 210 days after planting. Average yield is 65 quintal per hectare.

Mundaga: It is grown in Mysore. It has larger corms with thick large number of fingers.

Balaga: It is grown in Mysore and has small corms but they are many in number.

Yelachage: It is also grown in Mysore and has few small corms.

SEED AND PLANTING

It is always propagated vegetatively by fingers or rhizomes having one or two buds. It is reported that the mother rhizome is better than the off springs. In Andhra Pradesh, generally the mother rhizomes are preferred from which more vigorous sprouts are produced resulting in higher yields.

Planting time

The usual time for planting in India is May-June while in some parts of southern India it is planted in March-April.

Seed rate

Seed rate depends upon the distance of planting and size of rhizome used for planting. At 45 x 25 cm distance the average seed rate is about 17 to 20 quintal per hectare.

Method of planting

The crop can be planted on flat beds or on ridges. In Orissa, ridge planting at 22.5 x 22.5 cm gave the best yield as reported by Aiyadurai (1966), while in Andhra Pradesh the broad-ridge method of planting was found to be superior and more profitable than ridge and furrow methods. On largescale, potato planter can be used for its planting. Emergence takes place 2-4 weeks after planting.

MANURES AND FERTILISERS

It is a heavy feeder crop and requires much more nutrients than other seasonal crops. Generally, 200 to 300 quintals per hectare farmyard manure is mixed in the soil 25-30 days prior to planting. In addition to this 120 kg nitrogen and 55 kg each of P and K per hectare are applied by chemical fertilisers. Full dose of phosphorus and potash and half dose of nitrogen is applied at the time of planting and rest half nitrogen in two splits after 55 and 110 days of planting in the form of top dressing.

IRRIGATION AND DRAINAGE

Frequency of irrigation depends on weather and moisture retention capacity of the soil. Till sprouting is completed, irrigations at weekly intervals are essential. After sprouting, irrigations can be given at 10 to 15 days' interval in summer season. During rainy season, the crop does not require irrigation. It is very susceptible to waterlogging conditions, therefore, excess water during rainy season should be drained out otherwise it may cause rhizome rot.

WEED CONTROL

Weeds should be controlled manually or by chemicals. Early weeding may be avoided by the use of pre-emergence herbicides. Simazine @ 2 kg per hectare can be used as pre-emergence. Earthing up is also essential eight weeks after planting and may be repeated after sixteen weeks of planting. This operation also helps in weed control.

DISEASES AND THEIR CONTROL

Leaf spots

Leaf spots are caused by *Taphrina maculans* and *Colletotrichum capsici* found throughout India but it is a very serious disease in Tamil Nadu and Andhra Pradesh. Spots appear in greater number, are yellow in colour, about 1-2 mm in diameter and coalesce freely when caused by *Taphrina* sp. (Chattopadhyay, 1967).

When spots are caused by *Colletotrichum* sp., they are elliptic to oblong in shape, attain a size of 4-5 x 2-3 cm, appear on both surfaces of the leaf, are greyish-white in the centre with a brown margin and ill-defined yellow spots multiply during humid climate.

Control Measures

❖ Spray the crop with 0.2% solution of Dithane M-45, or Dithane Z-78, or Blitox at 15 days' interval.

❖ Spray the crop with Bordeaux mixture.

Root rot

Root rot in turmeric is caused by *Pythium graminicolum.* This disease has been reported recently in India (Chattopadhyay, 1967).

Control Measures

❖ Treat the tubers before planting with 0.3 per cent Agallol.

❖ Use disease-free tubers.

INSECT PESTS AND THEIR CONTROL

Shoot boring caterpillar (*Dichocrocis punctiferalis* Guen.)

The insect bores into and cuts the central shoots and the affected plants dry up (Sastri, 1950).

Control Measures

❖ Spray the crop with 0.2% solution of Sevin (50 W.P.).

❖ Remove the affected shoots in the initial stage of attack and destroy the larvae.

Thrips (*Panchaetothrips indicus*)

They are very small insects and suck the sap from the leaves.

Control Measure

❖ Spray the crop with 0.1% solution of Metasystox of Rogor.

HARVESTING

Turmeric takes about 8 to 10 months from planting to harvesting depending upon the variety and type of soil. When leaves fall down, remove them from the soil surface and remove the roots. All the adhering earth is shaken or rubbed off and the rhizomes are then washed well with water. Fingers are separated from the mother tubers. During harvesting, care should be taken that rhizomes are not cut or bruised.

YIELD

Turmeric yield depends upon the variety, soil, irrigation facilities and nutrients etc. Aiyadurai (1966) reported the yield of fresh raw turmeric from 168 to 224 quintal per hectare in the case of irrigated crop, and 67.2 to 89.6 quintal per hectare in rain-fed condition.

PREPARATION FOR MARKET

Turmeric is sold in the market in dried or processed form. In India, the curing method followed is the boiling or steaming the fresh and washed fingers in water, drying in sun and finally peeling or polishing. Generally, the pots used for "gur" making are also used for boiling turmeric while at some places deep earthenware pots, metal tanks or vats are also used for its boiling. The freshly harvested fingers are heaped in the pans or filled in the pots and sufficient water is added to it. The rhizomes are then boiled over a slow fire until they soften. The boiling takes about 3-4 hours. The rhizomes are then cooled and spread out to dry in the sun. The final operation in the processing of turmeric is polishing in which the thoroughly dried product is cleaned of the outer skin. This can be done by rubbing with hands or feet, or by putting them in gunny bags along with stones, shaking them or by rotating them in a polishing drum. After polishing it can be sold as such or in the form of powder. The yield of polished turmeric varies from 15 to 25 per cent of the fresh produce.

STORAGE

Freshly harvested rhizomes cannot be kept for more than one month at room temperature but the storage life can be increased by lowering down the temperature. It can be kept well for 16 to 24 weeks at the storage temperature of 5°C to 7°C.

The boiled, dried and polished turmeric can be kept at room temperature up to 3 to 5 years without any problem. Excess humidity, however, may reduce its quality and may cause some fungal infection during storage.

SEED PRODUCTION

It is a tuber crop, almost free from viral diseases, hence the production of quality seed is not a problem. Healthy and true to the type plant material is selected from the field and identified well on the basis of rhizome characters. The selected rhizomes are multiplied by following the recommended cultural practices.

GINGER

Botanical name	-	*Zingiber officinale* Rose
Family	-	Zingiberaceae
Synonymous	-	Aarda, Inchi, Shunti, Allamu

IMPORTANCE AND UTILITY

In Western countries, it is used for culinary purposes, in ginger-bread, biscuits, cakes, pudding, soups and pickles. In China, it is widely used as spice in Chinese cookery. Ginger beer and ginger wine are also prepared from it. After preserving with sugar, it is used in most of the countries. Its rhizomes yield 1-3 per cent pale yellow essential oil which is used for flavouring and in man's toilet water. It is used in medicine as a carminative and aromatic stimulant to the gastro-intestinal tract and externally as a rubefacient and counter-irritant. India produces about 50 per cent of the world's total genger and is the largest exporter. China, Taiwan, Nigeria, Sierra Leone, Jamaica, Thailand and Australia are the other ginger growing countries in the world. United Kingdom, United States and Saudi Arabia are the bigger importing countries. Edible portion of ginger contains 85 per cent water, 10.5 per cent carbohydrates, 1.1 per cent protein, 0.7 per cent fat, 0.05 per cent thiamine, 0.04 per cent riboflavin, Vitamin C and minerals in traces.

ORIGIN AND HISTORY

It originated from South-East Asia, but is nowhere known in a wild state. In Asia, it has been cultivated as spice since very ancient times.

BOTANY

It is a monocotyledon, belonging to the family Zingiberaceae in the order Zingiberales. The 2n chromosome number is 22. It is a perennial herb but is generally grown as an annual. The plant is 30-100 cm tall, with a robust branched rhizome borne horizontally near the surface of the soil. Rhizome is hard and thick, and usually pale yellow within. It is covered with small distichous scales with an encircling insertion. The inflorescence arises direct from the rootstock, is spicate and 15-25 cm long. The bracts are oppressed, ovate or elliptic, 2-3 cm long and 1.5-2.0 cm wide. The calyx is thin, tubular, spathaceous 1-1.2 cm long and three-toothed. The corolla tube is 2-2.5 cm long with three yellowish lobes. There are three stamens about 1.2 cm long and wide. The inferior ovary is trilocular with several ovules per loculus. The fruit, which is very seldom produced, is a thin walled, three valved capsule, with small, black arillate seed.

CLIMATIC REQUIREMENTS

It thrives well in hot, moist climate and can be grown successfully up to an elevation of 1500 metres. It does well at the average day temperature of 28°C to 35°C (Paulose, 1973) and where annual rainfall is 3000 mm, distributed 8 to 10 months during ginger growing season. In Himachal Pradesh and the hill tracts of Assam and West Bengal, the crop is grown under climatic conditions very different from those existing in the plains, with fairly low temperatures and rainfall. It can be grown as inter-crop in orchards.

SOIL AND ITS PREPARATION

It does well on medium loams with heavy supply of humus, particularly after cutting down forest or bush. In India' it is grown on a wide variety of soils such as sandy loams, clayey loams, lateritic and black soils, but better yields are recorded in loam soils. It is very sensitive to waterlogging conditions, hence lowlying areas are not suitable for its cultivation. Sloppy soils having hard pan are also not suitable for its cultivation. Soil should be prepared well by repeated harrowings followed by planking. At the time of soil preparation, residues of the previous crops etc. must be removed. If required, soil should be levelled well during its final preparation. Prior to planting, about 200 to 250 quintals of farmyard manure or compost or leaf mould should be added in the field.

VARIETIES

Wynad Manantody: It was reported by Paulose (1973) and is cultivated widely in Kerala, the state which produces the largest quantity of ginger in India.

Suprabha: This variety is found to be suitable for hills and is high yielding. It is resistant to soft rot.

Suruchi:- It is high yielding variety and tolerant to soft rot and good for plains and hills.

Surabhi: It is high yielding variety, resistant to soft rot and is most suitable for hills.

Maram: It is widely grown in Assam and was recently introduced in Kerala. It is high yielding variety and produces high percentage of dry ginger.

Rio-de-Janeiro: It was introduced to India from Brazil and cultivated in ginger growing areas. It has less fibre content but is not suitable for conversion to dry ginger on account of its high moisture content. Dry ginger of this variety has a shrivelled appearance.

China: It was introduced to India from China. It is high yielding variety with a fibre content of 3.43 per cent. Recovery of dry ginger from green ginger is only 13-15 per cent.

Canton: It is used for preservation purpose. It has more succulent and thicker rhizomes.

White or yellow ginger: These are commonly grown in Jamaica. Sometimes these two types are known as turmeric ginger and blue or flint ginger, in which the interior of the rhizomes has a bluish tinge, with harder, more fibrous rhizomes having poor quality and poor yield.

Burdwan: It is a local variety grown in West Bengal.

Following are the other varieties of ginger: Thingpui, Jorhat, Nadia, Thinladium, Wynad Local, Ernad, Thodupuzha, Kakakal, Narasapattam.

SEED AND SOWING

It is always propagated by the portions of the rhizome known as seed pieces or setts. Clumps of rhizome are separated which are about 2.5-5 cm long and weigh 28 to 56 g, each having at least one growing point.

Planting time

The usual time for planting in India is May and June. A number of experiments have shown that planting early in the season is beneficial. Randhawa and Nandpuri (1970) reported that the highest yield was obtained from Himachal Pradesh when it was planted in first and second week of May. Early planting ensures that the crop will make sufficient growth to tolerate heavy rains and will grow rapidly with the onset of heavy rains in July and August. At Ambalavayal in Kerala, Aiyadurai (1966) showed that planting in the first week of April was best and gave 100 to 200 per cent more yield than the local practice of late planting in May-June.

Seed rate

The seed rate varies from region to region, size of rhizome used for planting, and the methods of cultivation adopted. Paulose (1973) reported that in Kerala and other southern states of India, 1200 to 1400 kg seed rhizomes were required for planting one hectare, while in northern India, specially in Himachal Pradesh, 2500 to 3000 kg seed rhizomes were required, using bigger seed bits. It is reported by a number of workers that planting of large sized seed pieces gives significantly higher yield than the planting of small pieces.

Method of planting

Closer spacing in ginger gives higher yield than wider spacing. Aiyadurai (1966) reported that spacings of 15 x 15 cm, 15 x 23 cm and 23 x 23 cm gave better yields in India. Purseglove (1972) suggested that 30 x 15 cm was the normal spacing for ginger. Bed planting gives better yield than flat planting. Usually beds of one metre width, 15 cm height and of convenient length varying from 3 to 6 metres are prepared. The width of the channels between the beds is about 30 cm. Planting is done in 4-5 cm deep furrows on the beds at the distance given above.

MANURES AND FERTILISERS

It is an exhausting crop and requires heavy manuring for obtaining better yield and quality. About 200 to 250 quintal farmyard manure per hectare is incorporated in the soil 20 to 25 days before planting. About 120 kg nitrogen, 60 kg phosphorus and 60 kg potash per hectare should be applied in the form of chemical fertilisers. Half dose of nitrogen and full dose of phosphorus and potash should be applied at the time of planting. Remaining 60 kg nitrogen may be applied in two splits, the first about 40 to 60 days after planting.

MULCHING

Mulching is very essential in ginger cultivation as it helps to prevent drying of the soil and weed growth. Just after planting, a mulch of green leaves at the rate of 10000 to 12000 kg per hectare is applied. It should be repeated during the second and third month after planting at the rate of 5000 kg of green leaves each time. Aiyudurai (1966) reported that in mulched plots almost double yield was obtained as compared to unmulched ones.

IRRIGATION AND DRAINAGE

The total water requirement of the crop is 1320 and 1520 mm during complete crop cycle. The interval of irrigation depends upon the weather and the moisture retention capacity of the soil. Irrigation is given at fortnightly intervals during summer and from middle of September to November. Rainy season crop does not require irrigation. During rainy season waterlogging conditions should be avoided by providing better drainage facilities.

WEED CONTROL

In mulched crop, two to three weedings are generally given to the crop. The first weeding should be done before second mulching and should be repeated at one month interval. If mulching is not done, the crop needs about 5 to 6 weedings.

DISEASES AND THEIR CONTROL

Soft rot

It is one of the serious disease in India caused by *Pythium* sp. The affected plants become pale, the tips of leaves turn yellow, followed by complete yellowing and drying up of the leaves. The shoots fall and cease to produce rhizomes. The infection increases by high moisture content of the soil with insufficient drainage.

Control Measures

❖ Select a well-drained site for planting.

❖ Follow crop rotation to avoid·repeated planting of ginger in the same field.

❖ Use healthy rhizomes for seed purpose.

❖ Spray the crop with 0.2% solution of Dithane M-45 during rainy season.

❖ Treat the rhizomes with Dithane M-45 (0.2%) before planting.

Leaf spot

It is caused by *Colletrotrichum zingiberis* (Sundar) as reported by Chattopadhyay (1967). The fungus attacks the foliage only, forming round to oval light yellow spots which may coalesce to form large discoloured areas, often drying up in the centre to form a hole.

Control Measures

❖ Spray the crop with 0.2% solution of Dithane M-45 or Dithane Z-78 or Blitox at 15 days' interval.

❖ Spray the crop with 5-5-50 Bordeaux mixture.

Other diseases such as thread blight, root rot and dry black rot are also reported from different parts of the world.

INSECT PESTS AND THEIR CONTROL

Shoot borer (*Dichocrocis punctiferalis* Guen.)

Its larvae bore into the shoots. Sometimes the infection reaches 30 to 40% during humid season.

Control Measures

❖ Spray the crop periodically with 0.02% solution of Endosulfan (35 EC) at intervals of one month, starting from second month after planting.

❖ Spray the crop with 0.2% solution of Sevin (50 W.P.) at 15 days' interval during humid season.

Mealy bug (*Pseudococcus* sp.)

They cause little damage but may spoil the appearance of the sample.

Control Measure

❖ Fumigate the rhizomes with carbon bisulphide.

Scale insects (*Aspidiella bartii, A. spidiotus* sp.)

They damage the ginger plant by sucking the cell sap from the leaves. Affected leaves become pale and do not function properly.

Control Measure

❖ Spray the crop with 0.1% solution of Rogor or Metasystox.

Store beetle (*Sitodrepa panicea* L.) and Tobacco borer beetle (*Lasioderma serricorne* F.)

They damage the rhizomes during storage and may spoil the appearance of the produce.

Control Measure

❖   Fumigate the rhizomes with carbon bisulphide.

Root-knot nematodes (*Meloidogyne javanica* (Treub), *M. indica* R. and *M. incognita*)

They attack the crop through root infection and are reported from all ginger growing areas.

Control Measure

❖   Use DD or Nemacar nematicides in soil before planting.

HARVESTING

The optimum time for its harvesting is 210 to 260 days after planting. If rhizomes are allowed to remain in the field for longer period they become more fibrous reducing market value. For making preserved ginger, the harvesting should be done before they become fully mature i.e. about seven months after planting for dried ginger, the harvesting is done 8 to 10 months after planting, when leaves become yellow and stems begin lodging.

Harvesting is usually done by hand using a spade, hoe or digging fork.

YIELD

Ginger yield depends upon the variety, soil, irrigation facilities, nutrients and mulch application etc. Prentice (1959) reported that average yield of dry ginger is 1570 to 2000 kg per hectare. As reported from Central Horticultural Research Station, Ambalavayal, Kerala the yield per hectare of dry ginger is only about 1000 kg, with the lowest 940 kg in Kerala and the highest 1350 kg in Mysore. Bendall and Daly (1966) reported the normal yields in Queensland for the early harvest crop may be about 10,000 kg per hectare.

PREPARATION FOR MARKET

Three different forms in which ginger is sold in the market are fresh (green) ginger, preserved ginger in syrup or brine and dried ginger spice. For fresh ginger, consumed as a vegetable, the rhizomes are washed in running water thoroughly, put in baskets or in plastic containers and sent to the market. Preserved ginger is sold in the international market. It is washed first and soaked in cold water for two days, several changes of water being made. Then it is heated and boiled for 10 minutes and removed with fork. Later on it is boiled in sugar syrup for 45 minutes. For 100 kg ginger, 80 kg sugar and sufficient water is needed to cover the rhizomes. It is kept in syrup for two days and reboiled for 45 minutes after which it is packed in fresh syrup. The quantity of syrup used depends on the market for which ginger is intended.

The dried ginger spice is prepared by rhizomes. The peeled or unpeeled freshly harvested rhizomes are washed in running water thoroughly. Washed rhizomes are boiled for 30 to 45 minutes depending upon the variety. Later on it is kept in sunlight till it is dries completely.

STORAGE

Freshly harvested rhizomes cannot be stored for more than 20 days at room temperature but its storage life can be increased by lowering down the temperature. It can be kept well for 8 to 10 weeks at storage temperature of $5°C$ to $7°C$.

The preserved ginger can be kept at room temperature for 6 to 12 months while dried ginger can be kept in dry conditions at room temperature for two to three years.

SEED PRODUCTION

This tuber crop is almost free from viral diseases, hence, quality seed production is not a problem. Healthy and true to the type plant material is selected from the field on the basis on rhizome characters. The selected rhizomes are multiplied following the recommended cultural practices.

TAPIOCA

Botanical name	-	*Manihot esculenta*
Family	-	Euphorbiaceae
Synonymous	-	Yuca, Cassava, Manioc, Mandioc and Maravali

IMPORTANCE AND UTILITY

The tapioca tubers are used in the production of industrial alcohol. With the increase in the price of petro-chemical products, production of industrial alcohol from tapioca tubers is being closely examined in a number of countries. Apart from its industrial uses, it serves as a food source for millions of people. The crop is capable of producing more calories per unit of land than any other crop. It is also used in the production of starch, sagos, flour and chips.

At present, tapioca is grown over an area of 363,000 hectares with an annual production of 6371 thousand metric tonnes in India. The yield of tapioca tubers averages 175.42 quintal per hectare in our country. Seventy per cent of the total production of the world is used as food, 20 per cent as animal feed and 10 per cent for other industrial uses. Its tuber has the following composition (results expressed as per cent of dry matter). Dry matter 28.5 per cent, crude protein 2.6 per cent, ether extract 0.46 per cent, crude fibre 0.43 per cent, carbohydrate 94.1 per cent, Ash 2.4 per cent. Its 100 g edible fresh portion contains 59.4 per cent moisture, 38.1 per cent carbohydrates, 0.7 per cent protein, 0.2 per cent fat, 0.08 mg thiamine, 0.08 mg riboflavin, 12 mg Vitamin C and 1800 mg minerals.

In India, it is mainly grown in Kerala, Andhra Pradesh, Orissa, Maharashtra, etc. where it is used in place of potato.

ORIGIN AND HISTORY

It is a native of the eastern equatorial region of South America. In the beginning it was cultivated by the Red Indians in Brazil, Guiana and Mexico before the arrival of Europeans. Today, it is cultivated in about 40 countries of Africa, Latin America and Asia.

BOTANY

It belongs to the family Euphorbiaceae. The plant is herbaceous or semi-shrubby perennial reaching a height of about 1.5 to 4.5 metres. It has large spreading long stalked leaves, palmately divided. The plant possesses tall, thick straight stem marked along the length by numerous scares indicating position from where the leaves have dropped off. It flowers and bears fruit containing three seeds. The valuable parts of the plant are large, fleshy, cylindrical, tapering roots which are formed in clusters at the base of the stem.

CLIMATIC REQUIREMENTS

It can be grown from sea-level to an elevation of about 900 metres and can withstand drought extremely well but does not tolerate stagnant water. It thrives best in tropical warm humid climate with well distributed rainfall of over 900 cm per annum.

SOIL AND ITS PREPARATION

The most favourable soils for tapioca cultivation are loose textured and well-drained soils. In poorly drained soils, such as clayey or heavy textured soils, the tubers are deformed, subject to growth cracks and often not attractive in appearance. The best quality tubers and yield is obtained in sandy loam, silt loam and peat soils. Field should be prepared by one deep ploughing followed by five to six harrowings. Planking should be done for making the soil loose, friable and porous.

VARIETIES

The tapioca varieties are classified as sweet and bitter, based on the content of cyanogenic glucoside. The varieties differ in duration, shape, size and colour of leaves, colour of stem and tubers. Following are the main varieties of tapioca.

Travancore Red: Tubers are slightly red in colour and ready to harvest after 275 days of planting. Stem is slightly pink.

Sree Prakash: It is recommended for Kerala and Tamil Nadu. Plants are 1 to 1.5 metre long. Tubers are medium in size and ready to harvest 7 to 8 months after planting.

Co-1: It is recommended for Tamil Nadu. Tubers are white in colour. Average yield is 300 to 360 quintal per hectare. It is ready to harvest 8 months after planting.

Co.2: It is also recommended for Tamil Nadu. Average yield is 300 to 350 quintal per hectare. It is ready to harvest 9 to 10 months after planting.

Travancore white: Tubers are white, medium in size, sweet and ready to harvest after 290 days of planting. Stem is dark green.

M-4: It is introduced from Malaya. It has broad leaves and high yielding capacity.

AC-2380: It is a new selection. Its tubers are white in colour and ready to harvest after 300 days of planting.

H-2304: It is a hybrid released from Central Tuber Crop Research Institute, Trivandrum, Kerala. The average yield is 350 to 460 quintal per hectare.

H-1687: It is also a hybrid released from Central Tuber Crop Research Institute, Trivandrum, Kerala. The average yield is 325 to 450 quintal per hectare.

PLANTING

It is propagated by stem cuttings of about 15 to 25 cm length. The cuttings should be taken from the mature parts of the plant. After harvesting the crop, the stems are put in bundles and kept in a cool and dry place. At the time of planting, 15 to 25 cm long (containing 5 to 6 buds) cuttings are prepared. These stem pieces should be planted in shallow trenches or furrows at a depth of 5 to 10 cm. The cuttings are planted vertically or in a slightly slanting position leaving at least three nodes above ground. The rows should be made 90 cm apart and the cuttings planted at an interval of about 90 cm. At this distance about 12340 plants can be accommodated per hectare.

Time of planting

In northern region the planting should be done from March to May under irrigated conditions. In *Tarai* region, planting is done in February-March while in South India, the crop should be planted in April-May.

MANURES AND FERTILISERS

It is a long duration crop and requires much more nutrients than other seasonal crops. It requires on an average 150 kg nitrogen, 100 kg phosphorus and 250 kg potash in addition to 150 to 200 quintals of farmyard manure per hectare. Full quantity of farmyard manure should be mixed in the soil one month before planting while half dose of nitrogen and full dose of phosphorus and potash should be given as basal dressing at the time of planting. Remaining half dose of nitrogen should be given in two split doses, first after 75 days of planting and second after 150 days of planting.

IRRIGATION AND DRAINAGE

It is essential to irrigate the crop immediately after planting. Later on, irrigations can be given at an interval of 10 to 15 days during summer season. The roots develop near the surface, therefore, only light irrigations should be given. During rainy season the crop does not require irrigation at all. Excess water should be drained out immediately because it does not tolerate stagnant water.

WEED CONTROL

The roots develop near the surface, therefore, only shallow hoeing should be given. Weed control is important in early stages of plants. Later on, the plants completely cover the ground and then there is no need of inter-culture operations. Earthing should be done twice to get better quality tubers.

DISEASES AND THEIR CONTROL

Stem rot

This disease is caused by *Fusarium oxysporum* and is very destructive in many areas. The leaves of infected plants become dull in colour and then yellow between the veins and somewhat puckered. Yellowing is followed by wilting of the plant.

Control Measures

❖ Cuttings should be treated with 0.1% mercuric chloride solution.

❖ Drench the plants with 0.2% solution of Dithane M-45.

Soft rot

It is caused by *Rhizopus nigricans* and the infection generally takes place at wounds and waterlogging areas.

Control Measure

❖ Treat the cuttings with 0.2% solution of Dithane M-45.

INSECT PESTS AND THEIR CONTROL

Hairy caterpillar (*Diacrisia obliqua*)

It is an orange coloured hairy caterpillar and feeds on leaves of the plants in August-September.

Control Measures

❖ Collect and destroy the caterpillars.

❖ Spray the crop with 0.2 per cent solution of Melathian or Sevin (50 W.P.).

Aphids

They are very small insects found generally in groups on tender shoots and leaves of plants. They suck the cell sap and make the plants poor in growth.

Control Measure

❖ Spray the crop with 0.1% solution of Rogor or Metasystox.

HARVESTING

The crop takes 9 to 12 months for maturity. Yellowing and shedding of leaves are the main indications of maturity. The root tubers become fibrous, woody and poor in quality when harvesting of the the crop is delayed. On reaching maturity, the plants should be pulled out along with tubers by hand or the stems should be cut first and then the roots dug out.

YIELD

A tapioca plant carries one to ten roots weighing one to two and half kilograms each. The average yield is about 200 to 250 quintal per hectare. However, the long duration varieties, obviously, are more productive.

PREPARATION FOR MARKETING

The freshly harvested tubers are kept in partial shade for drying. Wash them in running water and sort out the damaged ones, and those thin and having uneven shape and put the better ones in baskets for market. Generally the tubers of medium thickness are preferred over others.

STORAGE

The tubers should be sold in the market immediately after harvest. Its storage life at room temperature can be extended to 16 days by coating the tubers with a fungicidal.wax emulsion. This may be done to prevent water loss from tubers through respiration. The tubers can also be stored in cold storage at a temperature of 0°C, at relative humidity of 85-90 per cent for a period of six and half months. The tubers, after harvest, should not be kept as such under room temperature. The raw tubers develop a poisonous cyanogenic glucoside which can cause giddiness, vomiting and restlessness.

SEED PRODUCTION

The best method of its multiplication is by stem cutting. Hence, seed production is not a problem. True to the types, healthy and disease-free desirable plant material is selected and cuttings are prepared from them.

BIBLIOGRAPHY

Anonymous, 1954. Fertilize your vegetables. Ind. Fmg. Aug.: 10-11 and 27.

Anonymous, 1967. Handbook of Agriculture, ICAR, New Delhi.

Anonymous, 1967. Red Bhindi: A choice variety for kitchen gardens. Madras Agric. J. 54-59.

Anonymous, 1978. Know your vegetable varieties. Seeds and Farms 4 (1-2) : 11-14.

Adriances, G.W. and F.R. Brison, 1955. Propagation of Horticultural Plants. McGraw Hill Book Co. Inc. New York and London. pp. 260-271.

Arora, P.N. 1967. Study of the effect of different dates of transplanting of onion seedlings on the bulb's development, percentage of bolting and yield of onion bulbs. Indian Jour. Agron. 12 : 332-334.

Arora, P.N. and Mathur, R.B.L. 1972. Note on effect of nitrogen and potash on the yield of carrots. Indian Jour. Agron. 17 (2) : 116-117.

Arora, S.K., Sharma, R.B. and Saimbhi, M.S. 1974. The performance of starter solution in brinjal. Jour. Res. Ludhiana 11 (3) : 239-241.

Arya. P.S. and Saini, S.S. 1975. Cabbage too needs proper care. Ind. Fmg Dig. VIII (10) : 17-18.

Audus, L.J. 1955. Plant growth substances. Leonard Hill (Books) Limited, London.

Avery, G.S. and Johnson, E.B. 1953. Hormones and Horticulture. McGraw Hill Co. Inc. New York.

Aykroyd et al. 1941. Health Bulletin No. 23 Published by Nutrition Research Lab., Koonoor.

Aykroyd, W.R. 1963. The nutritive value of Indian foods and planning of satisfactory diets. ICMR Special Rpt. Series No. 42.

Babu Ram and Tiwari, R.S. 1980. Know improved farming of cucurbits. Ind. Fmg Dig. XIII (1) : 9-12.

Bailey, L.H. 1930. Standard Encyclopedia of Horticulture. Vol. III. Mac Millan Co. New York.

Bailey, L.H. 1949. Manual of cultivated plants. The Mac Millan Co. New York.

Bailey, L.H. 1958. Standard Encyclopedia of Horticulture. Vol. III. The Mac Millan Co. New York, pp 3366-67.

Bavappa, K.V.A. 1974. Development and prospects of spice industry. Proceedings of a Symposium held at the C.F.I.R.T., Mysore.

Bealtic, W.R. 1938. Water melons, U.S.D.A. Farmers' Bulletin No. 1394.

Bendall, R.L. and Daly, R.A. 1966. Ginger growing in the ambour area, Queensland, Quarterly Rev. Agric. Econ. (19) : 83-96.

Bhalla, P.L. 1979. Towards bumper harvest of pumpkin and bottle gourd. Ind. Fmg Dig. XII (21) : 3-5.

Bhore, D.P., Bhapkar, D.G. and Chavan, V.M. 1967. Longevity of seeds in brinjal. Indian Jour. Agron. 12 (1) : 51-55.

Bid, M.M., Das P.K. and Dhua, S.P. 1971. Studies on the relative efficiencies of soil and foliar application of urea on brinjal. Technology Sindri 8 (3-4) : 261-264.

Brar, J.S. and Nandpuri, K.S. 1972. Cultivation of root crops. Punjab Agriculture University, Ludhiana. pp. 20.

Butani, D.K. and Verma, S. 1976. Pests of vegetables and their control—brinjal. Pesticides 10 (2) : 32-35.

Butani, D.K. and Verma, S. 1977. Insect pests of vegetables—tomato. Pesticides 11 (i) : 33-36.

Chandrasekharan, P. and George, C.M. 1973. Effect of NPK fertilizers in conjunction with 'Spartin' on the growth and yield of brinjal. Agric. Res. Jour. Kerala 11 (2) : 106-108.

Chatfield, C. 1949. Food composition tables for international use. F.A.O. Nutritional studies No. 3. F.A.O. Rome.

Chatfield, C. 1954. Food composition tables, minerals and vitamins for international use. F.A.O. Nutritional studies No. 11. F.A.O. Rome.

Chatterjee, S.S. 1966. Some hints on growing vegetables in the kitchen garden. Indian Horticulture 10 (2) : 7-10.

Chattopadhyay, S.B. 1967. Diseases of plants yielding drugs, dyes and spices. ICAR, New Delhi-1.

Chaugule, B.A. and Pandey, S.G. 1958. Hardening of seedlings for moisture in relation to growth, yield and irrigation requirements of brinjal fruit. Indian Jour. Agron. 3 (1) : 1-14.

Chauhan, D.V.S. 1968. Vegetable Production in India. Ram Prasad and Sons : Agra-3.

Choudhury, B. 1976. Vegetables, National Book Trust, India. New Delhi. Fourth Edition.

Choudhury, B. and Sirohi, P.S. 1975. Pusa Chetaki an early maturing profitable radish. Indian Hort. 20 (3) : 15-16.

Choudhury, B. and Ram Pal, 1961. Seed Production with regard to yield and quality in early cauliflower. *Brassica oleracea* var. *botrytis.* Indian Jour. Hort. 18 : 152-155.

Darlington, C.D. and Wylie, A.P. 1955. Chromosomes Atlas of Lower Plants. London.

Denisen, E.L. 1958. Principles of Horticulture. The Mac Millan Co. New York, pp. 70-82.

Desh Pandey, R.B. 1933. Studies in chillies. III. The inheritance of some characters in *C annum.* Indian Jour. Agric. 3 : 219-300.

Dhesi, N.S. and Nandpuri, K.S. 1968. Vegetable growing in Punjab. Punjab Univ. Farm Bull. No. 2.

Dhesi, N.S., Padda, D.S. and Malik, B.S. 1964. Effect of nitrogen, phosphorus and potash on the yield of squash melon. Punjab Hort. Jour 4 : 45-47.

Dhesi, N.S., Padda, D.S. and Kumar J.C. 1966. Response of bitter gourd to nitrogen, phosphate and potash fertilisation. Indian Hort. Jour. 23 : 169-171.

Dhurja, H.S. and Shukla, Vishnu, 1973. Foliar application of urea on tomato. Indian Jour. Hort. 30 (1-2) : 425-427.

Duruz, W.P. 1953. Principles of Nursery Management. A.T. Delamare Co., Inc., New York.

Dutta, O.P. and Singh, Sabhajeet. 1970. Annual Report of the Institute of Horticultural Research, Bangalore.

Dutta, O.P. 1971. Improvement of Okra through selection and hybridization. Mthly. Rept. Inst. Hort. Res., Bangalore.

Faulkner, R.P. 1955. Garden manures and fertilizers. W.H. and L. Collingridge

Ltd., London W.C.-2.

Gardner, V.R. 1942. Basic Horticulture. The Mac Millan Co. New York, pp. 12-13.

Gardner, V.R., Bradford, F.C. and Hooker, H.D. 1952. The fundamentals of fruit production. McGraw Hill Book Co. Inc. New York. pp. 571-633.

Gopala Swamiengar, K.S. 1935. Complete Gardening in India. The Hosali Press, Bangalore.

Grindle, E.W. 1960. Everyday Gardening in India. Taraporevala Sons & Co. Ltd., Bombay Fort.

Gupta, K.N. 1958. Udyan Vigyan Part I. Raja Ram Kumar Press, Lucknow.

Hanumantha, Rao and Purewal, S.S. 1957. Onion and Garlic Cultivation in India. ICAR Farm Bull. 3.

Joshi, S.N. 1961. Garlic is as good as any Indian Fmg.

Kamalanathan, S., Sundarajan, S. and Thamburaj, S. 1970. Studies on optimum spacing and manuring for Okra *Abelmoschus esculentus* (L) Moench. Madras Agric. J. 57 (1) : 10-17.

Kannu, K. and Nair, K.P. 1965. Jingiber officinale in Kerala. Madras Agric. J. 52 : 163-176.

Khandelwal, R.C. and Nath Prem, 1971. Effects of foliar application of urea on growth and yield of spinach beet. Fm. Jour., Calcutta 12 (11-12) : 29-32.

Khokhar, N.S., Singh, R.P. and Prasad Mahabir, 1970. Effect of different levels of nitrogen, phosphorus, potash and FYM on the yield of cabbage. Indian Jour. Agron. 15 (1) : 9-12.

Knott, J.E. 1955. Vegetable Growing. Lea and Febiger, Philadelphia.

Knott, J.E. 1960. Hand book for vegetable growers. John Wiley and Sons Inc. New York.

Kulkarni, C. and Patil, J.A. 1966. Niphad-53 improved strain of onion. Indian Hort. 10 (3) : 27.

Lal, Banarasi and De, Rajat. 1972. Fertilizers and moisture requirements of turnip. Indina Jour. Agric. Sci. 42 (2) : 156-160.

Lal Gulshan, 1973. Cultivation of onion, the improved way. Ind. Fmg Dig. VI (12) : 37-38.

Lal, Gulshan, 1975. Cauliflower — the queen of winter vegetables. Ind. Fms. Dig. VIII (9) : 79-82.

Lal, Gulshan. 1979. Tips for growing improved cucumbers. Ind. Fms. Dig. XII (2) : 11-14.

Lal, Gulshan. 1980. Okra, a popular rainy season vegetable. Ind. Fms. Dig. VIII (8) : 25-26.

Lal, Gulshan and Ram Babu, 1980. Grow chillies this summer. Ind. Fms. Dig. VIII (1) : 17-19.

Lal Gulshan, 1981. Tips for improved farming of winter season root vegetables. Ind. Fms. Dig. XIV (10) : 3.

Leopald, A. Carel. 1955. Auxins and Plant Growth. University of California Press. Barkleng Sons. Angeles.

Mac Gillivary, J.H. 1961. Vegetable Production. Mac Graw Hill Book Co. Inc., New York.

Maharana, D. and Singh, M. 1960. Effect of plant regulator and their methods of application on parthenocarpy in water melon. B.V. Jour. Agric. S.C. Res. 2 (2) : 12-16.

Mandke, D.V. and Arakeri, H.R. 1956. Consumptive use of water by onion crop for bulbs. Indian J. Agron. 1 (2) : 115-122.

Mathai, P.J. 1974. Raising a successful crop of bhindi. Ind. Fms. Dig. VII (5) : 41-43.

Mathur, R.B.L., Arora, P.N. and Prasad Mahabir, 1975. Effect of time of planting and fertilization on garlic. Indian Jour. Agron. 20 (1) : 46-47.

Mehrotra, O.N., Saxena, H.K. and Misra, P.H. 1972. Hunger signs in brinjals. Progve. Hort. 4 (3-4) : 93-100.

Mehta, Y.R. 1959. Vegetable growing in Uttar Pradesh. Bur. Agricu. Inform., U.P., Lucknow.

Misra, D.K. 1962. Melons on Sand Dunes. Indian Hort. 6(3).

Mital, S.P. and Srivastava, G. 1964. Seed yield in relation to bulb size and number of seed stalks in onion (*Allium capa* L.). Indian J. Hort. 21 (3-4) : 264-269.

Nandpuri, K.S. and Singh, Surjan. 1973. Three new tomato varieties. Punjab Agricultural University, Ludhiana. pp. 7.

Nandpuri, K.S., Singh, Surjan and Kanwar, J.S. 1977. Tomato 'Punjab Chhuhara'. Indian Hort. 22 (1) : 7-8.

Nath, Prem. 1976. Vegetables for the Tropical region. I.C.A.R. Low-Priced Books Series No.2, New Delhi.

Nath, Prem and Sachan, S.P. 1969. Studies on seed production of turnip. Allahabad Farmer XI (1) (4) : 267-270.

Nath, Prem and Dutta, O.P. 1971. New high yielding varieties in cucurbits. Indian Hort. 15 (4) : 11-13.

Ogura, H. 1968. Studies on the new male sterility in Japanese radish with special reference to the utilization of this sterility towards the practical raising of hybrid seeds. Mem. Fac. Agric. Kagoshima Univ. pp. 39-78.

Padda, D.S., Malik B.S. and Kumar, J.C. 1969. Response of musk melon to nitrogen, phosphorus and potash fertilization. Indian J. Hort. 26 (3, 4) : 172-175.

Pandey, U.B. and Singh, R.P. 1979. Cultivation of sweet potato. Ind. Fms. Dig. XII (8) : 39-40.

Parikh, H.S. 1974. Commercial production of tomatoes. Fin. Agric. 5 (4) : 31-37.

Patil, V.K., Gupta, P.K. and Thombre, P.G. 1973. Influence of pruning, mulching and nitrogen fertilisation on the growth and yield of staked tomato. Punjab Veg. Grower 8 (4) : 4-9.

Pathak, G.N. and Singh, B. 1950. Pollination and fruit setting in parwal. Indian Fmg. 9 (2) : 67-68.

Paulose, T.T. 1970. Development of ginger in India. Indian Species 7 (2) : 2.

Peter, K.V., Sarnaik, D.A. and Tyagi, S.D. 1972. Plant tomato and chilli varieties. Ind. Fms. Dig. XI (4) : 11-12.

Prasad. D.N. and Prakash, R. 1968. Floral biology of brinjal. Indian J. Agric. Sci. 38 : 1053-61.

Purewal, S.S. 1954. Production of chillies. Indian Fmg. 3 (12) : 20-23.

Purewal, S.S. 1957. Vegetable cultivation in northern India. I.C.A. Bulletin. 39.

Purewal, S.S. and Dargan, K.S. 1961. Effect of fertilizers and spacing on the development and yield of garlic. Indian Jour. Agron. 5 : 262-268.

Purewal, S.S. and Dargan, K.S. 1962. Fertilizer experiments with onion crop. Indian Jour. Agron. 7 : 46-53.

Purseglove, J.W. 1972. Tropical crops, Monocotyledons. Longman London.

Raghavan, T.S. and Venkatasubban K.R. 1943. Cytological studies in the family Zingiberaceae with special reference to chromosome number and cyto-taxonomy. Proc. Indian Acad. Sci. 17 : 118-132.

Ram, K. and Sharma, R.K. 1969. Effect of nitrogen supply on growth, yield and ascorbic acid content of cabbage. Poona Agric. College Mag. 59 (1-2) : 25-29.

Ram, H.H. 1981. Beans are better in spring. Ind. Fms. Dig. XIV (12) : 3-4.

Randhawa, K.S., Nandpuri, K.S. and Bajwa, M.S. 1972. Studies of the comparative efficiency of different sizes of seed and spacing on the yield of ginger. J. Res. India 9 (2) : 239-241.

Randhawa, K.S. and Nandpuri, K.S. 1974. Spacing and fertilizer requirements for new varieties of tomato. Progve. Fmg. 11 (1) : 23.

Rangaswami, G. 1975. Diseases of crop plants. Prentice-Hall India Pvt. Ltd., Second Edition.

Rao, H. and Purewal, S.S. 1953. Onion and garlic cultivation in India. I.C.A.R. Farm Bull. 3.

Relwani, L.L. 1963. Fertilizer investigation in chilli crop. Indian J. Agron. 7 (4) : 291-299.

Ridley, H.N. 1972. Spices. Mac Millan, London.

Sarnaik, D.A. and Peter, K.V. 1976. Tapioca a promising crop for Tarai. Ind Fms. Dig. IX (12) : 7-9.

Sastri, B.N. *et al.* 1950. The wealth of India. Raw Materials Vol. 2, New Delhi. Council for Scientific and Industrial Research. pp. 402-405.

Shekhawat, G.S., Sharma, D.C. and Jain, R.K. 1964. Response of peas to varying fertility and density conditions in Chambal Commanded area of Rajasthan. Indian Jour. Agron. 12 (2) : 103-107.

Singh, A.R., Jain, P.C. and Singh, S.M. 1958. Studies on transplanting of vegetable crops, effect of age and number of seedlings with and without starter solution and hardening on cauliflower. Indian J. Hort. 17 (4): 217-224.

Singh, H.B., Thakur, M.R. and Bhagchandani, P.M. 1962. Vegetable seed production of peas, lettuce, celery, parsley, onion, palak and spinach. Indian Jour. Hort. 19 : 147-154.

Singh, J.P. 1970. Elements of vegetable pests. Vora and Co. Publishers Pvt. Ltd., Bombay. pp. 275.

Singh, J.P., Gill, H.S. and Bullar, B.S. 1971. Pusa Chandrima, a high yielding turnip. Indian Hort. 16 (1) : 19-20.

Singh, N.P. 1976. Produce carrot, turnip and radish seeds on your farm. Ind Fms. Dig. IX (11) : 7-8.

Singh, N.P. and Singh, R.P. 1980. Effect of growth regulator, nitrogen levels and planting dates on growth, yield and quality of tomato. Thesis, G.B.P.U.A.&T., Pantnagar.

Singh, N.P. 1982. Grow Colocasia as summer crop. Ind Fms. Dig. XIV (4) : 25-26.

Singh, P.K. and Singh, J.P. 1974. All about cultivation of chillies. Ind. Fms. Dig. VII (5) : 45-46.

Smith, O. 1932. Relation of temperature to anthesis and blossom drop of the tomato together with the histological studies of the pistils. J. Agric. Res. 44 : 183-190.

Srivastava, B.K. and Singh, I.P. 1973. Plant garlic this way. Ind. Fms. Dig. X (10) : 41-42.

Srivastava, B.K. and Singh, B.P. 1974. Improved way to French bean. Ind. Fms. Dig. XII (1) : 27-28.

Swarup, V., Gill, H.S., Kalda, T.S. and Bhagchandani, P.M. 1968. Pusa Drum Herd a promising variety of cabbage. Indian Hort. 12 (3) : 66-67.

Thompson, C.H. and Kelly, C. William. 1957. Vegetable crops. McGraw Hill Book Co. Inc., U.S.A.

Tiwari, R.S. 1975. The world of cucurbita. Ind Fms. Dig. VIII (2) : 7-12.

Tiwari, R.S. 1976. Radish a crop of all the seasons. Ind. Fms. Dig. IX (1) : 17.

Tiwari, R.S. 1977. French bean a vegetable crop of great promise. Ind. Fms. Dig. X (2) : 41-42.

Venkataratnam, L. 1961. Apply boron to your early cauliflower crop. Indian Hort. 5 (4) : 25.

Vijay, O.P., Dutta, O.P. and Nath, Prem. 1971. A note on the improvement of brinjal. Indian J. Hort. 29 (1) : 67-68.

Walker, J.C. 1952. Diseases of vegetable crops. McGraw Hill Book Co.

Watts, R.L. and Watts, G.S. 1951. Vegetable Growing. Business, Orange, Judd Publishing Co., Inc. New York.

Work, Paul and Carew John. 1970. Vegetable Production and Marketing. Wiley Eastern Pvt. Ltd. New Delhi.

Wright, R.C., Rose, H. and Whiteman, T.M. 1954. The commercial storage Fruits, Vegetables, Florist and Nursery stocks. Agric. Hand Book No. 66. U.S.D.A.

Yawalkar, K.S. 1980. Vegetable Crops of India. Second Edition, Agri-Horticultural Publishing House, Nagpur.

Index